THE AMERICAN ANIMAL HOSPITAL ASSOCIATION

ENCYCLOPEDIA OF CAT HEALTH AND CARE

THE AMERICAN ANIMAL HOSPITAL ASSOCIATION

ENCYCLOPEDIA OF CAT HEALTH AND CARE

with Les Sussman

Special Consultant,
Alan Dubowy, DVM

Produced by The Philip Lief Group, Inc.

HEARST BOOKS
New York

Copyright © 1994 by The Philip Lief Group, Inc.

Illustrations by Emma Crawford
Photography by Mark McCullough

It is the policy of William Morrow and Company, Inc., and its imprints
and affiliates, recognizing the importance of preserving what has been
written, to print the books we publish on acid-free paper, and we exert
our best efforts to that end.

Library of Congress Cataloging-in-Publication Data
Sussman, Les, 1944–
    The American Animal Hospital Association encyclopedia of cat
health and care / Les Sussman.
      p.   cm.
    Includes index.
    ISBN 0-688-13454-8
    1. Cats—Health—Encyclopedias.   2. Cats—Diseases—Encyclopedias.
3. Cats—Encyclopedias.   I. American Animal Hospital Association.
II. Title.   III. Title: Encyclopedia of cat health and care.
IV. Title: Cat health and care.
SF447.S87   1994
636.8'089—dc20   94-6622 CIP

Printed in the United States of America

First Edition

1 2 3 4 5 6 7 8 9 10

Book design by Rhea Braunstein

CONTENTS

About the American Animal Hospital Association (AAHA)   *vii*

Introduction   *ix*

PART I. A GUIDE TO BREEDS AND TEMPERAMENTS

CHAPTER 1.   Breeds of Cats   3

CHAPTER 2.   Feline Behavior: Understanding Cats   21

PART II. CARING FOR YOUR CAT

CHAPTER 3.   Before You Own a Cat   47

CHAPTER 4.   Basic Cat Care   61

CHAPTER 5.   Vaccinations   79

CHAPTER 6.   When Your Cat Is Ill   81

CHAPTER 7.   Caring for the Older Cat   95

CHAPTER 8.   Saying Good-bye   99

PART III. THE ENCYCLOPEDIA OF CAT HEALTH

An At-a-Glance Guide to Signs and Symptoms 105

CHAPTER 9. Infectious Diseases 111

CHAPTER 10. Head and Neck Problems 125

CHAPTER 11. Skin and Hair Problems 147

CHAPTER 12. Respiratory System Problems 159

CHAPTER 13. Musculoskeletal System Problems 165

CHAPTER 14. Circulatory System Problems 171

CHAPTER 15. Nervous System Problems 175

CHAPTER 16. Digestive System Problems 179

CHAPTER 17. Urinary System Problems 191

CHAPTER 18. Cancer 195

CHAPTER 19. For Males Only 199

CHAPTER 20. For Females Only 201

CHAPTER 21. Caring for Kittens 217

CHAPTER 22. First-Aid Guide 231

   Emergency Procedures 232

   Common Emergencies 238

   Poison Control 255

Recording Your Cat's History 269

Resources 271

Index 275

ABOUT THE AMERICAN ANIMAL HOSPITAL ASSOCIATION (AAHA)

FOUNDED IN 1933, the American Animal Hospital Association is an international association of more than 12,000 veterinarians who treat companion animals, such as cat and dogs. Located in Lakewood, Colorado, the association sets widely observed standards for veterinary hospitals and pet health care, inspects and accredits these hospitals, and assists veterinary professionals in meeting these standards. AAHA hospital members are known throughout the world for providing the highest quality care for pets. There are currently more than 2,500 AAHA hospital members in the United States and Canada.

One of our organization's aims has always been to promote responsible pet ownership. Every companion animal deserves to have its most basic requirements, including food, warmth, and shelter, fulfilled. Every companion animal also deserves attention and affection, and to be cared for when ill. With this reference and its companion, *The AAHA Encyclopedia of Dog Health and Care,* we have aimed to disseminate sensible, practical information to pet owners in order to help build strong, loving, and mutually beneficial relationships between people and their pets.

For more information about the American Animal Hospital Association, write to P.O. Box 150899, Denver, Colorado 80215-0899.

INTRODUCTION

INDEPENDENT, CURIOUS, AND PLAYFUL, domestic cats are not only America's most popular companions, they are also among the most intelligent creatures on Earth. Cats are wonderful animals and exceptional pets, and with the right care they can live for many long, healthy years as companions to you and your family.

This book will help you provide such quality care. It will serve as a bridge between you and your veterinarian, presenting you with a broad spectrum of valuable information about the domestic cat that will greatly enhance your understanding and enjoyment of your pet.

Of the plethora of books about cat care on the market, many contain confusing medical phraseology or use elaborate scientific detail when discussing physical ailments and illnesses.

Others focus on only one facet of cat care, such as first aid or behavioral problems.

THREE BOOKS IN ONE

The American Animal Hospital Association Encyclopedia of Cat Health and Care is a unique and valuable addition to any cat owner's library. This single reference is actually three books in one: a guide to breeds and temperaments, a guide to caring for your cat, and an encyclopedia of cat health. Whether you are involved in the raising of kittens or are interested in knowing more about feline health, the special problems of elderly pets, or what to do in a feline medical emergency, you will find all this information and much more at your fingertips in easy-to-understand language. All the information in this book is up to date, authoritative, and culled from leading veterinarians and other expert sources.

A GUIDE TO BREEDS AND TEMPERAMENTS

In Part I, A Guide to Breeds and Temperaments, you'll learn about the long and ancient history of cats— which dates back to prehistoric times —as well as important data about many of the most popular breeds of cats, both long-haired and short-haired. Because each breed is so individual, information about the different personality traits of various purebred cats is provided. This will be especially helpful to you if you are thinking about purchasing a pedigreed cat.

You also will learn about the world of feline behavior. Cats are intelligent and aware creatures. They communicate, have a sophisticated social order, and are capable of letting their owners know when they are upset about something. If your cat is acting destructively, you may discover the answer why in this section, and you'll learn some simple techniques for dealing with a "naughty cat."

CARING FOR YOUR CAT

Part II presents six chapters that will show you how to become your cat's caretaker. You'll glean essential information about the responsibilities and obligations of cat ownership, from providing adequate space for your pet to community concerns, as well as information about how to choose the right cat, where to get a cat, and how to prepare for its arrival in your household.

Chapter 4 is a complete primer of basic cat care. It covers virtually every aspect of cat ownership, from the feeding of cats to such special situations as the best way to handle a cat on moving day. Other subjects discussed in this chapter include grooming, exercise, and cats' nutritional requirements.

Later chapters detail how to raise kittens, make certain that your cat or kitten is properly vaccinated, and provide general procedures to follow when your cat is ill, including feeding, monitoring a cat's temperature, and maximizing its comfort (including a list of medical supplies that should be on hand in every cat's home).

Anyone who owns a cat will ultimately have to deal with two stages of their cat's life that may not be the happiest of times: old age and death. Chapter 7 provides important information about the special needs of elderly cats, while Chapter 8 will help you consider the difficult issue of euthanasia and cope with those saddest of moments—the death of a longtime pet.

THE ENCYCLOPEDIA OF CAT HEALTH

This section begins with an At-a-Glance Guide to signs and symptoms and will quickly refer you to the disorders usually associated with a given symptom. For example: If you notice that your cat's abdomen is swollen, consult the symptom guide under the heading "Abdomen." The heading will then refer you to the pages in this encyclopedia that deal with the subject of swollen stomachs.

Chapters 9 through 21 present a comprehensive listing of illnesses and disorders most likely to beset your cats, from infectious diseases to cancer. In clear writing free of medical jargon, each disorder is discussed in terms of underlying causes, symptoms, and what treatments are available. These chapters are designed to be used as a general reference guide so that you can better understand and cope with any illnesses that may affect your cat's normal good health. This section, however, is *not* a substitute for getting veterinary help when your cat is ill.

Because male and female cats often have special medical problems that are gender-related, Chapters 19 and 20 focus on each gender's unique problems, such as urological infection in males or false pregnancy in females. The care, growth, and development of kittens (including raising them by hand) is discussed in Chapter 21.

Chapter 22 is divided into three sections designed to provide you with the information you need if an emergency befalls your cat. "Emergency Procedures" outlines techniques for approaching an injured cat, checking for breathing and pulse, and performing mouth-to-nose resuscitation. "Common Emergencies" advises on procedures for threatening situations, from burns to fractures to unconsciousness. Finally, "Poison Control" shows you how to respond if your cat has ingested a toxic substance. Such information can help you make the right choices in that critical period before your cat can receive veterinary help.

AN ESSENTIAL HEALTH AND CARE REFERENCE

More than 57 percent of American families own some kind of pet. According to the latest figures available, there are more than 57 million cats living in 30 percent of all households in the United States. The best way for these cats to receive all the loving care they deserve is for their human caretakers to be fully informed on all aspects of cat life. We hope this book will help the cat in your household live longer and enhance your enjoyment of this special family member.

PART I

A GUIDE TO BREEDS AND TEMPERAMENTS

1

BREEDS OF CATS

THE ANCESTRY OF THE CUTE creature curled up at your feet and purring contentedly can be traced back to a small, short-legged, weasel-like carnivorous mammal called *Miacis*.

The Miacis was a tree-living creature that lived in the Eocene period some forty to fifty million years ago. The Miacis looked something like the civet, with a long, fur-covered body, short legs, and a lengthy tail. This creature's catlike retractable claws enabled free movement in trees in search of food. The teeth of the Miacis were razor-sharp and well adapted for tearing and cutting flesh.

Every member of the cat family—including your household pet, *Felis catus*—is genealogically related to and evolved from the Miacis. So are many other carnivores, such as dogs, bears, raccoons, and hyenas.

The first cats were believed to have evolved about ten million years after Miacis made its appearance. It is estimated that this was probably ten or twenty million years before the dog as we know it today evolved.

Initially, the cats divided into two groups: large cats, such as the saber-toothed tiger, and small cats, such as the domestic cat. The time came, how-

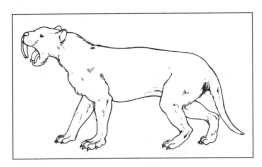

Large-toothed cats were too slow to catch nimble prey, and eventually became extinct.

3

ever, when the large, slow-moving cats' natural prey died out. These great cats were too clumsy to adapt to catching more agile animals, so they eventually became extinct.

Meanwhile, the smaller species of cats known as *Dinictis,* which were about the size of a lynx, were fast-moving, lithe, highly adaptable, intelligent, and strong. Their teeth were designed for stabbing and tearing, and their retractable claws gave them added speed and accuracy of movement while hunting. They survived the rigors of competitive existence, and from this species sprang our modern cats.

Little is known about the earliest relations between people and cats. People and dogs were probably living and hunting together 10,000 years ago, but it may have been several thousand years more before the wild cat became domesticated.

Did people capture and domesticate the cat? Or did the cat come in from the cold and adopt people? No one knows for sure. Evidence shows that the cat was already established as a domestic animal in ancient Egypt about 4,500 years ago, coinciding with the invention of the silo for storing grain. Cats were used for pest control both in grain-storage houses and in homes. Paintings and inscriptions from 2,000 B.C. and after also tell us that the Egyptians not only kept cats as household pets, but worshipped them as gods. One Egyptian tomb drawing from the Fifth Dynasty (2,600 B.C.) depicts a cat with a wide collar around its neck. Other ancient tomb paintings,

frescoes, and drawings portray Egyptian cats as elegant, slim creatures, often with large, pointed ears. The coat patterns of these cats, when they are indicated in paintings, show a spotted or mackerel cat with tawny or black markings on a lighter background. It is believed that the Egyptians domesticated several types of cat, and that one of them, *Felis lybica,* which came from the North African desert, may be the direct ancestor of today's domestic cat.

As we have already noted, the Egyptians, impressed by the cat's strength, agility, and cunning, deified their felines. One of the names for these sacred godcats was "miew." Many cat worshippers mummified cats after they died, and the animals' embalmed remains today give scientists great insight into the origins of domesticated felines.

A cat cult that developed in ancient Egypt lasted more than 2,000 years. The cat goddess Bast, or Bastet, was depicted as a tall, slender woman with a cat's head. She was worshipped as both solar and lunar goddess and represented the sacred eye of the God of Light. Bast was also known in Egypt as Pasht; it is believed that the word "puss" is derived from this name. Paintings of Bast or Pasht sometimes show her holding a basket of kittens in her arms.

This cult of the cat was taken quite seriously. The sacred animals were jealously guarded by their masters, and exporting or trading in cats was strictly prohibited. Eventually, however, cats found their way out of ancient Egypt. Sometimes they were stolen by traveling monks and Phoenician traders who sold the rare creatures in Europe and the East. Roman soldiers returning from campaigns in Egypt often brought cats back with them. Before the cat was introduced in Rome, Romans used stoats, weasels, and mongooses to guard their granaries.

Soon, cats similar to the ancient breed of Egyptian Kaffir cat were being domesticated in China and India. Some experts believe the cat arrived in the Far East as late as A.D. 400. These semiwild pets also were mainly used in vermin control.

The proliferation of cats continued. The ancient Greek cities of Carthage and Alexandria had a combined cat population estimated at 100,000. Eventually the Phoenicians, who traded with Cornish tin miners, brought cats to the British Isles, often bartering them for local goods.

Europe was late in acquiring the domestic cat, which was introduced there by the ancient Greeks and Romans as well as by Phoenician traders. The rarity of these domestic animals gave them great value, which they retained for centuries to come.

Cats were also worshipped by certain pagan cults in Europe—that is, until the Catholic Church waged war against the practice and claimed that cats were agents of the devil; many cats were burned alive as a result. By the eighteenth century, however, the antipathy against cats faded because of their usefulness, and felines once again became quite popular.

In ancient Egypt, cats were called by various names, such as Miw, Mau, Mau-Mei, Maau, or Maou. The word "cat" probably derives from the Nubian word *kadis,* which spread northward from Africa in its related forms through countries bordering the Mediterranean, the Baltic, and the Atlantic. Cats were known by similar names in all these countries.

There is no certainty about the origins of the American domestic cat. While a number of small wild cats, such as ocelots, roamed the American mountains, forests, and deserts, there are no records of any attempt to tame and breed these creatures. Native American folklore, however, hints that the Aztecs of Mexico may have kept a now-extinct breed of hairless cat.

We do know for certain that when the *Mayflower* moored at Plymouth Rock, one cat was among the hundred men and women aboard. It was probably brought to the American shores to guard the grain stores the New World settlers hoped to establish. As more and more ships arrived from Europe, each undoubtedly brought its complement of cats. Soon America's first feline colony was well under way.

BREEDS OF CATS

All pedigree, or pure breeds, of cat derive from various old or ancient breeds. Today there are more than a hundred recognized breeds and color varieties of pedigree domestic cats; although they number in the thousands, however, they represent only a small fraction of all cats in the United States.

Purebreds can be divided into five basic categories: Persians, other long-haired cats, British shorthairs, American shorthairs, and Oriental shorthairs.

If your cat does not fit into one of these categories, she certainly is not any less intelligent, charming, elegant, or desirable than her purebred kin—the characteristics of your cat are simply more a product of genetic luck than of carefully planned selective breeding. And although it is much more difficult to predict the future appearance and temperament of a mixed-breed kitten than of a purebred, nonpurebred cats nevertheless usually produce sturdy, intelligent offspring that possess the best qualities of their predecessors.

The concept of a purebred or pedigree cat did not exist until a hundred years ago, when cat shows in Europe first began to highlight the best results of breeding programs. Since then, programs have been developed so that cat fanciers can perpetuate and accentuate the best or most unusual features or strains of a particular breed of cat. Today, each country has its own associations that establish standards by which pedigree cats are judged. In the United States, if you are interested in any particular breed and want to know more about it, you should contact your local Cat Fanciers Association.

Some of the most popular breeds available in the United States are described here. The basic information provided about such characteristics as temperament may help you decide whether a particular breed is suitable as a family pet rather than for show purposes.

When reading the descriptions, remember that no two members of the same breed are identical. Within each breed there are substantial variations in size, color, hair length and texture, and a wide range of other physical characteristics. Personality can also differ from cat to cat within a particular breed. That's because every cat's temperament is shaped by many factors, including the type of home she was born in and the early handling and training she received.

Above all, avoid making spur-of-the-moment decisions in choosing a pedigree cat. There are many books at your local library that describe in detail the characteristics of any breed that may catch your fancy. Do your homework and become as familiar with the breed as you can before acquiring such a cat.

LONG-HAIRED CATS

Thirteen breeds of cat fall into the category of longhairs. Only six of these breeds, however, are officially recognized as championship stock by the Cat Fanciers' Association (CFA), the world's largest cat-registering association.

These six breeds are Balinese, Birman, Maine Coon, Persian, Somali, and Turkish Angora. The CFA includes the Himalayan and the Kashmir in its Persian category, but some other cat-fancier groups do not, and so list these two cats as separate breeds. Long-haired breeds that have not yet gained championship recognition by the CFA, but may eventually be added to the list, are the Cymric, Javanese, Norwegian Forest cat, Ragdoll, and Tiffany.

No one knows for certain how long-haired cats first developed. There are two schools of thought on the subject. One group of experts maintains that these cats arose through interbreeding in isolated mountain regions. Others speculate that long-haired cats developed in cold climates—possibly in a country like Russia.

Today's long-haired pedigree cats are mostly descended from cats brought to Britain from Turkey and Persia in the late nineteenth century.

BALINESE

HISTORY: The Balinese was developed in the 1950s from long-haired Siamese litters. This cat does not come from Bali, but was given the name to distinguish the breed from the Siamese.

DESCRIPTION: Like the Siamese, the Balinese has a long, svelte body, a wedge-shaped or triangular head, broad, pointed ears, and vivid blue almond-shaped eyes that slant to the long nose. The Balinese is a medium-sized cat with a soft erminelike coat. The long-plumed tail tapers to a point. The legs are long and slim, with the forelegs shorter than the hind legs. The paws are small and oval.

COLORS: White body shading to pale cream, with warm cream-colored points; white body that shades to apricot, with reddish-gold points; the white body may also be stippled with black, blue, or red; tabby patterns also occur.

PERSONALITY: Gentle and affectionate, with lots of curiosity. Like the Siamese, loves attention and wants to participate in every activity. Playful and intelligent, loyal and devoted to its owner. Has a softer voice and is less demanding than its Siamese cousins.

MISCELLANEOUS: Can be taught simple tricks like those taught dogs. The coat is shorter than a Persian's, requiring less grooming.

BIRMAN

HISTORY: A mysterious history and many colorful legends are associated with the Birman, which was known as "The Sacred Cat of Burma." One legend states that a pair of these cats were stolen from a Burmese temple and slipped to France on a yacht. The breed achieved recognition in France in 1925, but its championship status is relatively new. Only recently has the Birman been introduced into the United States.

DESCRIPTION: A large, stocky cat, long in build. The Birman has a narrow face and a pale, cream-colored body. With a long, silky coat, full mane, and long, bushy tail, the Birman is an impressive-looking animal. This cat has deep sapphire-blue eyes that are almost round and slightly slanted, and a head that is fairly round and broad, with full cheeks and a medium-sized Roman nose. The ears are medium-long, dark in color, and round-tipped.

COLORS: Cream-colored, gradually darkening on the back; face, ears, legs, feet, and tail are pointed with seal, blue, chocolate, or lilac; paws are tipped in white, and the back paws have white gloves in front and white gauntlets at the rear that finish in a point up the back of the legs.

PERSONALITY: Gentle, well-behaved, and very sociable. Very affectionate, also quite intelligent, with a small, pleasant voice.

MISCELLANEOUS: A very sociable cat who needs the company of other cats and people, and should not be left alone. Although the fur does not mat, the Birman requires daily grooming.

MAINE COON

HISTORY: It is believed that the Maine Coon was developed by the mating of American farm cats with Turkish longhairs brought to Maine in the nineteenth century by American seamen. Another theory holds that this breed is an offshoot of crossbreeding between early angoras and nonpedigree shorthairs. Folklore holds that the Maine Coon is the offspring of a cat who mated with a raccoon—but this is biologically impossible.

DESCRIPTION: This native American longhair has a heavy, shaggy coat that is almost short-haired in front but grows very long on the back and stomach. The Maine Coon is a sturdy and powerful cat with a large, wedge-shaped head, a medium-length nose, a squarish muzzle, and high cheekbones. Ears are large, pointed, and well-tufted, and set widely apart. The eyes are large, slightly slanted, and green; eyes can also be blue or gold. The body is large and muscular with moderately long legs and large, tufted paws. The tail is long, flowing, and bushy, and tapers to a blunt end.

COLORS: The Maine Coon comes in a variety of solid and mixed colors and patterns. Best known for the brown-striped and mottled variety, commonly known as the "tabby."

PERSONALITY: Active, intelligent, and quiet; particularly gentle with children. Has an easygoing attitude and a self-assured demeanor; makes an attractive, quiet chirping sound and adapts well to other animals.

MISCELLANEOUS: Unlike most longhairs, the Maine Coon is better suited for outdoor life than apartment living, needing space or access to a backyard or garden. The Maine Coon possesses great skill as a mouser and is also known for the peculiar habit of sleeping in strange positions and odd places. This cat's moderately long coat does not require much grooming.

PERSIANS

HISTORY: No one is certain about the origin of the Persian, although the breed is thought to have come from Persia (now Iran). The Persian is the most popular of the long-haired pedigreed breeds, boasting a fine-textured, silky coat that forms a full mane around the neck and back. The White Persians were the first long-haired cats to be introduced into Europe and are mentioned in some sixteenth-century texts. There are more than a dozen breeds of Persian cats, each with its own coat patterns or colors. The Himalayan and the Kashmirs are among these breeds, combining the thick, silky coat and full mane of the Persian with the colorings and markings of the Siamese.

DESCRIPTION: All Persians have a sturdy, rounded body with a round face and head, small ears, short, thick legs, a short nose, and large, almond-shaped, expressive eyes set on a slight angle. They have a powerful appearance due to a full chest and considerable girth. Their hind legs are longer than their front ones; these cats have heavily muscled thighs. They carry their long, flowing tail high. The exceptionally full coat consists of two types of hair—long, soft, and woolly undercoat hairs and slightly longer, coarser guard hairs that can be as much as four and a half inches long.

The guard hairs are attached to little muscles under the coat. A cat will fluff up guard hairs to trap warm air and remain comfortable in cold weather.

COLORS: Persians have various coat patterns or colors; they can be white, black, blue, cream, or red. Patterns include tabby, the spotted variety known as calico or tortoiseshell, which has a spotted brown or yellow coloring.

PERSONALITY: An affectionate, gentle, and intelligent cat, well-mannered and quiet. This breed loves attention and is playful but not demanding. An excellent show cat. May not be ideally suited to households with young children, because the Persian does not particularly like to be held.

MISCELLANEOUS: Requires daily grooming with a steel comb to prevent the coat from matting. Persians of show standards are very expensive.

SOMALI

HISTORY: The Somali achieved CFA championship status in 1978. The breed closely resembles and is a genetic offshoot of the short-haired Abyssinian cat. A complicated inbreeding program developed the Somali, which if bred with Abyssinians will produce a short-haired litter. Somalis must always be bred with each other to preserve breed characteristics.

DESCRIPTION: A medium-sized to large cat, lithe and muscular. The Somali has a softly rounded, wedge-shaped head, large and moderately pointed ears, and large, almond-shaped, expressive eyes that are either vivid green or gold. Except for the extremely soft, finely textured medium-length coat, the breed closely resembles the Abyssinian. The back is slightly arched, and the full, bushy tail is thick at the base and tapered at the end.

COLORS: There are two categories of colors: ruddy brown with darker shading of black on the tips of the ears and along the spine and tail; or deep red and ticked with chocolate brown that appears as the kitten matures.

PERSONALITY: An intelligent and active cat with a gentle, affectionate nature. Even-tempered, devoted, and friendly, with a soft voice. Easy to handle.

MISCELLANEOUS: Does not like being confined too closely. Needs freedom and lots of space for exercise. The breed prefers the company of another pet or a human to being alone.

TURKISH ANGORA

HISTORY: One of the oldest long-haired breeds. Like the Persian cat, the Angora was first introduced into Europe in the sixteenth century. Originally called Ankara cats, the breed comes from the province of Ankara in Turkey. This ancient breed nearly became extinct in Europe because of the popularity of Persian cats. Today, the Ankara Zoo oversees its breeding and exports only the white-haired version. The Angoras seen at shows in the United States are descended from cats first brought to this country in 1963.

DESCRIPTION: Small to medium in size, with fairly long, fine, silky hair that forms a ruff around the neck. Large, erect, tufted ears set high on a small to medium-sized, wedge-shaped head. Eyes are almond-shaped and orange in color; white Turkish Angoras may have blue eyes or one blue eye and one amber one. A fine-boned animal with a graceful torso and light frame, the Turkish Angora's legs are long and slim, with the forelegs slightly shorter than the hind legs. The rump is slightly higher than the front of the body, and the long, full tail is carried horizontally over the body when the cat walks.

COLORS: The breed comes in white, red, silver, brown, calico, black, and blue. The whites may be solid or tipped with black or blue. There are also tabby-striped Angoras.

PERSONALITY: An affectionate, intelligent, and playful cat. Polite, courteous, and quiet, these cats seem to understand their owners' desires. They are fastidious and love to play in water.

MISCELLANEOUS: The Turkish Angora thrives in a one-cat household.

Males are less nervous than females. They are good hunters and enjoy repetitive games and routines.

SHORT-HAIRED CATS

Twenty breeds of short-haired cats have been accorded championship status by the Cat Fanciers' Association. They are divided into four basic groups—natural breeds, hybrids, established breeds, and mutations.

Natural breeds are cats that have been documented as native to a specific geographical area. Over many years of mating with one another, they have produced a consistent type of cat with the same coloring or coat patterns. Natural breeds include the Abyssinian, American Shorthair, British Shorthair, Egyptian Mau, Japanese Bobtail, Korat, Manx, Russian Blue, and Siamese.

Hybrid breeds are the result of crossbreeding between two or more natural breeds. Among them are the Bombay, Colorpoint Shorthair, Exotic Shorthair, Oriental Shorthair, and Tonkinese.

Established breeds are cats that have been "manufactured" to meet ideal characteristics such as specific color, pattern, or physical type. The models they conform to are taken from variants of other breeds. These breeds include the Burmese and the Havana Brown.

Mutations are bred from cats that through some genetic inconsistency are born with unusual features. Among these breeds are the American Wirehair, Cornish Rex, Devon Rex, and Scottish Fold.

ABYSSINIAN

HISTORY: Although there is some disagreement over their ancestry, Abyssinian cats probably originated in Ethiopia (formerly Abyssinia) or Egypt thousands of years ago. They have a regal appearance and more than any other modern cat closely resemble the sacred cats depicted in ancient Egyptian carvings and paintings.

DESCRIPTION: Medium-sized, lithe, and graceful, with a firm, muscular, and well-balanced body, fine-boned legs and feet. The head is slightly rounded and wedge shaped. Forehead is wide. Almond-shaped eyes are gold or brown. Ears are large and broad at the base with pointed tips. Tail is fairly long. Coat is soft and silky. Each hair is ticked with two or three bands of darker color.

COLORS: Ruddy, red, and blue. The ruddy breed is orange-brown ticked with dark brown or black. The red is ticked with chocolate brown. The blue is a warm, soft blue-gray ticked with various shades of slate blue.

PERSONALITY: Extremely affectionate. Very intelligent and trainable. Active and playful. Good-natured with people, children, and other pets. Needs little grooming.

MISCELLANEOUS: Needs lots of room and outdoor space.

AMERICAN SHORTHAIR

HISTORY: A very old American breed. The American Shorthair's ancestors are believed to have been brought to the New World in the seventeenth century by early settlers. One story has it that these shorthairs arrived along with the Pilgrims and controlled the shipboard rat population during the voyage of the *Mayflower* and other early ships. Excellent mousers, these cats have always been popular on farms and in homes; even today they are considered working cats on many farms.

DESCRIPTION: A powerfully built, muscular cat of medium to large size, with a well-developed chest, heavy shoulders, and strong, heavily muscled legs. Paws are firm and rounded. The fairly long ears are set widely apart and are somewhat rounded at the tips. Head is large, with full cheeks, a square muzzle, and a well-developed chin. The round eyes have an open, sweet expression.

COLORS: There are thirty-four recognized colors and patterns. The most common colors are black, white, cream, blue, or red—either in solid colors or in any combination of patterns. The white may be tipped with black, red, or blue. Tabby, calico and tortoiseshell patterns are also found.

PERSONALITY: Loving and sociable, particularly hardy and strong. Intelligent; makes a wonderful house pet. Friendly with children and other pets. A great lap cat if you can bear the weight! Easy to groom.

AMERICAN WIREHAIR

HISTORY: A relatively new breed, produced by mutation. The first American Wirehair—a red-and-white male—was discovered in 1966 in an upstate New York barn, a spontaneous mutation in a litter of short-haired farm cats. Weasels killed all the litter except for this male.

DESCRIPTION: A well-muscled, medium-sized cat with a unique hard, wiry, tightly curled coat. The American Wirehair has a round head with prominent cheekbones and large, round eyes that are sometimes brilliant gold.

COLORS: The breed comes in thirty-four colors and patterns—the same as the American Shorthair. The most popular colors are black, white, blue, red, and tortoiseshell. The white may be tipped with black, blue, or red. The wirehair also comes in tabby patterns.

PERSONALITY: Affectionate, good-natured, and very inquisitive. Quiet and reserved, somewhat less receptive to strangers than the American Shorthair. Healthy, sturdy, and friendly with children and other pets. Easy to groom.

BOMBAY

HISTORY: The Bombay is a hybrid jet-black breed that was developed by crossing the Sable Brown Burmese with black American Shorthairs. The goal of this crossbreeding was to develop a cat that resembled the Indian black panther. The breed was first produced in 1958 and recognized by the CFA in 1976.

DESCRIPTION: A muscular, medium-sized cat with a pleasingly round head that has no sharp angles. Face is full, with rounded ears that tilt slightly forward and a short muzzle. Round, widely spaced eyes range in color from yellow to deep copper. The cat often assumes a semi-upright crouch.

COLORS: Jet black.

PERSONALITY: Intelligent, easy to train. Likes attention and companionship. Graceful and easygoing, with a charming personality. Good around children and other pets. A playful, sometimes mischievous cat that enjoys all sorts of activity.

BRITISH SHORTHAIR

HISTORY: This breed was developed in the late nineteenth century by crossing native British cats with Persians. Considered the oldest natural English breed, the British Shorthair may be descended from the domestic cats of Roman times.

DESCRIPTION: A medium-sized to large cat with a large head, a broad, deep body, and a short, dense coat; has a short, strong neck, prominent cheeks, and a short muzzle. Eyes are large and round. Depending on coat color, the eyes can be copper, green, yellow, hazel, or sapphire blue. The medium-sized ears are rounded at the tips. Tail is thick and tapering.

COLORS: There are eighteen recognized colors and patterns, although originally this cat's coat was blue. Popular colors are solid shades of black, blue, red, cream, or white; coat also may be tabby, tortoiseshell, or spotted.

PERSONALITY: Easygoing, intelligent, and devoted; strong and sturdy. Quite content to lie around the house; can be aloof. Quiet, soft voiced, and gentle, with lots of dignity and charm. The British Shorthair is a good mouser and friendly with children and other pets.

MISCELLANEOUS: So relaxed is this cat that you may need to encourage it to get involved in some activity. A great cat for people who don't like to fuss with their pets.

BURMESE

HISTORY: The Burmese originated from a single female named Wong Mau, brought over from Burma in 1930. She was subsequently mated with a Siamese, resulting in the breed we know today. The Burmese was recognized in 1936.

DESCRIPTION: A medium-sized cat with a compact, muscular body and rounded chest. The head is short and pleasingly round. Strong neck and shoulders. Rounded, expressive, slightly slanting eyes ranging in color from yellow to gold. Ears are large, widely separated, and slightly rounded at the tips.

COLORS: Solid sable brown, champagne, blue, and platinum.

PERSONALITY: Very social and affectionate, easy to train. A lively, alert cat that can be a clever clown. Intelligent, friendly with children and other pets. Can be somewhat vocal, but not as much as Siamese cats. Easy to groom.

COLORPOINT SHORTHAIR

HISTORY: The Colorpoint Shorthair was developed by crossing Siamese cats with other breeds, particularly American Shorthairs. This hybrid very much resembles a Siamese cat, except that the Colorpoint Shorthair has points on the mask, ears, feet, legs, and tail in seal, chocolate, blue, or lilac. These new colors were created in the breeding process.

DESCRIPTION: A beautiful cat with a fine-textured, glossy coat, dainty appearance, and an elongated, muscular body. The head is wedge-shaped; so is

the muzzle. Eyes are vivid blue and almond-shaped; ears are large and pointed.

COLORS: White-tipped with deep red, gray, or apricot; cream with brown points; blue-white tipped with blue-gray.

PERSONALITY: One of the most intelligent, affectionate, and compassionate breeds. Adores companionship and is always where you are. Active and demanding, easy to train, makes a good house pet. An extremely vocal cat with a distinctive voice that some people may find unpleasant.

CORNISH REX

HISTORY: There are two Rex breeds: the Cornish Rex and the Devon Rex, which are both fairly similar in appearance. The first Cornish cat was born in Cornwall, England, in 1950, appearing in a normal litter of farm kittens but looking somewhat different with its curly red and white coat. When this cat was mated with his mother, more curly coated kittens appeared in the litter, and the breed developed.

DESCRIPTION: The Cornish Rex has a long, narrow head with high-set, flared ears and a Roman nose. The medium-to-large oval eyes slant slightly upward. The whiskers and eyebrows are crinkled. The Devon Rex closely resembles the Cornish, except that the Devon Rex's head is less distinctly wedge-shaped and has pronounced cheekbones. The body of the Cornish Rex arches like a greyhound, with its torso tucked up to its waist. The body's most distinctive feature is short, curly fur completely devoid of guard hairs.

COLORS: There are twenty-eight recognized colors and patterns. Popular colors include white, black, blue, red, cream, chinchilla, and shaded silver. Cornish Rex cats also come in various tabby patterns in silver, red, brown, blue, or cream.

PERSONALITY: An extremely affectionate and devoted lap cat; enjoys being handled and projects warmth. Playful, inquisitive, and very people-oriented. Adores attention and is generally talkative. Excellent with children. Some shedding but easy to groom.

MISCELLANEOUS: The Cornish Rex is unusual because the coat lacks the coarse guard hairs of other cats. The breed's fine, curly fur produces little dander. People allergic to cats may be able to tolerate this breed.

EGYPTIAN MAU

HISTORY: Although the ancestors of the Egyptian Mau may have lived in ancient Egypt, this colorful and elegant breed was first developed in the United States when Egyptian cats were brought from Cairo in the 1950s. This is the only natural breed of spotted domestic cat.

DESCRIPTION: A medium-sized, powerfully built cat with a long, graceful body and slightly tapering tail. The graceful hind legs are proportionately longer than the front legs, which gives this cat an appearance of being on tiptoes when standing upright. Head is wedge-shaped. Almond-shaped eyes are light green or amber; they slant toward the ears, which are large, set wide apart, erect, and somewhat pointed. The medium-length coat is fine, silky, and lustrous.

COLORS: Silver, bronze, and smoke.

PERSONALITY: People-oriented, loving, and devoted. Intelligent, very active and playful, and good with children and other pets. Somewhat vocal with a soft, lyrical voice. Easy to groom.

EXOTIC SHORTHAIR

HISTORY: A hybrid developed in the 1960s by crossing the Persian with the American Shorthair. The objective was to produce a Persian-type cat with short hair.

DESCRIPTION: This striking cat resembles the Persian in conformation. The Exotic Shorthair has a large, round head, a short nose, full cheeks, and large, round eyes. Ears are small, wide-set, and rounded at the tips. This cat is deep-chested with a compact body, short legs, and a dense, plush coat. The eyes may be brilliant copper, green, or blue-green.

COLORS: Solid blue, red, cream, or white. White may be tipped with black, red, or blue. The cat also comes in tabby patterns, calico, and tortoiseshell.

PERSONALITY: Basically a quiet and contented cat, with a placid, unruffled manner, making it a good pet for children. Intelligent, healthy, and robust. Medium-length plush coat needs regular grooming, but not as frequently as the Persian.

HAVANA BROWN

HISTORY: This unusually intelligent and sweet-natured cat originated not in Cuba but in England. The Havana Brown is the result of years of selective crossbreeding of the black Domestic Shorthair with the seal-point Siamese carrying a brown gene. The result was a solid-colored brown cat. The deep, glossy, rich tobacco color resembles a Havana cigar, which earned the breed its name.

DESCRIPTION: A medium-sized cat with a firm, muscular body. A long, narrow head with a protruding, narrow muzzle. Vivid green oval-shaped eyes and brown whiskers. Large ears are pointed, tilted forward, and widely separated.

COLORS: A rich, even shade of warm brown.

PERSONALITY: People-oriented; can become very attached to its owner.

Affectionate, insists on intimacy, and hates to be ignored. Intelligent, active, and playful; good with children and other pets. Moderately talkative, but soft-voiced. Easy to groom.

JAPANESE BOBTAIL

HISTORY: Known for hundreds of years in Japan, this domestic cat has long been thought to bring good fortune. Since antiquity the Japanese Bobtail has been the subject of paintings, wood carvings, and statues. These cats are called Mi-Kee in Japan.

DESCRIPTION: A trim, muscular, medium-sized shorthair with high cheekbones and slanted eyes. The head forms an almost perfect equilateral triangle. The breed's most distinctive feature is the short, rigid tail that fans out in a sort of pom-pom. The soft, silky coat is almost nonshedding.

COLORS: The most dramatic and popular colors are red, black, and white calico patterns. Characteristically a tricolored cat, white with distinct patches of black and red-orange.

PERSONALITY: Quiet, elegant, very intelligent, loving, and devoted to its owner. Affectionate and good with children and other pets. Has a delicate voice; this cat is not particularly vocal.

MISCELLANEOUS: Unlike most cats, the Japanese Bobtail enjoys playing in water.

KORAT

HISTORY: An ancient natural breed, the Korat is the indigenous cat of Thailand. In its native country, this breed is highly prized and is a symbol of good luck. The Korat is rare, and ownership is restricted by the Thai government.

DESCRIPTION: A strong, muscular cat with a medium-sized build and a fairly short silver-blue coat. Head is heart-shaped, with a flat forehead, dark blue or lavender nose, and large ears that are rounded at the tips. The large and luminous eyes are green. The males look powerful and are renowned in Thailand for their prowess as fighters.

COLORS: Silver-blue, tipped with silver.

PERSONALITY: Intelligent and active, often becomes attached to one person. Responds to gentleness. The Korat is protective of family members and is friendly with thoughtful children and good-natured pets.

MANX

HISTORY: A tail-less cat, the Manx is the subject of many legends. One of the oldest known breeds, the Manx is believed to have originated on the Isle of Man, between England and Ireland. No one knows why the Manx has no tail, or how the breed first arrived on the Isle of Man; some cat lorists believe it was brought there on Eastern trading ships.

DESCRIPTION: A powerful-looking, compact cat with a short, arched back and exceptionally long rear legs. The Manx gives an overall impression of roundness, with a massive rump and an unusual double coat that is soft and thick underneath and glossy and somewhat harder on top. Has large, round eyes set at a slight angle toward the nose.

COLORS: All colors and mixtures, including blue, white, black, and red.

PERSONALITY: Lively and intelligent, loving and devoted. Playful and friendly with children, but often needs discipline because of a buoyant spirit. Healthy and adaptable, the Manx places few demands on its owner.

ORIENTAL SHORTHAIR

HISTORY: A highly stylized hybrid developed by crossing the Siamese with a number of other breeds. The breed was developed in England beginning in 1950.

DESCRIPTION: A medium-sized cat that resembles the Siamese. A long, slender body that is both graceful and muscular; a wedge-shaped head with a long, straight nose, almond-shaped eyes, and large, broadly pointed ears. Tail is long and whiplike. Eyes are vivid blue, green, or amber.

COLORS: Numerous colors.

PERSONALITY: An agile, acrobatic

cat; likes attention and is somewhat demanding. Curious, attentive, and affectionate; sometimes high-strung. Loves human attention and is friendly toward children and other pets.

RUSSIAN BLUE

HISTORY: The Russian Blue is believed to have descended from blue cats with beaverlike coats that once lived in northern Russia. This cat may have been brought to the West from Russia by British sailors around 1860.

CHARACTERISTICS: A sleek, graceful cat with a firm, muscular body, long, fine-boned legs, and a long, tapering tail. Head is wedge-shaped with large, pointed ears. The Russian Blue has a distinctive short, dense, beaverlike coat that stands out from the body. There is a lustrous sheen to this breed's blue coat—one of its hallmarks. The eyes are round, wide-set, and bright green.

PERSONALITY: Intelligent and devoted to people; a mild-tempered cat that likes peaceful surroundings. Hardy and active, but unusually quiet; an excellent apartment cat. Although quite talkative, the Russian Blue has a gentle voice.

SCOTTISH FOLD

HISTORY: A natural mutation discovered by a shepherd on a Perthshire, Scotland, farm in 1961. Since then, the Scottish Fold has been carefully bred to preserve the uniquely folded ears. The breed was established by crossing it with various shorthairs.

DESCRIPTION: A medium-sized cat with a short, well-padded body. A rounded head with prominent cheeks and whisker pads, and small, round-tipped ears that fold downward and forward. The Fold's expressive round eyes are separated by a short, broad nose.

COLORS: Solid black, blue, red, cream, or white. Also occurs in tabby patterns, tortoiseshell, and calico.

MISCELLANEOUS: Sweet temperament; friendly with people and other pets. Because their canals are very small, the ears require regular cleaning with a cotton swab to prevent infection. Otherwise easy to groom.

SIAMESE

HISTORY: No one knows for certain where this distinctive breed came from, although its origins are definitely Eastern. Siamese cats were highly prized in Siam (now Thailand) hundreds of years ago. They were first brought to England and the United States in the latter part of the nineteenth century. The first recorded American Siamese was owned by the wife of Rutherford B. Hayes, the nineteenth president of the United States. The Siamese are now the most popular of pedigreed breeds and are highly prized as show cats.

DESCRIPTION: A medium-sized cat: svelte, sinuous, elegant, and extremely refined. The coat is distinctively marked, fine-textured, and glossy. The wedge-shaped head is long and tapered. The ears are large and strikingly pointed. Deep blue, almond-shaped eyes slant toward the nose. Legs are long and slim; tail is long and tapered.

COLORS: This breed sports twenty-three possible colors and patterns. The special feature of Siamese cats is their unusual markings or points. Popular colors are seal-point, chocolate-point, blue-point, and lilac-point.

PERSONALITY: Affectionate and attentive; loves human companionship and dislikes isolation. An extremely demanding cat that is energetic, clever, and acrobatic. Highly intelligent and often unpredictable, the Siamese is the most talkative of cat breeds. The voice sometimes sounds like the crying of a baby. When the female of the breed is in heat, its voice can almost become unbearable to humans.

MISCELLANEOUS: A fearless and very independent cat, the Siamese does not respond to authoritarian human behavior.

TONKINESE

HISTORY: The Tonkinese is a hybrid of Siamese and Burmese. The cross-breeding took place in the 1960s and 1970s. To preserve the purebred line, Tonkinese should only be bred to other Tonkinese.

DESCRIPTION: The Tonkinese has a medium-sized torso and is muscular, solidly built, and surprisingly heavy. Females can weigh up to six pounds, and males average nine to twelve pounds. The breed has fairly slim legs, a head that is a modified wedge, and almond-shaped, aqua eyes. The coat is soft and minklike.

COLORS: Natural mink, champagne mink, blue mink, honey mink, and platinum mink.

PERSONALITY: A very intelligent cat with meticulous habits. Clever, active, fearless, and willful; tends to be mischievous. Very affectionate, friendly with children and other pets. Loyal and loving, the Tonkinese combines the best traits of Siamese and Burmese cats.

MISCELLANEOUS: This cat likes to show off. The breed is very acrobatic and gregarious and requires attentive owners.

Abyssinian

American Wirehair

American Wirehair

American Shorthair

Balinese

Birman

Bombay

British Shorthair

Burmese

Colorpoint Shorthair

Cornish Rex

Devon Rex

Egyptian Mau

Exotic Shorthair

Exotic Shorthair

Havana Brown

Himalayan

Japanese Bobtail

Korat

Maine Coon Cat

Manx

Oriental Shorthair

Persian

Persian

Ragdoll

Russian Blue

Scottish Fold

Scottish Fold

Siamese

Somali

Tonkinese

Turkish Angora

2

FELINE BEHAVIOR:
UNDERSTANDING CATS

UNDERSTANDING WHY CATS behave the way they do is not always easy. Many cat owners tend to interpret their cat's behavior anthropomorphically—they view their pet as a little human with whiskers and claws. Cats, however, are fundamentally different from human beings. Their motivations, attitudes, and social behavior are entirely catlike. No matter how much you may study its ways, even if you had nine lifetimes you'd never fully understand your cat's behavior.

Despite years of research into feline psychology, there remain many mysteries about the will and the ways of the domestic cat. In fact, if researchers have discovered anything at all conclusive about feline behavior, it is that cats make their own rules and define themselves as they go along.

What we do know about the basic behavior of domestic cats is that it is similar—if not identical—to the behavior of their kin in the wild. The major difference, of course, is that your pet has accepted her partnership with humans and human lifestyles. For example, wild cats will not come close to people, but domesticated cats love humans and the creature comforts we offer them—a bond that dates back thousands of years and is based on more than mere convenience.

With cats, however, there are bound to be behavioral problems at times. Some of these problems—and ways to prevent or resolve them—are discussed later in this section. But as a pet owner, recognize that your cat always will be dependent on you *and* independent of you, and will sometimes engage in behavior you may not understand or approve of. Remember that cats also vary in their responses to human emotions, much as people do. If you want a pet that will come running to you every time you whistle or give a command, perhaps you should think about getting a dog instead. Your cat will cooperate only if and when she wants to. That's exactly what makes cats so interesting!

INTELLIGENCE AND AWARENESS

Domestic cats are highly evolved, intelligent, and aware creatures. They may not speak our language, but they do communicate with us and with one another, think their way through problems, learn and remember the lessons they have learned, socialize, and adapt to their environment.

One excellent example of feline intelligence is hunting behavior. While all cats were once predators, today's domestic cat must be taught to hunt. If your cat is on the prowl for birds or mice, she learned to hunt from her mother or from another cat. In fact, if your female cat has never hunted, it is highly unlikely that any kittens in her litter will be hunters, either. But a mother cat who has learned to hunt will teach those skills to her offspring. Even if you have never seen your female cat exhibit hunting behavior before, the presence of kittens often intensifies what may be latent skills.

If your female cat is allowed outdoors, she will begin teaching her young how to hunt by bringing dead mice, birds, and other prey to the litter when the kittens are about four weeks old. You will see her eating the dead prey in front of her kittens while making growling noises. She does this to ward off competing predators. At first this behavior frightens the kittens, but eventually they become attracted to it.

If your cat is not allowed outdoors and cannot find any household prey to bring to her kittens within the first six to twenty weeks of their lives, the litter will not learn to hunt or kill prey from her. They may, however, learn these lessons with great difficulty later in life from another cat.

After first introducing dead prey to her litter, the mother next shows her kittens how to kill live prey. These lessons usually take place around nine to ten weeks. By now the kittens' instinctive hunting movements—lying in wait, stalking, pouncing, and the like—will have been perfected. The mother next needs to show her kittens how to make the killing bite.

Why do kittens kill? Animal behaviorists speculate that the kittens are stimulated to do so by the presence of live prey, by the rivalry between themselves and their mother, or by the rivalry among littermates.

All cats are intensely curious about scratchy and high-pitched squealing noises such as those made by mice. Cats will move quickly to the source of such sounds and investigate them. Cats also are attracted to any living animals their size or smaller.

Teaching and learning how to hunt is only one example of feline intelligence. There are countless other exam-

A kitten acquires its hunting skills from its mother. These skills include lying in wait, stalking, and pouncing upon prey.

ples; for instance, cats learn how to use litter boxes and even toilets. They learn to respond to their names and other commands. A cat will quickly learn how to drink water from a running faucet and figure out solutions to a variety of problems—especially if the end result advances her comfort.

In clinical tests for feline intelligence, researchers attached food to one of several strings. Before long, the cat under study had learned how to pull only that string to which a morsel of food was attached. In another intelligence test, the study subjects quickly figured out how to escape from intricate puzzle boxes and mazes.

Cats show their intelligence in other ways as well. For example, they remember things. Cats will remember how to open a door by jumping on the latch. They never forget how to find their way home. Once a cat learns how to get a human's attention—such as by tapping on doors or rattling objects—she retains these lessons. And the first time your cat learns how to scoop ice cream from a container or extract dry food from a packet, rest assured this is a lesson your pet will never forget!

Cats' intelligence is complemented by their high degree of awareness. The acuity of cats' senses exceeds that of human beings and many other animals. Their faculties of sight, hearing, touch, and smell are so finely developed that felines have earned the reputation of having a "sixth sense."

In addition to intelligence and awareness, cats possess such other traits as curiosity, determination, and dexterity. All these factors combine to make the domestic cat one of the world's most intelligent creatures.

COMMUNICATION

Human beings communicate with one another in more ways than we probably realize. We use different tones of voice for different situations, while subtle gestures contain a language of their own. Even odor plays an important role in the way we relate to each other, sometimes attracting or repelling us. We also communicate through eye contact—or avoiding it—and touch.

Similarly, cats have many ways to communicate with their own species and with the people in their lives. They constantly communicate with us and each other with every movement they make. They also express themselves through touch and through their sense of smell.

BODY LANGUAGE

Body language is perhaps the most complex way that felines communicate their rainbow of colorful emotions. They have a highly developed system of communication that uses most parts of their body—from ears to tail—to express what is going on in their minds.

Is your cat feeling contented? Frightened? Angry? By recognizing the following body signals, you'll be able to tell exactly what kind of mood your pet is in.

CONTENTED CAT

Cats commonly use body language to express their contentment, often in the way they sleep and arise from sleep. There is no better image of a creature at peace with the world than a cat snoozing away while curled tightly into a ball or stretched out upside down in the middle of your favorite armchair.

Upon awakening from a nap, a contented cat may yawn lazily and go through a luxurious series of stretching movements. These movements will be accompanied by heavy-lidded blinking of the eyes and gentle twitching of the whiskers.

The yawn really says it all. A long, slow, wide-mouthed yawn with a lot of teeth and a pink tongue is a sure sign that your pet feels safe and secure.

Here are some other ways a cat shows contentment:

1. The muscles will be relaxed.
2. The cat will be seated quietly with ears erect, indicating that she is alert and carefully watching what is going on.
3. Soft purring.
4. Washing with long, slow licks.
5. Upon seeing her owner, the cat will stand with her head lowered, hindquarters raised, tail held straight up. The tail tip is bent slightly forward and moves from side to side.
6. Rubbing of cheeks, whiskers, and tail against her owner. This marks a scent upon the owner's body.
7. The cat will wind between the owner's legs or jump onto his or her lap.

UPSET CAT (FRIGHTENED OR ANGRY)

Many situations can frighten or annoy a cat. You cat may become upset if she suddenly is placed in strange or unfamiliar surroundings, or if a strange cat or human approaches her.

In such situations, a cat will either sprint and hide until she feels more secure, or she will show how upset she is through the following body signals:

The frightened cat may crouch in a submissive position.

1. Body muscles will tense.

2. The cat will remain in a fixed position while she assesses the situation.

3. Her eyes will remain fixed on the stranger.

The angry cat's tail resembles a bottle brush.

4. If the cat is very anxious or afraid, the pupils of the eyes will dilate. The eyes will dart rapidly from side to side, looking for a way out. The cat may assume a submissive posture, crouching down with the ears flattened sideways across the head. The tail will be held low and the chin will be drawn in. She may roll on her back with a paw raised for self-defense, or she may try to make a dash for safety.

5. Each hair on the cat's tail will become extended until the tail looks like a bottle brush.

DEFENSIVE CAT

If the movements outlined above fail to defuse a disturbing situation, your cat's next reaction will be to stand her ground. She will continue to communicate the body signs described above, with more menacing additions:

The defensive cat, with arched back and bristling fur, makes herself look larger to ward off opponents.

The attacking cat bares her fangs and claws.

1. The defensive cat will growl, hiss, or spit.

2. She will arch her back.

3. The fur along her back will bristle.

4. The cat will display her fangs with her mouth wide open.

5. She will adopt a sideways stance and try to appear larger and more menacing.

6. The tail will be arched and bristling.

7. The ears will be flattened.

8. The whiskers will be bristling.

Attacking Cat

In an extreme situation, a frightened cat may prepare herself to attack. She will exhibit the following body signals:

1. The tail will be low and close to the ground, bristling and swishing.

2. The cat will crouch low.

3. The ears will be pricked and furled back.

4. The pupils will be reduced to slits, helping her to focus on her target.

5. The whiskers will bristle forward in order to sense all potential danger.

6. The claws will be extended.

7. The mouth will open wide with lips curled and fangs bared.

8. Snarls, hissing, and spitting will continue. The cat is ready to launch an attack by leaping at her adversary.

The Cat Who Is Ill

A cat who is not feeling well will usually not eat, will fail to wash herself, and may display the following body signals:

1. Her tail will be kept low.

2. She has a hunched-over appearance.

3. She will have a miserable facial expression. The eyes may be dull, the appearance of the face not bright, but depressed.

Desirous Cat

When your cat wants something from you, she will certainly let you know about it. If, for example, you walk into the kitchen and your cat bounds after you, persistently dipping and rubbing against your leg and trying to get your full attention, your pet is telling you that it is time to eat. Other body signals that indicate desire include the following:

A cat announces her desires by miaowing, stretching, and following her human companions.

1. Your cat will continue to gaze at you while miaowing.

2. She will perform a full body stretch and then touch you with her paw. She will repeat this motion until she gets your attention.

Keep in mind that while cats do not mind staring at you until they get what they want, they do not like being stared at. In fact, should your cat catch you observing her in some activity, she will either stop what she is doing altogether or continue in a more hesitant, self-conscious manner.

FACIAL EXPRESSIONS

Making faces is another way in which cats communicate their feelings. The shape of a cat's eyes and the motions of the ears and whiskers are rich in meaning. You might want to become familiar with some facial characteristics.

CONTENTED CAT

1. Perky ears.

2. Pupils bright and normal for prevailing light.

3. Relaxed whiskers.

The contented cat's face and whiskers are relaxed, her ears erect.

ANGRY CAT

1. Ears are erect but furled back. This change in ear position is one of a

The pupils of a cat's eyes become slits when she is angry.

number of body changes that signal to another individual that the cat is in an offensive stance.

2. Pupils constrict to slits.
3. Whiskers bristle forward.

FRIGHTENED CAT

1. Ears are flattened.
2. Eyes are wide open.
3. Whiskers are flattened.

A cat expresses fear by flattening her ears and whiskers.

PLAYING OR HUNTING CAT

1. Pupils are open.
2. Ears are pricked and thrust forward.
3. Whiskers are thrust forward in order to sense all possible stimuli.

VOCALIZATION

Cats possess an extensive vocabulary. In addition to commonplace sounds such as purring, hissing, and growling, up to sixteen distinct vocalizations have been identified. These range from suckling sounds that encourage kittens to take milk to a variety of "miaows" that express everything from pain to disapproval. Sometimes cats use facial expressions to accompany a certain tone of voice. When a cat wants something, for example, a "miaow" is usually accompanied by a questioning look on her face.

TOUCH

Cats also communicate by touch, very often using this sense to express interest and affection. The rubbing of noses and mutual grooming are examples of how cats use touch to communicate feelings.

Touch also provides the cat with a vital awareness of her immediate surroundings and serves to warn against injury or danger. Specialized nerve endings, or receptors, that respond to various sensations are found throughout a cat's skin. When stimulated, these nerve endings send messages rapidly through connecting nerves and up the spinal cord to the sensory areas of the feline brain.

The whiskers comprise the most important component of your cat's sense of touch. The whiskers, or vibrissae, are coarse, stiff hairs that stick out from the body and act like antennae. They also define the placement of an object near a cat's head by gauging changes of pressure created by movement. They translate the slightest contact with an object into sensory impulses.

THE LANGUAGE OF CATS

Basically, cat language consists of three general sound categories: murmurs, vowels, and strained, high-intensity sounds. Murmurs include purring and the soft sounds used for greeting, calling attention, acknowledgment, and approval.

There are several types of vowels, or the "miaow." They're used to demand, beg, complain, and express bewilderment. By the way a cat pronounces her "miaows," an attentive cat owner can recognize a small but impressive feline vocabulary. Pay close attention to your cat's "miaows," and you will soon become familiar with such concepts as "out," "in," "please," "thank you," "help," "food," "come here," and "no."

High-intensity, strained sounds make up a cat-to-cat vocabulary that ranges from snarls and growls to hisses and wails. These sounds are usually heard when your cat is confronted by a strange animal or human, is in pain, or is mating. And if you have ever seen a cat seated on a windowsill and unable to get at a bird perched outside, you may have heard yet another cat sound: the curious, tooth-rattling stutter of frustration.

Whiskers help communicate many things to your cat, such as whether a small opening is large enough to get through without injury. The vibrissae also are an important supplement to a feline's vision. If a cat is wandering around in the dark, for example, the whiskers are a great aid in preventing collisions with objects.

SMELL

The sense of smell is frequently used by cats to communicate. Cats have various scent glands that produce chemicals called pheromones, which convey information about themselves to other felines. Some of the scent glands that produce this chemical are located on the forehead and lips and around the anus.

When cats want to communicate with each other, they usually do so by scent-marking with urine, anal-sac secretions, and skin-gland secretions.

URINE MARKINGS

Male cats who are not neutered scent-mark by spraying urine. Because cats are territorial, such spraying is how tomcats (unneutered male cats) let other cats know who controls a particular patch of turf. Spraying also suppresses the competitive sexual behavior of other young tomcats.

ANAL-SAC SECRETIONS

While cats are well-known for carefully covering up their feces—whether in the litter box or in natural earth—they do use anal-sac odors to communicate. This can be observed when two strange cats investigate each other. They tend to spend a considerable amount of time circling each other and trying to smell each other's backsides.

Two anal sacs, or "scent glands," each about the size of a pea, are located under the cat's tail on each side of the anus. They mark the stool with an odor that identifies that particular individual and establishes her territory.

SKIN SECRETIONS

When your cat bunts—rubs the side of her head against you or a piece of furniture—she may be using a form of olfactory communication. Glandular secretions from your cat's face are being left on the object being bunted—a calling card of sorts. This is also true when your cat twines herself around the leg of a chair or around your legs. She is transferring identifying odors from her tail glands to the object at hand. The message is: "This is my turf. No trespassing."

SOCIAL BEHAVIOR

Cats are social animals. They have a well-developed social order, territorial rules and regulations, and prescribed sexual behavior. They play together, communicate, and are clearly capable of forming bonds with humans, other cats, and other animals.

Much has been written about the life and habits of the domestic cat. This section examines some of the more common forms of a cat's social behavior.

SOCIAL ORDER

Wild cats live in groups based on the mother-kitten unit. Occasionally, some mature males in such groups take on a paternal role. Most males, however, remain solitary nomads.

Domestic cats are much more social. If cats from completely different litters are introduced to each other as kittens, they will cohabit amicably. Cats with no other cats around generally direct their social urges toward their owners. If your cat is allowed to roam outdoors, she will soon become part of the community of cats in your neighborhood, block, or apartment complex.

This type of feline social club usually meets on neutral turf at night. The cats become an association; each cat knows all the other cats in this association, and they organize into a distinct hierarchy. Pity the strange cat that wanders into the neighborhood and wants to become a member of the club! Such a stranger will probably have to fight her way in before being allowed membership privileges.

While the makeup of the male social order is tightly structured, the hierarchical arrangement for female cats is very loose-knit and is based on motherhood. The unneutered female with the most kittens heads up the pecking order. Females who have been neutered after having borne litters experience a rapid social descent in this hierarchy.

Among males, the tomcat—the unneutered male—who is the roughest and toughest in battle against all comers becomes king of cats. Nor do unneutered males escape such trial by combat; they must fight several toms to establish a rank in the pecking order. These fights may even be spread out over several nights.

The dominant toms command the largest territories but do not necessarily mate with the greatest number of available females. In fact, sometimes females will choose to mate with cats who are lower in the hierarchy of neighborhood cats.

When a complete cat, or tom, is neutered, he gradually loses his standing in the hierarchy. Neutering weakens male sex hormone levels. Neutering aside, a dominant tom may lose his ranking if another cat proves to be stronger in combat.

Social order is also quickly established in households, barns, or other environments in which a large number of cats are forced to live together in a small space. In such a situation, a very rigid dominance order with a single leader usually emerges. The leader will have absolute priority over all the other cats for the best sleeping spot, first chance at food, and other privileges.

TERRITORIALITY

Yet cats are not generally known to be social animals in that they generally do not live in groups. Loners, they instinctively fight to protect their own territory, in order to ensure that they will have everything they need to survive. Whether you own an indoor or an outdoor cat, your pet is territorial by nature. Every cat has her own personal space—and will defend it if necessary. If your pet is an indoor cat, she will stake out a room, a chair, or a bed as her territorial zone. Should you have several indoor cats, they will jointly own their territory and defend it against any feline strangers. Outdoor cats, meanwhile, claim territory based on their hierarchical status.

Among outdoor cats, the stronger and more powerful the cat, the larger the territory she will claim. Toms control and defend the most territory, but neutered cats and females also will stake out turf and fight with even the toughest tom to keep it.

A cat's outdoor territory can vary in size. Dominant cats will stake out and mark huge tracts of land, including the gardens of catless households. Females

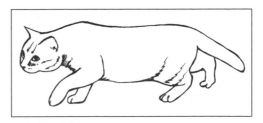

Once a cat has marked her territory, she will patrol it regularly.

HOW DO CATS IDENTIFY THEIR TERRITORY?

Most commonly they do so by spraying with urine to make "boundary posts." This usually consists of brief spurts of urination on vertical surfaces. Cats will also scratch visual signals with their claws on trees or fences, and they may rub their bodies against trees, posts, or fences.

with kittens will claim small amounts of territory and defend them fiercely. Female cats are especially intolerant of territorial intrusions from other females.

There is an exception to the territorial instinct among outdoor cats. They often establish a neutral meeting ground where males and females congregate on occasion—mostly to socialize and sometimes to mate. In such a setting, groups of cats sit peacefully but remain three to nineteen feet from one another.

Cats on their way to such nocturnal communal meeting grounds obey strict rules of passage. No cat will intrude on the private territory of any other cat while heading toward this neutral zone. If fact, cats establish major "highways" to such meeting places. Any cat moving along this route has right of way against any other cat approaching from a different direction, whatever the approaching cat's hierarchical community standing may be.

AGGRESSIVE BEHAVIOR

For both indoor and outdoor cats, the approach of a strange feline with hostile intentions is certain to set the scene for a noisy and nasty confrontation.

In approaching each other, both cats will walk on tiptoe with their tails slowly lashing from side to side. They will turn their heads from side to side and make direct eye contact. All these gestures are designed to be threatening and intimidating. The goal of each cat is to bully the other into submission. Sometimes all this body language works: One of the cats decides that an adversary seems a bit too much to handle and slinks off.

More often than not, however, neither of the two cats will give any ground despite all the hissing, snarling, and menacing body language. The two felines will continue to approach each other cautiously.

Cats bent on such a collision course will slowly walk past each other. The aggressor will then spring, trying to get a grip on her rival by the nape of the neck.

The cat that has been attacked will immediately assume a defensive posture, throwing herself on her back for protection. The two adversaries will then lie on the ground, belly to belly, and claw, bite, and yowl at each other.

This combative behavior will continue until one of the cats—usually the attacker—jumps free. This gives the opponent several options. It can move into another defensive position, launch an attack of its own, or simply run away. If the opponent decides to flee, the victor will usually pursue it.

SEXUAL BEHAVIOR

An integral part of feline social behavior revolves around the cat's sexual urges and need to mate. For cats as for almost any animal, success in reproduction is the key to species survival, which is why so much feline behavior is linked to sex.

Sexual development in cats begins at puberty, when the female's ovaries mature and male's testicles begin to produce sperm and sex hormones. Cats enter puberty somewhere between three and eighteen months. Females generally mature sexually at three to nine months, males at seven to twelve months. Feral, or wild cats, may not mature sexually until they are fifteen to eighteen months old.

Females usually go into "heat"—the desire to mate—several times each year, in late winter to early spring, and again in late spring to early summer. Males go through a period of springtime sexual excitement, or "rut," which diminishes to low sexual activity during the autumn. When choosing a cat, this schedule of sexual activity may help you decide whether to select a male or female (see p. 51). You will also want to read about the pros and cons of spaying or neutering your cat in the section on responsible ownership (see p. 48).

You can easily tell when your female cat is in heat. She will become exceptionally affectionate, rubbing herself more than usual on your legs and household objects, often with her chin down along the floor. During this period she undergoes gradual buildup of hormonal levels. If your cat begins to push herself along the floor with her head to one side, then flips over into a roll, rubs her head on a paw, or grooms herself, she is in heat. She will also spend a lot of time in a head-down crouch with her rump elevated and her hind legs moving as though treading water. As if all this activity weren't distracting enough, there will be a low, throaty vocal accompaniment to all this unusual behavior.

This constant motion and vocalization can be irritating, but if you let your cat out in this condition, she will undoubtedly return pregnant. The best way to avoid the problem entirely is to get her spayed.

You can tell if your unneutered male cat is in rut when he begins spraying with a backing motion and a shaking of the tail. Your neutered cat may also go through these motions, but is less likely to actually spray.

When a female cat goes into heat, most of the male cats in the neighborhood know about it. They can smell and hear her condition. In this attracted and aroused state, the male cats begin to assemble around the needy female.

Her need may even attract cats from outside the neighborhood, often provoking noisy, bloody catfights between the locals and outsiders.

All this commotion among toms may last a few days, because females come into heat several days before they are ready to mate. The victorious male usually mates with the female.

Courtship between male and female cats is very ritualized and may last for several hours before copulation takes

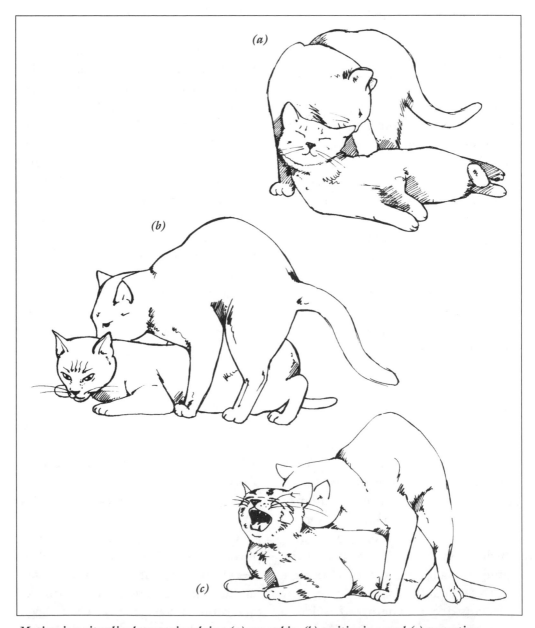

Mating is a ritualized process involving (a) courtship, (b) positioning, and (c) mounting.

place. Cats about to mate engage in a traditional pursuit and avoidance behavior.

Once the female is ready to consummate the relationship, she will crouch and rub her body against the ground. She may begin to knead with her feet as she lowers the front of her body and raises her posterior in a submissive posture.

At this point in the mating process, the female shifts her tail to one side, giving the male complete access to her vulva. Little hairs around the vulva become erect to make the target more visible.

The male cat must know exactly when the female is ready. A premature attempt to mount her may result in a vigorous attack.

When both parties are ready, the male grasps the female by the skin over the nape of her neck. This is done to immobilize her during the sexual act. Ejaculation and ovulation take place within five to fifteen seconds and involve a few deep pelvic thrusts by the male.

At the moment of ejaculation, the female releases a loud, piercing cry followed by an almost explosive separation as she turns upon her mate.

EATING

Eating is very much part of a cat's social behavior. Cats usually make a great production about it—especially in terms of letting you know that they are hungry.

Cats like to eat many small meals during the course of a day, sometimes as many as twelve. Even if a large quantity of food is placed before them, unlike dogs they will rarely devour all the food in one sitting. Instead, they will keep coming back for seconds and thirds.

Felines are also notoriously finicky eaters. Although they are classified as carnivores, most cats prefer fish to meat. They also get bored with a steady diet of the same food and prefer novelty.

If your cat's intake of food increases or decreases during certain months of the year, do not worry. Your cat's appetite will increase during cold weather and decrease when the weather turns warm. Cats also gain and lose body weight in cycles of several months' duration.

However, should your cat continue to lose weight or experience a persistent loss of appetite, and there are other symptoms of disease, consult your veterinarian.

PLAY

Every living creature needs to play, and cats are no exception. Play for cats is a release of pent-up energy. When kittens play together or with their mother, they are also preparing for adult life by learning all the movements necessary for attack and defense.

If you have two cats at home and they are playing together, what may look to be a rough-and-tumble game really is not. Your cats are well aware that their game of combat is not in

Play provides a nondestructive outlet for stored energy.

earnest, and they will not harm each other. Watch this behavior and you will see that when the dominant cat is holding her mate, if that hold causes any pain, a certain growl will make the aggressive cat let go.

Kittens begin to play at about three weeks of age. This play starts off with the kittens gently pawing at each other. As their coordination improves, they begin biting, chasing, and rolling.

Social play increases from four to eleven weeks of age and then rapidly declines. By this time, the kittens seem to pair off during play periods, which usually takes place four times a day. At nine weeks, kittens spend almost an hour each day playing.

WASHING

There is no more pleasurable and relaxing sight than to watch your cat wash herself. Animal behaviorists believe that the action of light and warmth on a cat's coat sets off this reflex.

In washing, your cat uses her tongue, paws, and even teeth to clean most of her head and body. The tongue of your cat is covered with tiny projections—called papillae—that are used to wash and comb the coat.

When your cat wakes up or finishes eating, she will first lick her mouth and lips. She will then lick a paw until it is damp and use that paw to clean one side of her head, ears, eyes, and nose. The cat will continue washing until she feels clean. Then she licks the other paw and begins to wash the other side of her body. Next, your cat will lick each shoulder and foreleg, followed by a washing of her sides, flanks, hindlegs, the genitals and tail.

Should there be tangles or burrs in her coat or between her toes, your cat will use her teeth to bite them out. This meticulous grooming will conclude with a careful removal—with her teeth—of dirt or mud on the pads.

If you have two cats or a mother

Two cats who share the same home will often wash each other.

CATS AND DREAMS

Do cats dream? Watch your pet sleep; she certainly can *appear* to be dreaming. Paws and claws move. Ears flick, whiskers twitch. At times your cat may even talk in her sleep. Some scientists believe that in the deep sleep stage, cats do indeed dream. But researchers are certain that whether asleep or awake, cats are constantly receiving and programming information from environmental stimuli.

and kitten, you will see the mother wash her kitten or the two cats grooming each other as a sign of affection.

Young kittens start washing themselves at about three weeks of age. At about the age of six weeks, when they are eating solids, they will already be able to wash their paws and faces quite well and clean up their tail ends each time they use the litter box.

SLEEPING

Cats like to spend a lot of time sleeping. Studies have shown that cats sleep an average of sixteen hours a day, usually in the form of short "cat naps." Experts believe that a cat's great delight in rest and relaxation is inherited from her wild relatives, who use up all their energy hunting at high speed but in short spurts.

Cats like to sleep where it is warm, so do not be surprised to find your cat contentedly curled up on top of your stove, a nose-length away from a sizzling radiator, or in your bedding when you wake up in the morning.

PROBLEM BEHAVIOR

Cats in the wild can choose their own company, remove themselves from situations in which conflicts arise, and develop their own cycles of daily activity. The urban domestic cat does not always have these options, yet her basic physiology and behavior are closely linked to those of her wild cousins.

Even the best-mannered cat may at times suddenly develop strange behavioral problems. When stress begins to build, like people your cat needs some kind of outlet for it. Experiments in

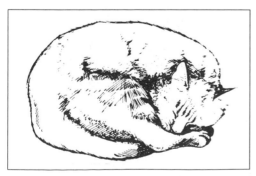

Cats spend an average of sixteen hours per day asleep.

animal psychology do seem to indicate that domestic cats exposed to irreconcilable conflicts not only develop severe behavioral problems but also become physically ill, often with psychosomatic disorders—in other words, disorders that have no physical causes.

Before you go rushing off to obtain the services of a pet psychologist, however, remember that most of your cat's common behavioral problems are treatable, often without your needing to enlist the aid of such an expert.

Keep in mind that all feline misbehavior is nothing more than the response of your pet to some stressful situation in her life. You may not understand why your cat is suddenly acting the way she is, and you certainly may not approve. But if your cat could speak, she would probably tell you exactly why she has begun to behave differently.

If your cat is acting badly, using force to try to change the cat's behavior simply will not work. Physical punishment will not rectify the problem but will offend your cat and will cause her to dislike and distrust you. This is particularly true if you mete out your punishment more than a few seconds after your cat has misbehaved. Your cat simply will not make the connection between her actions and your punishment if, for example, fifteen minutes have passed since the deed was done.

It is also a mistake to constantly scold your cat. Such behavior on your part will have no effect other than turning a happy, loving pet into a sulking, fearful creature.

The best approach to dealing with a cat who has begun to misbehave is to use psychology rather than punishment. It's wise to anticipate trouble and head it off. For example, if your cat leaps onto the kitchen table while you and your family are eating dinner, don't angrily shoo her away. Instead, experts suggest that you feed your cat well just before you eat. Cats like to sleep immediately after eating. So while you and your family are enjoying your meal, your well-fed cat will be enjoying a nice snooze.

Another common example of bad behavior that can be rectified simply is the strange taste for electrical cords cats sometimes develop. If you see your cat chewing on a cord, don't yell at her. A much better solution is to coat the electrical cords in your home with "Bitter Apple Jelly"—a repulsive-tasting product available in most pet stores.

Stress contributes to a domestic cat's misbehavior, but behavioral problems are also caused by a cat's inability to find a release for all her instincts and energies. Most naughty behavior is simply your cat's way of burning off excess energy.

For example, if a household cat with a hunting instinct has no prey to pursue, she will redirect her energies into chasing or ambushing you as you walk from room to room. You can easily rechannel this impulse into more constructive behavior by attaching a ball to a ribbon or a string and letting your cat chase it around the room.

A good workout is also the best way to calm down an overactive pet—especially one that lately has been devastating the house after you leave. Involve your pet in strenuous exercise just before you leave home. The exercise will use up excess energy and help keep your cat fit. It will also provide your cat with the attention she may crave. More likely than not, your cat will peacefully sleep away the hours until you return.

DESTRUCTIVE SCRATCHING

Your cat's razor-sharp claws can cause serious damage to your furniture, curtains, and other household items. If your cat has been engaging in such destructive behavior, you should first understand that your cat is not intentionally trying to be bad. All cats

If you find your cat frequently scratching at curtains and furniture, consider purchasing a scratching post.

scratch objects as a way to groom themselves. They groom their claws by catching the outer, worn part on a rough surface and drawing it through the material until the old claw flakes off. This exposes the new claw underneath.

The solution to this problem may be as simple as buying a scratching post. In fact, if you have a scratching post in your home from the day you obtain your pet, the chances are a destructive scratching problem will never develop in the first place. When you purchase a scratching post, make certain that it is an upright stand with carpeted covering that is not overly dense or too soft. A good rule of thumb is that the post be tall enough so that your cat can reach up to the top of it while standing on her hind legs.

If you have just obtained a kitten, keep the post near the kitten's sleeping quarters. You can train your kitten to use a scratching post by taking her to the post several times a day. Stand the kitten up against the post and run her paws down along it. While doing this, murmur encouraging words to your new pet so that she sees that you approve of this activity.

If your adult cat ignores the scratching post, try sprinkling some catnip on or about it and she will soon get the idea.

DECLAWING

If scratching becomes insufferable, declawing is an option. You should be aware, however, that declawing is a surgical procedure that involves the removal of the entire last joint of each toe. The toes are then stitched or bandaged tightly to keep them from hemorrhaging.

This procedure requires use of a general anesthesia and means several days of hospitalization for your young pet or pets. After the stitches or bandages are removed, your kitten's feet will be rather painful for at least a week.

Many cat lovers claim that declawing is inhumane and causes behavioral changes in cats. Many veterinarians, on the other hand, say that declawed cats can live normal lives without any problem. Many veterinarians also suggest that only the front legs of cats be declawed, because hind legs rarely cause any damage.

If you decide to declaw your kitten or cat, the animal must never be allowed to go outdoors. A declawed cat is a defenseless cat. Consider the matter carefully, and discuss it with your veterinarian. If you can get your cat or kittens to use a scratching post instead of destroying expensive furniture, that should always be your first choice. If you have a kitten and want to declaw her, try to have the procedure done as early as possible.

ever, a cat's attraction to houseplants is simply a result of extreme curiosity. Cats will frequently nibble at greenery just to find out what it is.

Such curiosity, however, can be extremely hazardous to your pet—particularly if the plant nibbled on is a poisonous one (see Poison, p. 264). If you notice that your cat is developing a plant-nibbling habit, try to dissuade her from doing so immediately.

One simple way to do this is to purchase a water pistol. At the moment your cat approaches a plant, squirt her with water. Since most cats dislike water, your pet should quickly learn to avoid the plant. You may also want to place plants where your cat cannot reach them.

If your plants are outdoors and your cat is allowed outside, fencing them off may be a good idea. By the way, studies show that outdoor cats are much less interested in nibbling at plants than their confined counterparts are.

Another suggestion is to visit your local pet store and purchase plants that are safe for your pet to chew on—such as live catnip—while removing your more decorative houseplants from her reach.

EATING PLANTS

Cats are carnivorous animals, so why do they like to eat plants? One answer is that plants—and the chlorophyll in them—can aid digestion. Mostly, how-

SOILING

One of the most serious problems among household cats is house soiling—urinating and defecating outside the litter box.

Something is obviously wrong when your cat begins to engage in such behavior, because cats learn early in life how to use a litter box. Before trying any behavioral techniques or consulting with a pet psychologist, you should first make an appointment with your veterinarian.

Soiling can be a symptom of serious health problems such as cystitis, a bladder infection that is more likely to affect male cats than female ones (see Urinary System Problems, Chapter Seventeen). Symptoms of this disease include leaving small amounts of urine around the house, blood in the urine, frequent urination, or straining over the litter box with no results.

If your male cat suddenly begins to spray urine against the walls, he may not be ill but simply expressing some type of territorial, competitive, or sexual drive. In most of these cases, spraying will stop within a few weeks if you get your cat neutered. Female cats in heat also may spray for similar reasons.

Other common reasons why cats soil include the following:

1. The litter box is not clean enough. Try removing stools from the litter with a scooper twice a day. Wash the litter box and refill it with fresh litter weekly.
2. The litter box is too small or too flimsy. Replace it with a larger, stronger box. If your cat is a deep digger and spills litter all over the place, covered litter boxes are available at most pet stores.
3. The location of the litter box is not private enough. This is often sufficient reason for your cat to seek out an alternative site. Find a more private location for the box.
4. The litter box is too far removed from where your cat likes to spend most of her time. It does not make any sense to put a litter box in the basement if your cat spends most of her waking hours in an upstairs area.
5. If a litter box is too close to where your cat eats her meals, your pet may decide not to use the box.

Other reasons why your cat may be soiling the household include her objection to a new brand of litter, refusal to share her litter box with a newly arrived cat (there should be at least one litter box per cat in your household), or resentment at being left alone for too long.

Cats sometimes experience anxiety and insecurity. If emotional factors are behind this misbehavior—such as resentment at being left alone or jealousy over the arrival of a new cat or baby in the house—you must give your cat extra attention and support until she feels reassured. If your cat becomes overly anxious, you may want to ask your vet to provide a short-term supply of tranquilizers.

If "accidents" happen and the culprit is an elderly cat, try to be understanding. Aging cats sometimes have a difficult time getting to the litter box when they have to go.

Wherever soiling takes place, it is important that you quickly remove all traces of the urine or feces or your cat will become attracted to that spot and will repeat the behavior. After the area is cleaned, spray it with a cat repellent or odor counteractant, both available at most local pet stores.

DEALING WITH AGGRESSION

If you find your cat stalking, pouncing, and nipping at your feet as part of her play, she is probably acting out predatory instincts.

This behavior may be amusing at first, but it can also become a problem if the nipping causes an injury or if the surprise attack causes you or someone in your family to fall and get hurt. In such a case, the cat's aggressive behavior must be immediately curtailed.

Cats often behave this way because they are left alone too long and have not been played with much by their owner. You can resolve this problem several ways.

One obvious solution is to purchase a second cat to keep your pet from being lonely and feeling neglected. If another cat is out of the question, try purchasing moving, active toys that will engage the interest and energy of your pet. Such toys, of course, do not operate by themselves. You will need to spend some time winding the toys up or otherwise setting them in motion.

If the sudden pouncing behavior is getting on your nerves, and you know your cat is waiting to spring at you from under the table, try wiggling a string with a ball attached to it. This will not only divert your cat's attention from attacking your feet, but will also help teach your cat to play with inanimate but moving toys.

Perhaps the simplest solution of all is to take time to play with your cat.

To stop your cat from nipping or biting, one effective method is to startle your cat with a water gun or plant sprayer. Whistles can also be used. Such punishment is also effective because it will not cause your cat to dislike you. Your pet will not directly associate either the water or the sound of the whistle with you.

If your cat nips at you irritably while being stroked, or displays aggression by taking hold of your hand in a mock bite position, you should immediately reproach her with a firm "no" command. If that fails to loosen your cat's grip on your hand, flick on the top of her nose with your thumb and forefinger. Any feline that displays such irritability or aggressive behavior upon being petted should be stroked more gently and for shorter periods of time.

If your cat's aggression is directed at a second household pet—especially if there is hissing, spitting, growling, biting, scratching, and other hostile behavior—you must immediately remove the two cats from each others' sight completely.

Because cats are curious creatures, after a few days of separation each will begin wondering what happened to the other one. After this cooling-off period, you may gradually begin to reintroduce the two cats to each other.

Do this at mealtime, with the cats in separate carriers or cages at opposite ends of the room.

At each day's feeding time, gradually move the cats in their containers closer together. The idea is to try and teach your pets that they will be rewarded with food only in the presence of each other.

Only when both cats in their containers can eat together peacefully and side by side—no hissing or growling—is it safe to attempt to let them play together again.

PART II

CARING
FOR
YOUR CAT

BEFORE YOU OWN A CAT

NO OTHER CREATURE is as charming, graceful, and irresistible as a cat, which is why a special relationship between people and cats has existed for thousands of years. Whatever the type of cat and for whatever purpose they come into our lives, felines always exert a positive influence on their human owners.

Before you set out to get a cat, however, you should be fully aware of the responsibilities you are about to undertake.

RESPONSIBLE OWNERSHIP

Owning a cat means being willing to spend time with your new pet. You will have to show him kindness and make certain that he is eating right. As a cat owner, you must make sure that the animal is regularly groomed and kept healthy; that includes scheduling routine veterinary checkups and making certain that your cat is properly vaccinated (see Vaccinations, p. 79).

Other responsibilities include providing your new pet with essentials, such as fresh water daily and a litter box in which the litter is changed regularly. If you have problems scooping out fecal waste each day or cleaning a litter box, a cat may not be the right pet for you.

Owning a cat also means providing other basics for his comfort and care: scratching posts, carrying cases, food bowls, and toys. Bear in mind, as well, that while cats can be left alone for longer periods than dogs, they do get lonely and need human companionship. If you travel often, cat ownership may not be for you.

Cat owners are responsible for the health of their pets. If you have never owned a cat before, you should call some local veterinarians to get ballpark figures for such expenses as vaccinations, spaying, declawing, and routine examinations, to ensure that you are fully informed of the possible medical costs. If you are thinking about owning a cat but find you cannot afford vaccinations, you should strongly consider opting for a less expensive pet. Owning a cat is a financial responsibility: Out of fairness to your pet, research expenses in advance and be certain you will be able to meet them.

While most cats do not require as much room as dogs, they do need enough space to play and exercise. Do you have the room and the time to play with your cat? If you are worried about your expensive household furnishings being scratched, you should think twice about obtaining a cat. Cats can frequently test your patience. They are often up to some mischief, such as digging in flower pots. Are you the type of personality who might flare angrily at such behavior?

Cat ownership also brings a new responsibility to the community you live in. If you do allow your cat to go outside, you must make certain that he doesn't wander freely and disturb other people and their pets. If you live in an apartment building, you must first determine whether you will be permitted to keep a cat.

Another important responsibility concerns the issue of unregulated breeding. It's very important not to add to the feline homeless population by allowing your cat to have unwanted kittens. Many pet owners turn such kittens out on the streets if they cannot find someone to adopt them. If you are not willing to keep the kittens or to find them homes, you need to be prepared to spay or neuter any cat you may acquire.

These are only some of the things to consider before obtaining a cat. If you are willing to manage the responsibilities involved, your new pet will probably be quite happy in your household.

CHOOSING THE RIGHT CAT

Once you have decided to own a cat, you must decide what kind to get. Should you purchase a pedigreed cat or adopt an ordinary house pet from the animal shelter? Do you want a kitten or an adult cat? A male or a female?

If you have your heart set on a purebred, the first thing you should do is begin gathering information on the various breeds. You can begin your homework by rereading the section on breeds in Chapter 1. Next, check the bookstore or public library; you will find many excellent books on the subject. (See also the Resources section at the back of this book.)

It's important to use common sense in choosing a purebred cat. If you live in a city apartment with no access to the outdoors, select a breed that is quiet and does not require large exercise areas. If you are a country or suburban dweller with plenty of yard space, a lively breed that enjoys the outdoor life—such as the Somali—is an excellent choice.

Are there children or other pets in your household? Then make sure that the breed you select is good with kids (most are) and other animals. Purebreds often require grooming, but if you do not want to groom your cat each day, a short-haired breed is preferable to a long-haired one.

If your only consideration in choosing a cat is finding one to love and care for, and who in return will provide you with affection and companionship, then you should make a trip to your local animal shelter, which is filled with cats of all ages in desperate need of a good home. These cats are usually devoted and loving creatures who would otherwise be put to death.

PET SHOPS VERSUS BREEDERS

If it is a pedigreed cat that you want, your next step is deciding where to get him. Many purebred kittens are sold through pet shops or breeders. Sometimes you can even find older pedigreed cats waiting for adoption in animal shelters.

Breeders keep the strongest, healthiest cats, however, and are usually your best source for pedigreed kittens. While it is possible to buy a good-quality kitten from a pet store, keep in mind that these shops generally buy their pedigreed cats from local breeders or commercial breeders. If these kittens were as desirable as the breeders wanted them to be, they probably would have sold them themselves. Also, pet store owners are not familiar with the temperament, health, or background of the kittens' parents. It is best that you not buy a pedigreed kitten from a pet store until your veterinarian first examines him. You should also avoid any breeder or pet store owner who tries to rush you into making a purchase, and be wary of any "cut-rate" or "bargain" kittens.

BREEDERS

The object of most reputable breeders is to raise friendly, intelligent, mild-tempered pets. Reputable breeders also will not sell sick cats.

How do you locate breeders? Many of the best breeders advertise in newspapers. Cat shows are another excellent source for contacting breeders. There are also magazines—such as *Cats* magazine—that carry ads from breeders.

Breeders charge more for the cats they sell than pet shops do, but you are getting a better quality cat. If you buy a pedigreed cat from a breeder (or pet store, for that matter), make certain that you will be allowed to return the kitten within a given period if he does not pass a veterinarian's examination.

Also make certain that you get the cat's "papers"—especially the registration certificate that tells you that the cat's records and his pedigree are on

---

PAPERS TO ASK FOR UPON PURCHASING A PEDIGREED CAT

- **Registration certificate**
- **The kitten's pedigree or family tree**
- **Proof of vaccinations**
- **A complete health record**
- **A record of the health and temperament of the kitten's parents**
- **A list of foods the kitten has been eating**

---

file with one of the cat fancier's associations—when you pay for the cat. (See the Resources section for the names of some of the major associations.)

ANIMAL SHELTERS

If nonpedigree cats are more your cup of tea, an animal shelter is often the best place to adopt one. Shelters operated by various anticruelty societies are filled with adorable kittens and older cats just waiting for a loving owner. You can find the phone number for your local anticruelty society in the telephone directory.

Most animal shelters will simply ask you a few questions to make certain that you understand the responsibility of pet ownership. The cost of purchasing a kitten or cat from any of these shelters is quite low, and you can rest assured that any cat you adopt has already been properly vaccinated. Many shelters provide affordable spaying, neutering, and preliminary vaccinations; some even give complimentary ID tags and cat food to new pet owners.

ADOPTING A STRAY

You may not be thinking about getting a cat at all, and suddenly you come across a stray who changes your mind. While homeless cats may be rather shy and reserved, they are no less friendly than any other cats, and there is no good reason not to adopt such an animal.

If the stray cat or kitten you find looks well-fed and is tame, there is a strong likelihood that he belongs to someone in the neighborhood. You should not take such a cat home without first trying to locate his owner.

On the other hand, if the cat looks thin and ragged, or if you discover him hanging around your house on the lookout for scraps of food, you may assume that he either escaped from some household or was abandoned.

Once you have decided to adopt a stray, your first order of business is to have him undergo a thorough veterinary examination. Cats who roam freely often suffer many physical forms of neglect. They also frequently suffer from various illnesses, especially ringworm and toxoplasma, which is another good reason to have a veterinarian examine him. Exercise some precautions before taking your cat to the veterinarian; if you suspect external parasites, you may want to wear gloves when handling him.

KITTENS VERSUS CATS

When you acquire a grown cat, you know exactly what you are getting. His personality and habits have already been established, which can be a benefit or a drawback, depending on the cat's temperament. Additionally, a mature cat requires less supervision and training than a kitten does. What you will miss is the opportunity of affecting his personality while he is growing up.

Kittens, while charming to watch, require lots of attention. Not only do you have to feed them more than once a day, but they keep erratic schedules and require constant supervision. You may have a greater opportunity to help in the development of a kitten's personality, but unlike well-trained adult cats, they do not know how to conduct themselves properly in a household. If you already own a cat and want a second one, however, it is best to acquire a kitten, who may be less threatening to your current cat.

MALE OR FEMALE?

Your choice of a male or female cat is a question of personal preference.

There are no sex-linked character differences between male and female cats. Both male and female cats are loving and companionable. An altered cat may become an even more attentive and affectionate pet; male and female cats that have been altered will not roam in search of sexual gratification or to work off hormone-induced aggression. They tend to be much more content with their human owners. If, however, you wish to breed and exhibit cats, it is best to buy a female.

LONG-HAIRED OR SHORT-HAIRED?

Whatever cat you own, some grooming will be necessary. Short-haired cats, of course, are much easier to groom. Long-haired breeds require daily combing and brushing because their coats quickly become matted when not cared for.

If you suffer from allergies, it might be wiser to purchase a short-haired cat, which tends to shed less. Also, if you don't want to spend hours vacuuming up cat hair, then a short-haired cat should be your choice.

LITTERMATES: PROS AND CONS

If you already own a cat and are planning to get a second one, remember that cats are very jealous and territorial. There is bound to be some animosity in the beginning. Even if it is a kitten that you bring into your household, your older cat is likely to hiss, slap, and gen-

CATS AND THE ELDERLY

There is no better therapy for loneliness than a feline companion. Research has proven that cats introduced into the lives of elderly persons who live alone cause remarkable improvement in their emotional, physical, and psychological well-being.

If you are a senior citizen who is living alone, or if you know an elderly person who may benefit from a feline companion, you should know that humane societies often have programs to provide well-mannered cats to the elderly free of charge.

Many humane societies also sponsor "Animal-Assisted Therapy" programs, in which animals such as cats and dogs are brought into senior-citizen centers, hospitals, and various types of convalescent centers on a regular basis. The success and popularity of these programs is so great that in many areas there is often a long waiting list of nursing homes and other institutions who want to participate.

erally give the new kitten a hard time. If you are to have two male cats in your house, it is wise to be sure they are both neutered. (Neutering should be done at seven to ten months of age.)

On the other hand, a second cat will, over the long run, provide company for your pet. The two cats will eventually work things out and enjoy each other. You can also consider bringing a puppy into your house. Contrary to popular belief, dogs and cats are not natural enemies. Your best bet is to establish a cat-and-dog relationship when both are in the kitten and puppy stages.

CATS AND CHILDREN

While cats and children can coexist happily, you should think twice about getting a cat for a very young child. Cats are, by nature, very sensitive creatures. They don't like rough handling, loud noises, and hasty movements. A very young child may handle a cat roughly without meaning to, or may ruffle his nerves with too much noise and activity. Cats like to spend much of their day resting, and a small child simply may not understand that.

Most cats are tolerant of a child's antics—although they would not put up with the same kind of behavior from an adult. If you do bring a cat into a household where there is a child or children, however, you have a responsibility to teach your youngsters to respect the rights of their new feline friend. This is generally not a problem with older children. They may even want to take over the responsibility for raising the new pet—something you should encourage. In doing so, they will learn important lessons about the personalities of animals and the rewards and responsibilities of caring for them.

How to Choose a Healthy Cat

When you are selecting a kitten or a cat, you must be alert to important clues about the animal's health and well-being. While purebred cats purchased from breeders are almost always in good health, a cat of any age obtained from the pound or a pet store requires a careful evaluation.

When you enter a pet shop or cattery, the first thing you should pay attention to is the sanitary conditions and the way cats are kept. If you see any cats or kittens with diarrhea, hear cats coughing, or observe cats with eye or nose discharges, shop for your new pet somewhere else.

Regardless of where you get your pet—whether from a breeder, shop, or animal shelter—the checklist on pages 54–55 will help you choose a healthy animal.

If you are choosing a kitten from a litter, the most important thing to remember is that a healthy kitten is active. He plays and runs around, wrestles with his siblings, and is responsive to you and all stimuli. Nor should a kitten shy away from you. A healthy kitten will approach you playfully and purr when you pet him.

Next, be alert to the kitten's physical health, checking every area indicated on the checklist.

It is not a good idea to obtain a kitten who is less than eight weeks old and not fully weaned. And while you may be tempted to buy a sick animal out of pity, do not do so unless you are willing to spend the time and money necessary to restore him to good health. If the kitten dies, you will also suffer heartbreak.

Finally, no matter where you obtain your new pet, make certain that you have him examined and vaccinated by a veterinarian as quickly as possible. This is especially important if you have any other cats in your household. Some shelters will provide this service as part of the purchase price.

INTRODUCING YOUR CAT TO HIS NEW HOME

Even before you bring your new pet home, you should be making preparations for his arrival. Unless you have selected a mature, well-trained cat who can be trusted anywhere in your house, choose an area where the new arrival can be temporarily confined in safety and comfort.

Give this area a safety check. Any electrical wires that can be chewed should be removed or hidden. Rid the area of any toxic chemicals or other materials that can be swallowed, along with breakable objects such as vases or glassware.

Keep in mind that cats are curious animals who will investigate every nook and cranny of their new environment, often scaling your furniture as

SIGNS OF A HEALTHY CAT OR KITTEN

- The eyes should be clear, bright, and wide open. There should be no discharges.
- The eyelids should be free of scales. Scales could indicate ringworm (see Ringworm, p. 156)
- The ears should be clean, with no signs of infection. Head-shaking or ear-scratching may indicate mite infestation. Ear mites (see Ear Mites, p. 127) look like gritty black dirt specks. (Note: ear mites can be easily cleared up, and this condition alone should not dissuade you from adopting a kitten.)
- The tongue and gums should be a healthy pink. If healthy, the small baby teeth will be clean and bright.

Check a kitten's eye for discharge.

Scales on the eyelids or around the face may indicate ringworm.

Look for black specks inside your cat's ears. These specks usually indicate that the cat has ear mites.

part of this inspection tour. If you are concerned about sustaining damage to your furniture, consider moving pieces you are particularly worried about out of your cat's reach, and cover other furniture with sheets or fabric until your cat has had time to adjust fully.

If you have brought home a cat who is not yet housebroken, make certain that the entire floor in the area you select is covered with several layers of newspapers. Place your cat's bed in this room, along with a litter box and a few toys, such as a catnip ball or a mouse. When you introduce your new cat or kitten to the area, place him in the litter box so he knows where it is located.

- The nose should be cool and dry and free of discharge. The cat should not be sneezing.
- The coat should be shiny, with no bald patches or flakes. The fur should be soft, fluffy, and glossy.
- The skin should be without sores, fleas, or other signs of irritation.
- The abdomen should not be distended. A distended abdomen could indicate the presence of parasites.
- The anal area should be clean and free of all fecal matter. Diarrhea leaves dirty traces on the fur, suggesting an ill cat.

Check inside the mouth for signs of gum disease and tooth decay.

Check the skin for fleas and other external parasites.

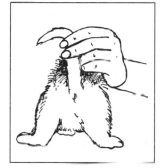

Check for traces of diarrhea on the fur surrounding the anus.

ESSENTIAL SUPPLIES

The majority of kittens available from pet shops and breeders are between the ages of two and four months. Before bringing your kitten home, make certain that you have the following equipment and supplies on hand. None are difficult to find. Pet shops and the pet sections of supermarkets are the best places to obtain them.

CAT BED

Beds can range from expensive models to a simple cardboard carton with an opening cut into the side. Line it with a washable pillow, a blanket, or any other soft and cozy material that the cat will enjoy relaxing and sleeping in. Place the bed in an area that is quiet and removed from drafts.

FOOD AND WATER DISHES

Make certain that each cat in your household has an individual feeding dish and water bowl. Feeding dishes can be made of anything from stainless steel to pottery. A good rule of thumb is to select bowls that are easy to clean, do not slide across the floor while the cat eats, and do not tip over easily. Shallow bowls rather than deep ones are best; cats do not like to eat out of deep bowls.

LITTER BOX, LITTER, AND SCOOP

Think of a cat's litter box as a sanitary indoor toilet. It is an essential item in the life of any indoor cat. Make sure the tray is made of nonporous material such as plastic, stainless steel, or baked enamel so that it is easy to clean. The most common type of litter box—one that is available at most pet shops—is a shallow, rectangular-shaped box measuring twelve by eighteen inches. If you are getting a young kitten, be certain that it is shallow enough for the kitten to climb over the edges.

Kitty litter can be purchased in any pet shop or grocery store. Fill the pan with two to three inches of litter. You may also use sand, sawdust, or shredded newspapers. Litter material should be changed every three or four days. You will also need a slotted scoop to remove fecal waste from the box so that you don't have to handle soiled litter. Fecal matter should be removed from the box daily.

To help control odor, sprinkle half a cup of baking soda on the bottom of the litter pan. Wash the litter box thoroughly with soap and water each time you change the litter.

SCRATCHING POSTS

As was discussed in the behavioral problems section of Chapter 2 (p. 39), scratching is a deeply ingrained and normal feline instinct, as distressful as it may be to you if you live in a household filled with expensive furnishings. A scratching post is one of the most effective ways of dealing with this naturally occurring behavior. There are a variety of models available on the market, from twelve-inch-high scratching posts to those that extend all the way to the ceiling. The ideal scratching post is sturdy, covered with a rough surface, and, again, tall enough to let a cat stretch to his full height to claw at it.

TOYS

Up to now, your kitten probably got most of his exercise frolicking and engaging in mock battles with his littermates. Now new sources of amusement will be required to make certain that he gets enough exercise. Toys are excellent items for amusing cats, and your pet store will be loaded with them.

Your only concern should be that

the toy not easily come apart and possibly get caught in your kitten's throat or be swallowed. Avoid toys with glued-on parts that can come apart or be easily removed by your cat. If you don't want to spend money on toys, then improvise. Golf balls, cardboard toilet-paper tubes, wadded-up aluminum foil, and even an old pair of socks can give endless hours of enjoyment to your new pet.

THE FIRST FEW DAYS

A new environment can be stressful for a cat, so try your best to make the adjustment period for your new pet an easy one. Make sure that everyone in your household, including your children, understands the situation. Loud noises, sudden movements, or too much handling should be avoided in the first few days. Let your new pet take his time exploring his new surroundings without too many interruptions. Permit the new household member to

quietly get over any uncertainties that he might be experiencing.

If you have a dog or another cat in the household, make preparations to keep them elsewhere until after the adjustment period. Don't do anything drastic, like putting your older pet out of the house. Rather, confine your new cat and his more-established housemates to separate parts of the living space. After a few days, a supervised meeting of all the pets in your household can be arranged.

When you bring your new cat home, it's best to leave the cat in his carrier with the exit door open, so he can venture into his new environment when he is ready. The cat will most likely curiously peer out of his carrier and then slowly begin to explore the area, cautiously keeping his body close to the ground. Your new cat may even make a dash for safety and hide under an armchair, sofa, or bureau until he feels secure enough to come out. Never corner a cat in hiding or try to yank him out by force.

For both cat and owner, the first day

HELPING A CAT ADJUST TO HIS NEW HOME

Here are a few steps you can take to comfort your cat during his first nights in a new home:

1. **Leave the light on in the room where your cat will be sleeping.**
2. **Leave the radio on softly. Music and the sound of human voices can be very soothing to a nervous cat.**
3. **If the cat is particularly distressed, allow him to sleep in a room with humans.**

is usually the most challenging. Simply try to leave your new pet alone. Give him a bowl of water, a small amount of food—perhaps some cooked hamburger or a semimoist cat food—and let him begin to work things out. Do not worry if your new pet does not eat. This is a normal reaction to all the sudden excitement in his life.

Be warned that you and your family may miss a few winks of sleep that first night. A new cat in the household will probably prowl and cry throughout the evening hours. Be patient. Your new cat or kitten will eventually settle down and your normal sleeping routine can be resumed.

As the adjustment period proceeds, your cat will soon become the outgoing, playful, and affectionate creature that you hoped he would be.

If you live in the country or suburbs and have a backyard, you may want your cat to spend much of his time outside. Cats enjoy being outdoors regardless of the temperature; it feeds into their sense of adventure. Before you release your cat into the backyard, however, a number of precautions should be taken:

1. Do not allow kittens who are less than three months old outside. Kittens this young are not yet fully vaccinated and have very little immunity to contagious feline diseases.

2. Before you let him go outdoors, teach your cat his name. Get him to learn to come when you call him. One way to do that is by rewarding him with food each time he responds to his name.

3. Make sure your cat's first exposure to the outside world is supervised and of short duration, especially if he's a young cat. The time he is allowed to remain outdoors should be gradually lengthened.

4. Your cat may encounter other cats, so make certain he is properly vaccinated before being allowed outdoors.

5. In order to prevent unwanted litters, it is wise to have your cat spayed or neutered before permitting him to roam outside.

For an apartment cat, the most important thing in his life is his relationship to another being, whether that being is animal or human. Also, indoor cats need much more affection and entertainment than do outdoor cats, so make certain that you allot plenty of playtime for your new pet. Make sure that your new pet is socialized; let it interact with humans and other pets in a friendly manner. An animal that is forced into a solitary lifestyle may develop behavioral problems.

The general rule for handling a feline newcomer to your household—*after* he has become adjusted to his new surroundings—is to do so often and regularly. Make certain that you and your family handle your cat or kitten gently so that he does not become frightened or wary of human beings. Lift your cat carefully and place him down tenderly. Stroke him down the back and under the chin so that he senses your friendliness. If a cat is teased or dropped, he can become

THREE WAYS TO SOCIALIZE YOUR NEW CAT OR KITTEN:

- Make sure your cat gets plenty of physical attention, including petting and cuddling.
- Feed her in a room frequented by familiar people.
- Play with her. Favorite play equipment may include a ball made of aluminum foil or paper for fetching and string or rope for dragging.

frightened of human contact, or even injured.

You may also want to get your kitten used to having her feet and legs handled, by stroking them in a gentle and playful manner. This acclimation will come in handy later on if you need to trim her claws (see Nail Trimming, p. 70).

HOW TO CHOOSE A VETERINARIAN

Ideally, you should take your new pet for a complete veterinary checkup within forty-eight hours of bringing him home. He must be vaccinated against such deadly diseases as distemper and pneumonitis.

You may already have chosen your veterinarian—but if not, how do you go about finding the right one? Begin by asking cat owners who they would recommend. The American Animal Hospital Association—(800) 252-2242, or (303) 986-2800 in Colorado—can also give you the names of qualified veterinarians in your area. Other sources are the local veterinary

association or humane society. Don't just ask for names. Be specific with your questions about these animal doctors and their specialties.

Find out whether the veterinarian recommended to you works in an animal hospital near your house, in case there is an emergency. Does he or she make house calls? Is it possible to obtain emergency care after hours, or on weekends and holidays?

Before selecting a veterinarian, meet with the doctor and ask to be shown around the facility. Is the facility bright, clean, and pleasant-smelling? If not, you do not want your new cat treated there.

If the veterinarian you are interested in does not take the time to answer all your questions and address your concerns, or if you detect a reluctance to allow you to tour the hospital, he or she is not the professional to whom you should entrust the care of your cat.

When you bring your cat in for his first examination, bring along any vaccination or health records from the place you bought or adopted him. Also bring a fresh stool sample with you in a plastic bag so that your veterinarian can check for signs of internal parasites.

A kitten should have his first checkup when he is about six or eight weeks old. The veterinarian will take the cat's history and give him a general examination. The kitten will also receive the first in a series of vaccinations to guard him against several serious illnesses.

Even if your new cat seems perfectly healthy, he should receive an examination along with the necessary vaccinations. Annual examinations and booster shots should follow. Whenever you take your cat for his yearly exam, remember to bring along a fresh stool sample.

4

BASIC CAT CARE

THE BEST WAY for you to give your cat the care she requires is to learn all about her many needs. This chapter will explore all of the fundamental aspects of cat care, from handling and feeding to exercise and grooming. You will learn how to help your cat become a responsible and welcomed member of your community. You will also find out how to help your cat adjust to special situations like travel and moving from one home to another.

YOUR CAT'S EATING HABITS AND HOW THEY EVOLVED

Despite thousands of years of domestication, cats remain predators by nature. When cats were living in the wild, they ate the entire body of their prey—including the fur and the entrails. It was a way for cats to obtain a balanced diet with muscle and organ food and roughage.

Today's domestic cats, whether ordinary or pedigreed, may no longer hunt for food, but they still display the eating habits of their wild ancestors. Feed a cat a piece of meat the size of a mouse and watch what your pet does with it. Unless she is very hungry, the cat will pull the meat off the plate, shake it, throw it up in the air, and swallow it without chewing. The cat will then regurgitate the meat and sometimes hide it. Even young kittens instinctively defend their prey. They will hiss, growl, and guard a small piece of meat from their siblings. This behavior does not occur when you feed your cat dry or mushy food or liquids. In

61

fact, cats will often share such foods from one dish without any display of antagonism.

If they have been taught to do so, cats also enjoy hunting and sometimes eating mice. Even the most well-fed and well-mannered cat will often catch mice. If your cat decides she does not want to eat the mouse, she may deposit her prey at your feet as a present.

YOUR CAT'S NUTRITIONAL REQUIREMENTS

It is your responsibility to see that your cat gets the proper kind of diet. For good health, appearance, vitality, and long life, that diet must include the right amounts of protein, carbohydrates, fat, vitamins, minerals, and other nutrients.

These requirements can be met by a good commercial cat food with the addition of high-quality protein, such as milk, egg yolk, poultry, fish, or cheese. The daily food intake for the average adult cat should be between six and eight ounces, plus water or milk. Vitamin and mineral supplements will be discussed later in this section.

Cats, like people, require variety in the food they eat. Try varying your cat's diet about every fifth day. You may feed your cat something entirely different, or you may offer the same basic commercial food with additional foods added. Table scraps are acceptable once in a while, as long as they aren't overly fatty.

PROTEINS

Protein is found in meat, fish, poultry, eggs, cheese, and milk. No other nutrient in your cat's diet is as important as protein, because it is responsible for the growth and development of body tissue and for the maintenance of optimum health.

Proteins exist in a number of forms. They are composed of smaller molecules known as amino acids. Cats require twenty-three essential amino acids for good health. When proteins are taken in through the digestive system, they are broken down into their constituent amino acids, which are then reassembled in the form of new protein. Surplus amino acids are burned as energy.

A cat's requirement for protein is much higher than that of a dog. This is one good reason to feed your cat commercial cat foods rather than table scraps alone, because such foods contain the levels of protein that your pet requires. Other than this, there is really no qualitative difference between any of the good commercial and professional cat foods.

CARBOHYDRATES

Carbohydrates are food substances that supply energy to the body. They also provide fiber necessary for the intestines to function properly. Good sources of carbohydrates in food are starches, sugars, and cellulose. Do not worry about your cat getting enough carbohydrates in her diet; she will get all she needs from a good-quality commercial cat food.

FATS

Fats are broken down in the body into fatty acids and glycogen. The body then transforms glycogen into glucose, a body fuel. Fats also add taste and texture to a cat's food, while adding certain essential fatty acids necessary for healthy skin and glossy coats. They provide your cat with important vitamins, such as A, D, E, and K. Commercially prepared cat foods contain all the fats your cat requires.

VITAMINS

Your cat's needs for vitamins are not necessarily the same as people's. Vitamins are accessory organic substances that are needed for metabolism and are essential to life and growth. They are not produced by the body and must be furnished in the diet. Vitamins are divided into two categories: the water-soluble vitamins, which include the B-complex group and vitamin C, and the fat-soluble vitamins (A, D, E, and K).

Generally, commercial cat foods contain sufficient vitamins for the average adult cat. Some veterinarians advise vitamin and mineral supplements for pregnant cats, kittens, and older cats. Do not add nutritional supplements to your cat's diet without first checking with your veterinarian, because vitamin overdoses can cause serious problems.

MINERALS

Minerals regulate the body's chemical balance and act as catalysts for a number of biological reactions. They help maintain the body's fluid balance and the movement of fluids through cell walls. They also help make up bones, soft tissues, muscle, teeth, and nerve cells. Cats get the minerals they require from the ash in commercially prepared cat foods. Too much ash, however, can cause problems such as the formation of bladder stones in cats (see Bladder Stones, p. 194). Read the label on the brand of cat food you purchase. Ash content should not exceed 4 percent in moist cat foods, 12 percent in dry foods. Do not give your cat mineral supplements unless you are advised to do so by your veterinarian.

LIQUIDS

Clean, fresh water is an essential part of your cat's diet. It should be available at all times, especially if your cat is on a dry or semimoist cat food diet. Although cats are not avid water drinkers, a minimum amount of fluid is necessary each day for the proper functioning of the kidneys and to avoid dehydration. Discourage your cat from drinking water from the toilet bowl or from flower vases. The water in toilets may contain disinfectant chemicals, while water in vases may be toxic from the flowers.

Some pet owners believe that milk is a good substitute for water. This is incorrect. Milk is actually a food and is not to be substituted for water. While milk contains many valuable nutrients and is an excellent source of calcium, your cat should be getting all the nutrients she needs by eating a balanced diet. Milk should be an occasional treat for your cat, not a steady staple.

TYPES OF CAT FOOD

There are so many varieties of cat food that deciding which one to purchase for your cat can become a confusing ordeal. Basically, there are three types of cat food: dry, semimoist, and canned.

DRY FOOD

Cats need a certain amount of dry food each day. These abrasive, bite-sized nuggets are excellent for your cat's gums and teeth. They help prevent tartar buildup and gum disease. Dry cat food is economical and contains all the vitamins and minerals your cat may require. Dry foods are low in fat, however, and some essential nutrients are destroyed by the high heat used in the manufacturing process. You can compensate for this by adding a little butter or a bit of meat to the food. Make certain that the ash content does not exceed 12 percent, and that you provide your cat with plenty of water.

SEMIMOIST FOODS

Soft-moist, or semimoist, cat foods are packaged in airtight cellophane bags that do not require refrigeration. Once opened, however, the food must be eaten by your cat or discarded; thankfully, many semimoist foods come packaged in single-meal portions. Soft-moist foods are combinations of meat, poultry, fish, and their byproducts. This type of food is especially palatable to cats. Portions are premeasured for easy use. Although these cat foods are not as deficient in fat as the completely dry brands, your cat will benefit if you add an extra bit of fat to her diet each day.

Semimoist foods tend to be more expensive than canned or dry cat foods. If you plan to make semimoist food your cat's main diet, vary the flavors and beware of overfeeding. Some cats tend to overindulge in semimoist food, and need careful monitoring.

CANNED FOOD

Canned cat foods are combinations of meat, poultry, fish, and their by-products, with cereals or grains, fats, and vitamins and minerals added to make them nutritionally complete.

Most canned foods are about 25 percent solid food and 75 percent water, and contain about 500 to 600 calories per twelve-ounce can.

When you purchase canned cat food, be aware of the content analysis. The ash content should not exceed 4 percent. The cheaper brands of canned cat food usually contain too much ash and low-quality proteins, such as gristle, entrails, and skin. Try to avoid these inexpensive brands because the heat used in processing destroys many essential vitamins. If canned cat food is your pet's staple, strive for variety. Do not serve your cat the same type of food each and every day. Your cat may even like it if you vary the brand of food you serve. This is fine so long as the food is uniformly nutritious and balanced.

FEEDING YOUR ADULT CAT

When should you feed your cat? Adult cats usually need to be fed once every twenty-four hours, although many cats prefer to be fed twice a day. Growing kittens and pregnant cats should be fed several meals a day. Remember that cats are creatures of habit. Once you establish a feeding schedule, stick to it or your cat will become upset. Similarly, if your cat gets used to a varied diet, sustain it.

Another important question is how much food to provide. About four to seven ounces of food a day will sustain the average cat very well. An adult cat's stomach will hold four and a half ounces of food or more. Most cat food labels recommend the amount to feed. Follow the manufacturer's suggestions and you won't go too far wrong. Serve your cat's food at room temperature, never hot or cold. Put any leftover food in the refrigerator or throw it out.

SPECIAL DIETS

Cats who suffer from heart disease or kidney, liver, or intestinal problems often require special diets. So do obese cats. If your cat suffers from some ailment or has gained too much weight, consult with your veterinarian, who will recommend a special diet for your pet.

SNACKS

If your cat has been eating well-balanced meals, there is no reason why you should deny her a special treat once in a while—but only if her appetite for regular meals is good. Such treats are available in most pet shops and supermarkets, and are specially prepared to be palatable to cats.

It is not harmful to serve your cat small amounts of other types of snacks as well. Cats enjoy cheese, cake, chili, bread, and many of the foods that people eat—just don't overdo it. Snacks are no substitute for well-balanced meals. If your cat prefers snacks to cat foods, discuss the matter with your veterinarian.

FINICKY EATERS

There are many reasons why a cat will balk at eating her food—sometimes even her favorite dish. Odor is usually at the top of the list. A cat's sense of smell is so acute that a repugnant odor, or a lack of odor, could result in a refusal to eat.

Another frequent reason a cat becomes a finicky eater has to do with food consistency. Some cats simply prefer dry food and others moist. Also, if your cat has a sore mouth or tongue, she may eat food very gingerly or not at all. Many cats will not eat if there is noise or too much activity around them at mealtime. Instead, they will scurry off to a quiet, secluded spot. Food that is too cold also may be given a wide berth by your cat.

Should your cat refuse food for more than forty-eight hours, something is definitely wrong, and a phone call to your veterinarian is in order.

OBESITY

If your cat is gaining too much weight, the amount of carbohydrates must be lowered and higher-protein food, such as eggs, meat, and fish, should be given to him to cut down his caloric intake. Obesity is the source of many serious health problems for your cat. It can shorten his life by hastening such conditions as congestive heart failure and respiratory or kidney problems.

An overweight cat should first be examined by a veterinarian to determine whether plain overeating is the problem, not some other ailment. If overeating is the reason for weight gain, your veterinarian will establish a diet that will reduce your cat's weight.

In any weight-reduction program there will probably be no significant loss of weight for at least two weeks. This is the time it takes for your cat's body to use up excess fluid. Weigh your cat once a week. If there are no evident results by the third week, get in touch with your veterinarian.

EXERCISE

Exercise is an important way for your cat to stay in shape and avoid becoming overweight. Continuous confinement without regular exercise is extremely bad for your cat's health because neither her appetite nor her circulatory system is being properly stimulated. If you have an indoor cat and she has no playmates to wrestle and romp with, you should set aside a play period together. If there are children in your household, your cat will not be lacking for exercise—in fact, you may have to curtail the amount of time that your children will want to play with her. Most cats get sufficient exercise through their natural tendency to explore and climb, even within the confines of the smallest apartment.

HANDLING YOUR CAT

The most important element in handling a cat is gentleness. The right sort of handling is gentle, deliberate, and quiet. You should apply a minimum of physical restraint while stroking and petting the animal, and always speak in a soft voice. If you are boisterous, abrupt, or handle your cat roughly, she will become frightened and may hiss and bite or even scratch you.

The best way to pick up your cat is to approach her from the side, placing one arm around her forelegs and the other around her hind legs or beneath her abdomen. Hold your cat comfortably in your arms as you would a baby, with just enough restraint so that the animal is not prompted to escape. Another effective way to pick up a cat is to place the flat of your hand under the cat's chest and between her forelegs, using the other hand to support the rear section of the body from below. This gives good support to your cat's body and she will not try to squirm free.

When you are ready to put your cat down, do so gently. Make sure all four feet touch the ground at the same time to prevent strain.

GROOMING

Ordinary house cats require no special grooming; they are quite capable of doing so themselves several times a day, using their tongues to wash themselves and keep their fur shiny and free of dust. Some cat owners, however, enjoy the process of grooming their cats. Rare is the cat who will complain about all this pleasant attention she is getting. Remember that the aim of grooming is to maintain a full, glossy coat. Grooming can be helpful during peak shedding season (late spring and early fall), and can help eliminate clumps of hair that could cause hairballs.

FIRST STEPS

Cat grooming does not require a lot of time or professional training. It is best to begin grooming when your cat is still young; this will get the cat used to being brushed and handled. Establish a regular routine—a certain time of day when you will be brushing your pet or doing other grooming tasks. Special cat brushes and combs can be purchased at pet stores.

BRUSHING AND COMBING

Regular brushing provides much better care for your cat's coat than the

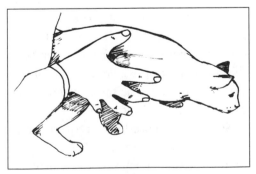

Place your cat back on the ground with all four feet touching down at the same time.

BATHING A CAT

1. Make sure bathing is done indoors. The bathing area should be warm and free of drafts. It helps to close the bathroom door.

2. Use baby shampoo or buy a shampoo at a pet store.

3. The tub should contain several inches of lukewarm water.

4. Put on a pair of gloves and then carefully place your cat in the tub. Do not frighten your cat by running or spraying water on her. Scoop up some water from the tub in your hand and pour it over the fur.

5. Do not submerge your cat's head in the water, even for a second.

6. Keep soap out of your cat's eyes.

7. Make sure the fur is thoroughly rinsed of soap to prevent irritation of the sensitive skin beneath.

8. After the bath, gently pat the cat dry with a towel.

9. When the fur is completely dry, give your cat a good brushing. This helps remove loose hairs and restores luster to the fur by spreading natural oils throughout the coat.

animal can give herself. Three types of hair coats have to be considered in grooming: short hair, long hair, and semilong hair.

The fur of the short-haired cat lies close to the body. All dead hairs have to be removed. Start at the head and work down toward the rear, brushing and combing in short strokes. Brush your pet's fur for at least five to ten minutes each day, and brush the hair in the direction of growth.

Long-haired cats require more time to be groomed. They need to be combed thoroughly at least once a week, especially in the spring and fall, when shedding takes place and new fur grows in. You must also gently comb the undercoat—the belly and between the legs—of long-haired cats to keep the fur from getting matted. It is important to untangle matted hair. Try to accomplish this as gently as possible, using your fingers. If you think the tangle needs to be cut out, take your cat to a groomer.

Semi-long-haired cats require more grooming care than shorthairs and less than longhairs. They should be brushed and combed until the coat has the desired silky sheen.

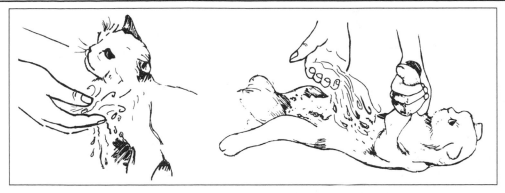

Make sure the fur is rinsed thoroughly to prevent irritation to sensitive skin underneath.

Use extra caution when cleaning fur around the eyes.

When the fur is dry, brush to remove loose hairs and to restore luster.

BATHING

Cats are innately clean animals and normally do not need baths, which in any case most do not enjoy at all. Sometimes, however, a cat will get dirty and not be able to clean herself thoroughly. She may become excessively dirty or smelly as a result of an encounter with a skunk, or may need to be bathed because of some parasitic infection or other health reason. Kittens under six months should not be bathed at all unless absolutely necessary, because they might catch cold.

If you must bathe your cat, expect a lot of resistance. You may need the help of an assistant to carry out this task, because your cat will make every attempt to get out of the water.

PROFESSIONAL GROOMERS

Some pet owners simply do not have the time to groom their cats—particularly if they own a long-haired cat that requires lots of careful attention. Many pet stores provide cat and dog grooming services; there are also individuals who do this professionally. Ask your pet store owner, veterinarian, or pet-owning friends about qualified groomers.

NAIL TRIMMING

There are situations that may prompt you to have your cat's nails trimmed, especially if your cat is inadvertently inflicting painful cuts with those nails on your or other pets. Nail clipping, however, is a difficult procedure. You may be better off to have your cat's nails clipped by your veterinarian.

EAR CLEANING

Your cat is naturally fastidious. This is why you need not go overboard in cleaning your pet's ears. Once a week, however, you should examine the flaps of your cat's ears. If there is an excess amount of wax, dirt, or debris in the ears, you should clean them. Such an accumulation of matter in the ears may also suggest an ear infection.

Also, if you repeatedly discover dark little clumps of matter in your cat's ears and the cat keeps shaking and scratching her head, there may be ear mites present (see Ear Mites, p. 127). If so, consult your veterinarian.

When cleaning your cat's ears, do not use alcohol or other solvents, and do *not* clean farther inside the ear than you can see. Simply moisten a cloth, cotton wad, or cotton swab with water or mineral oil. If you are using a cloth, wrap it around your little finger. Care-

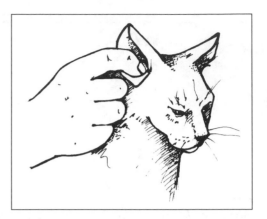

Clean the ear with a cloth moistened with mineral oil or water. Use any finger for the outer ear, but switch to your little finger to clean the ear canal.

fully insert your finger into the ear canal. Gently wipe the surface to remove dirt, excess wax, and debris.

If you do not like the idea of putting your finger in your cat's ear, first remove loose wax and debris from the ear canal with cotton swabs. Then follow with cotton balls moistened with warm water or mineral oil.

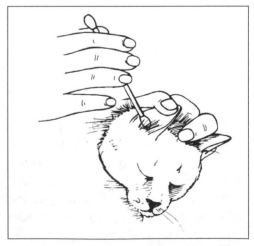

Exercise caution when using a cotton swab to clean the ear.

To remove loose wax and debris from the folds and crevices of your cat's ears, use dry cotton swabs. Use a gentle, rotating motion and cotton swabs moistened with warm water or mineral oil.

EYE CLEANING

You should be familiar with some simple steps about taking care of your cat's eyes. If crusty material appears in their corners, use a piece of cotton or a paper tissue moistened with some water to remove the dried discharge. Always wipe away from the ear and toward the nose.

Some breeds of Persian cats suffer from a condition that results in the narrowing or plugging of the tear ducts. This causes the eyes to tear up frequently, leaving yellow stains on the fur. If this is the case with your Persian, you should wipe her tears off several times a day with clean, soft paper tissue. Consult with your veterinarian, who may prescribe eyedrops.

CARE OF YOUR CAT'S TEETH

There should be no problem with your cat's teeth if she is kept on a healthy diet. Nonetheless, a yearly checkup of teeth and gums by your veterinarian is in order. To prevent dental problems, you should also feed your cat some dry food daily (see Types of Cat Food, p. 64) and allow her to chew bones that do not splinter.

Large bones with a little meat left on them, such as lamb and beef marrow-bones, are good selections. Avoid chicken or pork-chop bones, as well as any long bones like ribs.

It is also a good idea to wipe your cat's teeth and gums weekly with a salt-and-baking-soda solution. One teaspoon of salt and one teaspoon of soda in a cup of water makes for an excellent oral antiseptic and teeth cleanser (see Periodontal Disease, Prevention, page 140).

TRAVELING WITH YOUR CAT

Many people think that cats do not make good traveling companions, but sometimes they do, especially if they became accustomed to traveling as kittens. Even if your cat is not an experienced traveler, however, life on the road can be made easier for both you and your cat by following these tips:

1. A veterinary checkup prior to departure is essential. Make certain that your cat is in good health and that she has all her required inoculations and booster shots.

2. Have a suitable carrier that can withstand a long trip—and one in which your cat can ride in comfort and safety. A small cardboard box, gym bag, or even a bowling bag (with an adequate air supply) may be great for an occasional trip to the animal hospital, but for extended travel a wire cage is a much better idea.

Wire cages are an especially good idea in warm or hot weather because they allow air to circulate. If you keep your cat in the cage instead of allowing her to roam about the car, you can also keep your windows lowered a few inches when you stop for food or to use the restroom.

Whatever type of cage you may choose, make certain that it is well ventilated, easy to clean, and sturdy. A lightweight blanket on the floor of the cage will add considerably to your cat's comfort.

TRAVELING BY CAR

With a little help from you, a cat can quickly become acclimated to traveling in a car. Here are some steps you can take to smooth the ride:

1. Before you leave home, introduce your cat to her carrier. Put it in the middle of the room with the door open. Place some of her favorite food or a favorite toy inside and encourage her to enter, speaking in soothing, positive tones. Once she is in the carrier, carry her around the house at first for a few minutes. Later, try carrying your cat around the block in the carrier.

2. Take a few short car rides with your cat so that she becomes accustomed to the sound and motion of the automobile.

3. On long trips, do not forget to bring along the litter box, food, and plenty of fresh water. Spillproof water bowls are available.

4. While many cats will curl up and sleep during a long car ride, your pet may have an excitable personality. If that is the case, ask your veterinarian to prescribe a tranquilizer. This will not only help your cat to get to sleep, but will also prevent vomiting or drooling. Both nausea and fear can cause a cat to salivate. (See Motion Sickness, p. 188.)

5. On long trips, stop every few hours to exercise your pet. A leash or harness should be part of your travel equipment. Make certain your cat has a collar with an identification tag.

6. If you are the only person in the car, your cat should be in her carrier. If others are along for the ride and your cat is not in her carrier, she should wear a pet harness, which you can purchase at most pet shops. These harnesses come with leashes and should be under the control of someone in the car. Do not allow your cat to roam about the car while you are driving. Many an accident has been caused by a driver who was suddenly distracted by his cat.

7. Never leave any pet in a parked car on a hot day. If it is absolutely essential that you must do so, find a shady spot to park your car in and leave a window cracked open.

8. Feed your cat only at the end of the day's journey, but allow her to drink water whenever she wishes.

9. Many inns and hotels permit feline guests, so there is no reason to leave your cat in the car overnight. Always call ahead to make reservations, and to make sure cats are allowed.

GETTING USED TO A LEASH

Cats are often resistant to a leash, collar, or harness, especially at first. The best way to acclimate your cat to this important equipment is to do so gradually and patiently. First, place the collar or harness on your cat and allow her to play with it — to get used to the new accessory on her own terms. Watch her to be certain she doesn't get hurt.

Then attach the leash to the collar or harness. Again, let her play with it at first. After a few minutes, gently pick up the end of the leash and slowly start to walk with it. *Do not drag or force your cat to walk.* Speak soothingly to her, and be sure not to leave the leash on for too long in the beginning, just a few minutes at a time. Your cat may never love walking with it, but she will probably cooperate after she gets used to the idea.

For a listing of motels or hotels in the United States and Canada that accept pets, an inexpensive booklet is available from Gaines Professional Services. Send $1.50 to Gaines "Touring with Towser," P.O. Box 1007, Kankakee, Illinois, 60901.

TRAVELING BY PLANE

There are advantages to traveling with your cat by plane, the most important of which is that this mode of transportation cuts down on travel time. But while most cats are good fliers, it is not a good idea to put a pregnant, elderly, or ill cat on a plane.

Rules and regulations for pet transport by air vary from airline to airline, so always check carefully to find out the regulations of the airline you are traveling on. Some airlines will not allow you to book a seat for your pet, insisting that she ride in the baggage compartment, while other airlines will do so providing the carrier is small enough to fit under the passenger seat. Whatever the case, be certain to apprise yourself fully of the airline's official policy.

You may consider using a shipping service. These services, while expensive, nevertheless take the headache out of pet air travel. Pet shipping firms arrange for pickup and delivery of your cat to the airport, take care of the necessary documents, and book the flights. They will also pick up and deliver your pet to her destination point.

If your cat is going by air, feed her a light meal and give her water about four hours before the trip. If your cat is excitable, ask your veterinarian to prescribe a tranquilizer. If you ship your cat, make certain her health certificate and other pertinent documents are securely attached to her carrier.

CAMPING

One in ten American families goes camping every year, often with the family cat.

Cats are welcome in almost all national parks and forests, as well as in most state parks. There are, however, a few states that do not allow pets in their parks: Florida, Maryland, New Jersey, Pennsylvania, and Rhode Island.

To ensure that cats remain welcome at state and national parks, it is important that both you and your feline friend be considerate of other campers. Do not let your cat roam free. Pack a litter box or a scoop and some plastic bags, so your cat's feces will not be left behind.

While cats may not be as adventure-some as dogs, they nonetheless also like to explore new places. If you decide to take your cat for a walk through a forest or other natural attraction, however, make it a short one and be sure to use a leash. Cats are easily frightened by new environments, and too long a walk can become stressful and/or tiring for your pet. Additionally, many indoor cats might be terrified by the vast environment of the outdoors, so they should be gradually acclimated to such a venture. Try taking your cat into an area that resembles your camping grounds for a one-day outing at first.

LEAVING YOUR CAT BEHIND

BOARDING

Going on vacation often means having to leave your cat behind. Boarding a cat used to mean leaving him in a small cage at a kennel. Today, however, the pet-boarding industry has put on a new face and has turned the experience into something more pleasurable for animal and owner alike.

Ask for recommendations from your veterinarian or from friends who have boarded cats. Your Yellow Pages may also have an extensive listing of boarding establishments.

Capable boarding facilities are usually well-booked—especially during the summer months, weekends, and holidays—so plan ahead. If your cat is not used to being away from home, bring along some of her favorite toys, her bed, and her blanket. Perhaps an old T-shirt of yours will help as well, as your scent will comfort and soothe her. This will make your cat's adjustment to her temporary home a lot easier.

Do not forget to tell the boarding establishment if there are any special requirements for your cat or if she has any medical conditions. Leave the name and number of your veterinarian, along with a number where you can be reached in case of an emergency.

PET SITTERS

When the cat's away, the mice may play. But what do cats do when you are away?

If you are gone for too long, your cat may become depressed and even fall ill, which is why it is a good idea to ask a friend to come over and feed your cat, or hire a cat-sitting service if you plan a prolonged vacation or business trip.

Before you use such a service, ask for references and phone numbers. Call the people listed and ask for candid opinions about the service. Cat sitters provide a variety of services, from feeding and exercising your pet to administering medicine. Some services come directly to your home. Others place your cat in another pet lover's home until you return—an excellent alternative to boarding.

Ask friends, look in the newspapers, or check the Yellow Pages to find a pet-sitting service.

SPECIAL SITUATIONS

Certain events may occur requiring decisive, caring action on your part. In these situations, you yourself may be distracted (for example, moving from one home to another) or distressed (if your cat has wandered off), making it

difficult to think things through clearly. Read on to prepare yourself for special situations that may occur, in order to give your cat the best care you can.

LOST CAT

A cat that somehow strays and manages to get herself lost is a tragedy. That is why many pet owners are having their cats tattooed and listed with one of the several pet registries now in operation throughout the country. According to experts—including many humane societies—pet tattooing may be the best way to make certain that a lost cat is returned to you.

The procedure is quick and absolutely harmless, although some veterinarians may choose to administer a mild sedative, just to help your cat through the process. An identifying serial number (your Social Security number is highly

WHAT TO DO IF YOUR CAT IS LOST

If your cat has run away, you must act calmly and rationally to try to find him. Here are some helpful steps to take:

PLACES TO CONTACT
- **The local police department**
- **The animal control officer**
- **Local shelters**
- **Local veterinarians**

PLACES TO POST NOTICES
- **The lost-and-found sections of your local newspapers**
- **Supermarket bulletin boards**
- **The local post office, if they allow such notices to be posted**

recommended) is tattooed on your pet's inner flank. The number is then listed with a pet registry. Most police departments and animal shelters know how to reach the major registries. Ask your veterinarian or local animal shelter about this and other pet identification techniques, such as implanting a microchip inside a pet's body.

MOVING

Americans are part of a mobile society; one out of every five families moves its household each year. Moving is not only a disruption for the family, it can be terrifying for your cat. Cats are creatures of habit and do not like abrupt changes of environment.

If you are planning a move, prepare your cat for the transition to her new home. Confine your cat to a room in your household with her litter box and plenty of water until the tumult of moving is over.

Once you bring your cat over to your new house or apartment, let her explore her new setting. Make some of her old toys available; these familiar items will help comfort her. You may wish to keep all doors and windows shut, because some cats have a tendency to wander off and try to return to their more familiar settings. The American Humane Association suggests that because of this tendency, if your cat is accustomed to going outdoors you should keep her confined to the house for several weeks until she is acclimated to her new turf. Try to sur-

round her with comforting objects from your old home, including pictures and furniture. Then, let her explore her new surroundings, giving her the option to return to the room you first put her in if necessary.

VISITORS

If your cat tends to misbehave, or if visitors to your home are allergic to cats or afraid of animals, you may want to keep your cat confined to another part of the house when you have company. Also, if your guests are bringing children with them, it may be a good idea to keep your cat out of sight so that she is not annoyed by the children, who will surely want to play with her. Make certain she has plenty of water available, as well as toys to keep her occupied.

If your visitors have no objections to cats, it might be a good idea to feed your cat just before they arrive. A good meal may put your cat to sleep and keep her out of harm's way until the guests depart. The cat may in fact decide on her own to leave the scene until it's safer to emerge.

REDECORATING

Like moving, redecorating can wreak havoc on your cat's nerves. Follow the suggestions given in the above section on moving. Common sense would dictate that you keep your cat from being underfoot while the decorators are at work. This will prevent any accidents between worker and cat, as well as protect your pet from exposure to fumes, nails, tacks, glue, and electrical equipment.

YOUR CAT AND THE LAW

One would never expect the stern Puritans to be concerned about the rights of animals, but they were. In fact, while most people in the New World considered any type of animal to be mere property, to be used or abused at whim, the leaders of the Massachusetts Bay Colony were busy drafting the first anticruelty law.

In 1641 the Puritans had their first legal code printed. Entitled "The Body of Liberties," it carefully spelled out a hundred legal statutes. Interestingly enough, number ninety-two specifically refers to animals. It reads: "No man shall exercise any Tirrany or Crueltie towards any bruite Creature which are usualie kept for man's use." This may very well have been the first stirrings of the animal-rights movement in America.

Three hundred years later, despite the best efforts of animal welfare groups, cats continue to be the target of persecution and exploitation. They are thrown out of homes by owners who have grown weary of them and are abused in other ways.

Despite such abuse, each year a number of progressive laws are passed by local, state, and the federal government to protect the rights of all animals. If you are interested in learning

more about the abuse of animals and legislation to deal with it, write to the Humane Society of the United States, 2100 L St., N.W., Washington, D.C., 20037.

For urban-dwelling cat owners, one of the biggest problems are restrictive laws that allow landlords to refuse to rent an apartment to someone who owns a cat or dog. In addition, an increasing number of states have passed laws that limit the number of pets per household. If you want more information on how to oppose such legislation, contact the Humane Society.

If you believe a landlord is discriminating against you because you own a cat, contact your local Humane Society, which may refer you to an attorney who specializes in such cases.

PREVENTIVE HEALTH CARE

Preventive health care for your cat is as simple as taking your pet for annual veterinary checkups. Regular checkups and a well-balanced diet will help your cat maintain good health throughout her life.

Regular trips to your veterinarian are important because such periodic examinations allow the veterinarian to monitor your cat's health, and design a program of care geared specifically for him. Remember, it is easier to prevent a disease than to treat one—and less expensive, too.

As we've emphasized throughout this book, the best time to begin a preventive health program for your pet is as soon as you get one. Your cat will be vaccinated (see Vaccinations, p. 79) and tested for worms, and will be well on her way toward good health.

PET HEALTH INSURANCE

Pet owners in the United States spend more than $6.9 billion yearly to care for their 109 million cats and dogs. Should your cat become ill, pet health insurance might come in handy. Health insurance for animals works very much like it does for people. It is designed to pay for that expensive and unexpected feline medical emergency. Most policies cover surgery and hospitalization costs, but like human health insurance plans, premium costs vary. So look for a policy that fits your pocketbook.

To obtain information on pet health insurance, contact your veterinarian, insurance company, or your local Humane Society.

SAFETY

Making your home a safe environment for your pet can prevent injuries. Prevention is a very simple procedure. If there are hanging cords attached to any-thing that can come crashing down, remove them. Electrical cords should be kept hidden or out of reach of your cat.

Cats love to crawl into dark, secluded places, which include ovens, dishwashers, and clothes washers. Make certain that you keep the doors to any of these appliances securely shut. Because cats love to sit on windowsills and sun, if you are living in a high-rise apartment, screens are essential so that your cat does not go bounding over the ledge in pursuit of some passing sparrow.

Most households are filled with little items that are scattered about—pins, needles, rubber bands, string, paper clips. Kittens or cats on the prowl for something to play with may get one of these small items lodged in their throats. Try not to leave such items lying about.

Cats are among the world's most curious creatures. They will climb atop the highest bookcase in your home for the satisfaction of finding out what is up there. If there happens to be an expensive vase on the top of your bookcase or anything else that is breakable, that item can easily come crashing down along with your cat, who is more likely than not to land on the shattered pieces.

By making a weekly safety check of your home, you will help your cat avoid many hazards.

5

VACCINATIONS

YOUR CAT'S BODY has the ability to produce natural protective substances called antibodies that can ward off certain infectious diseases. Your cat can also be given a disease-fighting capability through vaccinations.

When your pet is vaccinated, he is exposed to heat-killed germs and germ products that stimulate his immune system to produce antibodies against specific infection-causing organisms.

The most common vaccinations are against distemper, upper respiratory infections, and rabies. If your cat goes outdoors, it is especially important that he get a rabies shot, if for no other reason than the danger this disease poses to humans. Combination vaccinations are available that can give your cat protection against rabies as well as other infectious diseases. Consult your veterinarian on the benefits of this type of vaccine.

The usual age for your cat's first series of vaccinations is about two to three months, with annual booster shots after that. For the vaccination to be effective, kittens have to be free of parasites (see Intestinal Parasites, p. 183). You should have your kittens dewormed (see Intestinal Parasites, p. 183) or examined to see if they have worms before having them immunized.

If you have just acquired an adult cat, your first responsibility is to take him to the vet for a checkup and appropriate vaccination shots. If you know who owned the cat previously, ask the former owner for his vaccination record card.

If you adopt a stray, especially if he is malnourished or otherwise in poor physical condition, more than one series of vaccinations may be needed to restore the cat's immune system to a

TYPICAL VACCINATION SCHEDULE

Type of Vaccination	Age of Cat	How Administered
Distemper	8 to 12 weeks old	Two or three vaccinations two to four weeks apart; booster shot every year.
	12 weeks or older	Most likely one vaccination; booster shot every year.
Rabies	8 to 12 weeks old	Two vaccinations two to four weeks apart; booster shot every year.
	12 weeks or older	One vaccination; booster shot every year
Upper respiratory infections	Any age	Two or three vaccinations two to four weeks apart; booster shot every year.

state where it can develop its own anti-bodies. A cat in such poor shape may have to be revaccinated later.

If your cat is already suffering from some infectious disease, a vaccination may be too little too late. Also, if you vaccinate a kitten less than twelve weeks old, a second series of vaccina-tions may be required, because the vaccines injected into his system can be destroyed by antibodies acquired from the mother and still present in the kit-ten's body.

Keep a record at home of all vac-cines your cat receives (see Recording Your Cat's History, p. 269).

6

WHEN YOUR CAT IS ILL

A DAY MAY COME when you notice changes in the behavior or habits of your cat. These changes can be subtle. Your usually affectionate cat, for example, may suddenly want to be left alone. Or your ordinarily undemanding pet becomes inexplicably more demanding of your attention and affection. Your cat may also suddenly become a picky eater or start demanding an unusual amount of food or water.

You certainly need not become obsessed about monitoring your cat's every action, but it is important that you know your cat well enough to observe any such out-of-the-ordinary behavior. If you do suspect that something unusual is going on, your best bet is to take your cat to your veterinarian for a complete physical checkup.

There may also be an occasion when there is little doubt that your cat is not feeling well. There may be obvious signs of illness, such as sticky eyes, runny nose, coughing, vomiting, or diarrhea. Of course, in such circumstances an immediate trip to see your vetcrinarian is in order so that your pet can get prompt medical attention. Before you transport your cat, however, you might try calling your veterinarian to request a house call. This will make life easier for both you and your pet.

In this chapter you will learn the basics of what to do if your cat is ill—or if you think your cat is ill. It is important, for example, that you be familiar with how to take your cat's temperature and pulse, how to collect a urine sample, and the best way to restrain your cat when attempting all this. This chapter also provides helpful information on various bandaging techniques, something you should know in case your cat injures her paw or tail.

If you bring your cat to an animal clinic and she must remain there, she will be getting the best care possible, and there is little else you will have to do for her. In many situations, however, your cat will be sent home with instructions on how to care for her.

Should this occur, you must nurse your cat. You may be required to medicate her; force her to take food, water, or medication; take her temperature; and perform other sick-room tasks. In doing so, you will need to be persistent and patient—especially patient, because nursing an ill or recuperating cat is often an around-the-clock job.

This chapter will describe in simple detail various common home-nursing techniques that you may be called upon to perform. In many instances, you will use the techniques in conjunction with specific instructions given by your veterinarian. Never hesitate to ask your veterinarian about any procedures you do not understand.

If your cat does not cooperate, do not give up. Ask your veterinarian for help. Sometimes all that is required is a simple change, such as a different type of medication. If you continue to have problems nursing your cat at home, you may have to bring her to the veterinarian for certain treatments, or your veterinarian may recommend tranquilizers or some other approach to help you treat her.

Above all, never feel guilty if you encounter problems in nursing your cat at home. Cats are not easy patients; they are very proud and independent. And always follow your veterinarian's advice. Some cat owners disregard such advice or try to take shortcuts. This is not fair either to your cat or to your veterinarian, who may be blamed unjustly if the animal doesn't recover because you did not follow instructions carefully.

YOUR CAT'S FIRST-AID KIT

Unless you own a cat with a specific and recurrent health problem, there is no need for an elaborate pharmaceutical supply cabinet. Certain essentials should be readily available, such as tweezers and a thermometer, along with any medications prescribed by your veterinarian for your ailing cat.

Cats do have accidents, so "be prepared" is always a good motto for pet owners. Before trouble strikes, the prudent cat owner will have on hand medical supplies that may be needed in an emergency or for general medical purposes.

Your feline first-aid kit should be kept in a clearly labeled box or carton, its location known to every member of your family. If you take your cat along on vacation, bring the first-aid kit with you.

HOW TO TAKE YOUR CAT'S TEMPERATURE

You may be asked by your veterinarian to take your cat's temperature and report any fluctuations. A cat's normal temperature is between 100 degrees and 102.5 degrees. If your pet's tem-

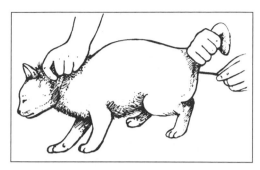

Try to have someone help you restrain your cat while you take her temperature.

perature is above 103 degrees or below 100 degrees, call your veterinarian immediately. A temperature below 100 degrees is usually an indication that your cat's body is weakening; a temperature above 103 degrees should be regarded as a fever.

In taking your cat's temperature, you may use a standard human rectal thermometer. Never put a thermometer into your cat's mouth. It's a good idea to have someone assist you in restraining your cat while you take her temperature. A cat's rectal muscles are quite strong, and she may struggle against this procedure, so you could use some help.

The method for taking your cat's temperature is as follows:

1. Speak soothingly to your pet and gently get her to stand. Grasp her tail and hold her upright. This will prevent her from sitting.

2. Shake the thermometer down and lubricate it well with petroleum or K-Y jelly, available at your local pharmacy

3. Gently insert the thermometer up to one-third of its length into the rectum. Once the thermometer is inserted a little bit, your cat should relax and stop resisting it.

4. Gently push the thermometer in about one and a half inches. Keep it in place for approximately two minutes and hold on to the exposed end. It is rare that the thermometer will break off; if this happens, usually it's because the cat tries to sit down. Do not attempt to find and extract the broken end. Notify your veterinarian immediately.

HOW TO TAKE YOUR CAT'S PULSE

The normal pulse rate of a cat is 150–240 beats per minute. To take your cat's pulse, grasp the chest just behind the elbows with one hand while supporting the cat with the other. Move your hand until you detect a heartbeat. Count the number of beats in twenty seconds, and multiply that number by three. For example, 50 beats in 20 seconds would be 150 beats per minute.

You can also take a cat's pulse by feeling for the heartbeat on the inside of the back leg where it joins the body. Use the above beat count.

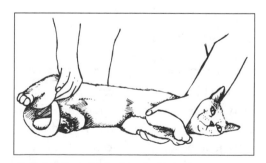

Feel for the pulse inside the back leg.

YOUR CAT'S FIRST-AID KIT

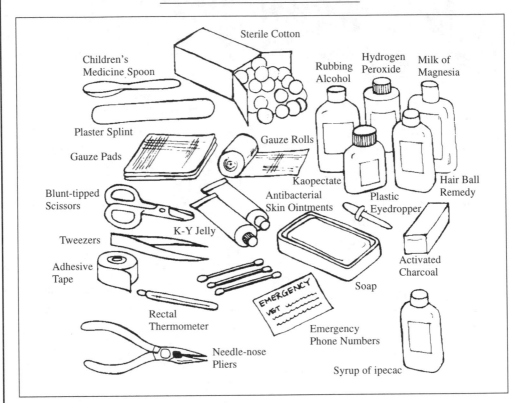

The kit should be stocked with the following items :

1. **Activated charcoal to absorb poisons.**
2. **Adhesive tape (a one-inch-wide roll).**
3. **Antibacterial skin ointments to soothe minor rashes and burns.**
4. **Blunt-tipped scissors.**

COLLECTING URINE SAMPLES

If you have only one cat, the simplest way to get a urine specimen is to remove most of the litter from the pan and just wait. Once your cat has urinated in the pan, simply use an eyedropper to collect a sample.

Make sure that you've thoroughly cleaned the pan before taking a urine sample. Rinse the tray thoroughly so that the sample is not contaminated with disinfectant.

Refrigerate the sample until you can take it to your veterinarian. If you have more than one cat using the litter box, it will probably be neces-

5. Children's medicine spoon or syringe (with needle removed; ask a veterinarian to provide this) for administering liquids.
6. Emergency phone numbers: Keep your veterinarian's phone number handy, taped inside the lid of the kit. Some cities and towns have pet emergency ambulance services; keep that number in the kit as well.
7. Gauze pads (three by three inches).
8. Gauze roll (three-inch roll). Used for compresses, bandages, and tourniquets.
9. Hair ball remedy (check with your veterinarian for the most effective commercial product).
10. Hydrogen peroxide (the 3 percent solution is good for use as an antiseptic and to induce vomiting).
11. Kaopectate (for control of diarrhea; also good for coating the stomach to prevent the absorption of poison).
12. Milk of magnesia, liquid or tablets (these are used as laxatives; good for preventing absorption of poison).
13. Needle-nose pliers (to remove objects that are caught in your cat's throat).
14. Plaster splint.
15. Plastic eyedropper for administering liquid medication.
16. Rectal thermometer (either the type used by veterinarians or the hospital type).
17. A tube of K-Y jelly or petroleum jelly for taking temperature rectally.
18. Rubbing alcohol (effective for removing ticks).
19. Soap for cleaning wounds.
20. Sterile cotton (used for removing ticks, cleaning ears, and as a cushion under bandages).
21. Syrup of ipecac to induce vomiting in case of poisoning.
22. Tweezers for tick removal.

sary for you to take your cat to your veterinarian to obtain a urine sample.

RESTRAINING A CAT

Cats seem to have a sixth sense about when you are going to give them some medication or apply a treatment. At such times, they usually make themselves very scarce.

Be aware of this and plan ahead. Begin by confining your cat to one room well ahead of time. It is a good idea to have someone help you. Even the best-natured cats are reluctant patients and need to be held while you administer medication.

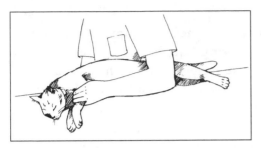

Stretch your cat out and restrain her by holding her hind legs in one hand and the scruff of her neck in the other.

Should no assistant be available, place your cat on a counter or table. This confuses and distracts the cat and prevents her from escaping easily; on the floor, you have less control and your cat has more room to maneuver. Stretch the cat out so she does not scratch you with her rear claws; hold her down with one arm while medicating with the other.

If you do have help, stretch the cat out on the table. Grasp her by the hind legs and the scruff of the neck while your assistant takes care of medicating or applying other treatments.

Even if you own a good-natured cat, be gentle in handling her. Too much restraint or sudden, rough movements will frighten your pet: the result will be an uncooperative patient. When you place a good-natured cat on the counter or table, hold her gently in the stretched-out position. Speak soothingly to her. If your cat wants to grasp the edge of the counter or table with her front feet, allow her to do so.

In the case of an extremely uncooperative cat, protect yourself and anyone who may be assisting you by wearing heavy gloves and long sleeves.

BANDAGING A CAT

Bandages keep wounds clean and dry, thus reducing the chances of infection. However, they are more difficult to apply to cats than they are to dogs. And rare is the cat owner who after finally applying a bandage later finds it still in place. If your cat sustains the type of injury (such as a paw, limb, or tail wound) that requires a bandage, you should first firmly but gently restrain your cat (see Restraining a Cat in this chapter).

FOOT WOUND

Apply sterile gauze pads to the wound. Insert cotton balls between the toes. Wrap the foot snugly with adhesive tape to hold gauze pads and cotton balls in place.

NOTE: If your cat sustains an injury requiring bandaging, it is always wise to consult with a veterinarian. He or she will confirm whether the wound requires professional attention, or whether you will be able to administer care at home.

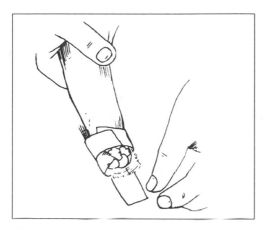

When bandaging a paw, place cotton between each toe.

LEG WOUND

Wrap the leg as described on page 86. Apply several sterile gauze pads to the wound. Keep the pads in place by binding them with strips of adhesive tape. Wrap the tape around the leg, but not too tightly. If the dressing remains on for some time, periodically check for swelling.

TAIL WOUND

Apply adhesive tape to support the tail until you see your veterinarian (see Fractures, p. 246).

EYE WOUND

Your veterinarian may prescribe an eye bandage for your cat as part of the treatment. Place a sterile gauze square over the affected eye and keep it in place by taping around the head and under the chin with one-inch adhesive. Do not tape too tightly, and keep the ears free.

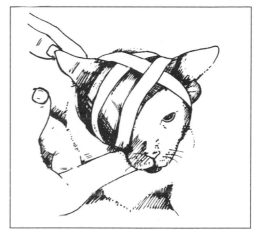

When bandaging an eye, always keep the ears free.

EAR WOUND

These dressings are difficult to apply. Most ear injuries can be left exposed. Consult your veterinarian.

If your cat is scratching an area of her skin that is being treated for some wound or disorder, you can wrap her hind legs with gauze, bandage, and tape, making sure that the claws are covered. This will allow the affected area to heal properly.

If the lesion or wound is on the body around the chest or rib cage, you can wrap an old T-shirt, portion of a pillowcase, or a towel around your cat and pin it securely; this will keep her from licking or scratching the affected area.

ELIZABETHAN COLLARS

There may be an area that cannot be bandaged. In such a case you can make an "Elizabethan" collar, which resembles the fashion style popular in sixteenth-century Elizabethan England. This ingenious apparatus will prevent your cat from turning around to lick the problem area.

Pet supply stores as well as veterinarians often keep vinyl Elizabethan collars in stock. However, they are also fairly simple to make at home using cardboard or plastic.

Take a circular piece of cardboard or plastic and cut a hole in the middle just wide enough to allow your cat to slip her head through. Punch two parallel arcs of eyelets through the bottom of the circle, each running along the circle's circumference. Run string through these eyelets and fasten the string to your cat's regular collar. If you have made the Elizabethan collar the right size, it should now be secure. Remove by simply untying the strings and slipping the collar over your cat's head.

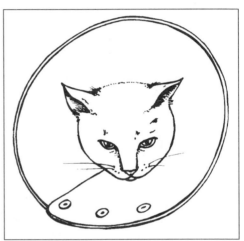

An Elizabethan collar keeps the cat from scratching or biting wounds and infected or irritated areas.

Elizabethan collars are also good to keep your cat from scratching an ear wound.

NURSING A SICK CAT AT HOME

When nursing an ill cat at home, use many of the precautions you would apply to a human patient. Your objectives are simple: to prevent infection or reinfection, to provide optimum conditions for recovery, and to make your sick pet's life as pleasant as possible.

DEPRESSION

Cats who are ill often become depressed. If you are nursing a cat who is ill or recuperating from an illness, you should spend as much time as you can with her.

Speak soothingly to her. Stroke her gently and make sure that she is getting proper nourishment and is grooming herself. Should you need to leave the house, remember to turn on the radio to help keep your cat company. A news or talk show is better than music, because cats feel comforted by human voices.

Do not involve your cat in any energetic play, but certainly provide her with a favorite toy so that she gets some exercise.

BED

Rest and warmth are essential to ill cats. The "sick room" should contain a comfortable bed of easily laundered materials. The bed should be in a corner free from drafts and out of the way of strong sunlight. The sick room must have a warm, even temperature and be adequately ventilated. A sick cat tends to chill quickly, so heating pads and electric blankets or hot water bottles are all good warming elements. Be careful, however, that hot water bottles and heating pads do not burn your cat. Always cover the heat source with a towel, making sure its surface never touches your cat's skin. Never leave a heat source on when you are not at home.

PEACE AND QUIET

Cats who are ill or recovering from an illness need rest. If you have children in the household, try to keep them reasonably quiet and don't do anything to worry or annoy your cat.

EXERCISE

Try to discourage your patient from wandering about, and under no circumstances should you allow a sick, convalescing, or injured cat to go outdoors. If possible, place the sick-room within sight and sound of interesting household goings-on. The idea is to keep your cat resting but interested in the outside world. When they become ill, cats have a tendency to withdraw. They fare better psychologically if they receive human attention and affection.

FOOD

Cats who are not feeling well sometimes avoid food. You will have to try various ways to make sure that your cat gets some nourishment. Unless your veterinarian disagrees, feed your cat only small amounts of food she can digest easily. If your cat is having difficulty keeping regular cat food down, try strained foods for babies or some nourishing bland dishes such as tepid beef broth, cottage cheese, or soft-boiled eggs. If your cat is recovering from an illness, she will probably be on a special diet prescribed by your veterinarian. Check with your veterinarian if the cat is refusing that special food.

FORCE-FEEDING

Sometimes a cat who is not feeling well will shun food and water. If your

HOW TO FORCE-FEED YOUR CAT

1. Hold your cat's head. Using one hand, squeeze the side of her cheeks with your thumb and forefinger to open her mouth.

2. Place some of the nutrient preparation (in paste form) on the index finger of your other hand.

3. Put the paste on the roof of your cat's mouth.

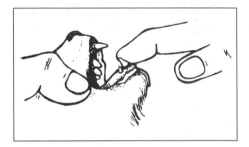

Force-feeding may require two people. One person can open the cat's mouth and insert food, while the other keeps the cat's head steady.

cat is not on a special diet, one way to get a cat to eat is to provide her with very strong-smelling, fishy foods. Don't be afraid to experiment with other kinds of food. Special treats or food that she is rarely fed may whet your cat's appetite. Some rare roast beef or expensive canned salmon might just do the trick.

If your cat still refuses to take any nourishment, you may have to force-feed her. A nutrient preparation in paste form is available through your veterinarian. Or you can concoct your own recipe using some of this paste and adding canned cat food. Then follow the steps outlined in the above box.

Never give too much food too quickly; this could cause gagging and vomiting. A good rule of thumb is to give your cat about two ounces of food every couple of hours during the day.

To feed your cat liquid food or water, follow the procedures for giving liquid medication.

HOW TO GIVE YOUR CAT MEDICATION

TOPICAL MEDICATIONS

Topical medications come in three basic forms: liquid drops, ointments, and creams.

HOW TO GIVE YOUR CAT LIQUID DROPS

When giving liquid medication to your cat:

1. Hold your cat's head up at a forty-five-degree angle.

2. Make a pouch in the corner of the lip fold by pulling the cheek outward.

3. Use an eyedropper. Slowly pour the liquid into the pouch.

4. If your cat does not swallow the liquid, jiggle the pouch slightly or tap the flat surface of your cat's nose with your finger. This will cause her to swallow. Make certain that your cat's head

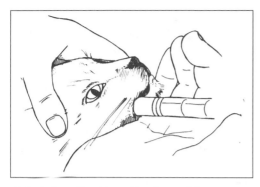

Administer liquid medications with an eyedropper.

remains tilted at a forty-five-degree angle until the liquid is swallowed.

An alternative method is to grasp your cat by the scruff of the neck. Pull back so that the head is tilted backward and the mouth is open. You may then use an eyedropper to administer the liquid drop by drop, letting it run down the tongue.

ADMINISTERING OINTMENTS AND CREAMS

Cats frequently lick a medication off their skin as soon as it is applied. To prevent this from happening, when you apply the ointment or cream rub it well into the skin and allow it to be absorbed for several minutes, using your hands to keep your cat's mouth away from the medication.

HOW TO GIVE YOUR CAT PILLS

Giving pills to a cat can be an exasperating experience. Unlike dogs, in whose

TO ADMINISTER A PILL

1. Tilt the head backward, with your thumb and fingertips on either side of the jaw.
2. Open the mouth by pushing on the front of the lower jaw with your other index finger. Have your assistant place the pill as far back on the tongue as possible.

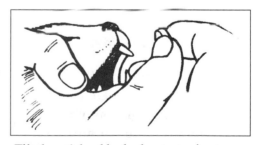

Tilt the cat's head back when preparing to administer a pill.

3. Close the mouth and start stroking your cat's throat in order to stimulate the swallowing reflex.

If you don't have an assistant, hold the pill or capsule in your hand between your thumb and index finger. With your other hand, tilt the cat's head back at a forty-five-degree angle and gently press open the corner of the mouth. Move your fingers around to the front teeth and press the lower jaw down until the mouth is open enough to pop the pill in; place it as far back on the center of the tongue as possible.

case you can hide pills in food, cats will usually find the pill and push it aside.

In order for a cat to swallow a pill, it must be placed in the back of the cat's mouth, the mouth held closed, and the chin stroked until the tongue comes forward and the pill is swallowed.

Giving a cat a pill may require sev-eral attempts. Do not give up out of frustration. It's perfectly normal for your cat to try to spit out the pill she so badly needs. You can aid the process by speaking soothingly to your cat and stroking her. But be sure to act swiftly and with authority, assuring your cat that you know exactly how to accom-

---

APPLYING EAR AND EYE MEDICATION

HOW TO APPLY EYE MEDICATION

Liquid drops or ointments are usu-ally used to treat eye disorders. To apply such medication:

1. Place one hand on top of your cat's head to tilt the head upward.
2. With your free hand, place the drops directly over each eye. Ointments should be squeezed in a fine line on the inside of the lower lid.

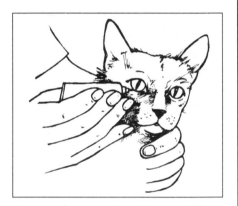

Squeeze ointment along the lower lid.

HOW TO APPLY EAR MEDICATION

Eardrops or ointments are fairly easy to apply:

1. Hold cat firmly. Using your index finger and thumb, gen-tly manipulate ear until ear canal is exposed.
2. Squeeze recommended dosage into ear.
3. Hold edges of the ear closed and gently rub the base of the ear so that the drops are dis-tributed inside. Try to keep your cat from shaking her head and spraying drops.

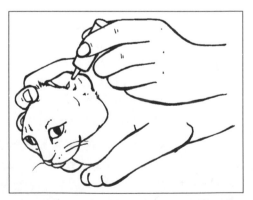

Apply ear medication directly into ear canal.

plish your goal. Praise your cat when the task has been completed successfully. With patience and a little practice, you should soon master one of these methods.

AFTER SURGERY

A cat that has just come out of surgery requires constant supervision. Some critical cases require intensive care and must remain in a veterinary hospital. Other cats may be sent home after a day or two of observation. If your veterinarian believes that your cat will not respond to anyone but her owner, he or she will recommend home recovery. This may involve bringing your cat back to the hospital daily or even twice daily for treatment.

Make sure your recovering cat gets plenty of rest. Recovery time depends upon the reason for surgery and the areas affected. The cat will be tired and weak at first, which is actually beneficial —it will enable her to get plenty of much-needed peace and sleep. Keep her to any recommended dietary restrictions. Check for any problems with the incision area; if there is any swelling, pus, redness, or if the wound emits a foul odor, call your veterinarian. Also call if a fever occurs, or if your cat refuses to eat. Keep all appointments with your cat's doctor.

DISABLED CATS

A severe injury or bone infection can sometimes result in the amputation of a limb. Cats can adapt quite well to getting around on three legs and often make the adjustment to a missing leg better than people do. Veterinarians report many cases in which the amputee is walking around the day after surgery. In a few days they are running and playing —even climbing—as if nothing has happened. Disabled cats can lead normal lives for years to come, so there is no need to fret about your cat if she has lost a limb.

7

CARING FOR
THE OLDER CAT

WITH PROPER CARE and good luck, your cat can live quite a long time—more than twice as long as a dog. Cats sometimes survive for seventeen or more

The older cat may appear to have lost weight and muscle tone.

years, although it is rather uncommon for a cat to reach his twentieth birthday.

The feline year equals about four human years, which means a cat is well into middle age by his eighth birthday. As is the case with people, the threshold from middle age into old age varies, pretty much depending on care, diet, and heredity.

The life span of uncared-for stray cats is much shorter. Such wanderers live approximately two years. Roaming toms are the least likely to make it to middle or old age.

There is not much evidence regarding the longevity of different breeds. The general rule seems to be that any cat that has been closely inbred is likely to have a shorter-than-average life span.

THE AGING PROCESS

As cats age, their bodies start functioning less efficiently. The older cat becomes less active and less adaptable. Loss of muscle tone on the elderly cat's frame means that the cat loses strength and stamina.

The elderly cat is thinner than a young cat, and his appetite sometimes lags. He seeks warm spots and sleeps more. The coat of an older feline may be thin, and there is usually some graying around the muzzle.

As is the case with elderly humans, an aging cat's sight and hearing may become less acute. An older cat also may show less concern about keeping himself clean. Elderly cats often suffer from bowel problems, such as constipation. They also occasionally lose control of their bowels and bladder.

Dental disease is quite common in geriatric cats, as are eye and ear problems. A cat's chances of developing cancer also increase with age, as cancer-causing products accumulate in the body or the immune system becomes impaired.

Old age is probably most noticeable in breeding cats, especially queens. If not spayed, the elderly female cat will still come into heat and mate, but the litters become smaller after the age of eight years. At age eleven or twelve, breeding females often fail to produce kittens even after mating has occurred. This is not the case with toms. Elderly toms may retain their potency into ripe old age, sometimes siring kittens at fifteen years of age.

An elderly cat's greatest need is affection. Although he may not play as much as he used to, he wants attention more than ever.

If you want to add years to your cat's life, give him extra attention and treat him with gentleness, tenderness, and the dignity befitting his years.

Old cats require special care. That care should begin with regular checkups every three to four months. In addition, it is important that you be alert to any problems that your cat may be experiencing.

Take simple precautions with your feline senior citizen. Make sure his bed is away from any drafts. If you allow your cat outdoors, limit his activities during cold weather. In hot weather, air conditioning is a great benefit to geriatric cats.

Another thing you can do to make an elderly cat feel more comfortable is to place litter pans in various rooms in case your pet should lose bladder or bowel control. Be understanding of accidents; your elderly cat is not misbehaving on purpose.

If you own an elderly long-haired cat, he may require some assistance with his grooming. You may also want to keep your cat's nails trimmed, since his reduced exercise level may cause them to grow too long. If your elderly cat begins to lose interest in grooming himself, it may become necessary for you to regularly clean his face and anal region with warm water.

Because old cats prefer comfortable routines and do not adapt well to new situations, avoid sudden or unexpected

ACCIDENT-PROOFING AN ELDERLY CAT'S HOME

As cats age, they often become more accident-prone. Loss of agility, muscle tone, and failing eyesight all increase the likelihood that your cat may occasionally bump into something, perhaps causing damage to an object, or more seriously, inflicting damage upon himself. Here are some tips on making a home accident-proof for the elderly cat, and in helping your cat be as comfortable as possible:

- Become even more vigilant about wires and furnishings that may cause injury. Keep all wires taped to the floor under carpets and rugs.
- Keep rugs securely fastened to the floor.
- Try to help your cat avoid jumping on to or down from high places.
- If your cat has become sight-impaired, you must also make certain that he is not allowed outdoors.
- Keep your cat's food, water, litter box, scratching post, and bed in places that he is familiar with.

changes in your environment. If you must go away for an extended period of time, make detailed arrangements for the care of your pet while you're away. Older cats often have a difficult time adjusting to a new environment, so the best option for care while you're out of town is to ask a friend or neighbor to look in on your cat each day. If possible, choose someone who your cat already knows. In addition to ensuring that your cat is well and properly fed, this surrogate caretaker should also give your cat love and attention — a few minutes of warm petting should impress upon your cat that everything is fine, even though his loved ones are temporarily absent.

Try to avoid other situations that may cause your geriatric feline stress. For example, try to avoid bringing strange pets into the home, or moving your cat out of the home too frequently.

DIET

Your elderly cat's diet should include high-quality protein food such as fish, meat, and poultry. Your cat should also be given a vitamin-mineral supplement. Consult with your veterinarian about the best types of feline supplements for aged cats. According to the National Research Council, a properly fed elderly cat should be taking in about thirty-two calories per pound of body weight daily.

If your cat's appetite decreases and strong-smelling food fails to whet his appetite, consult your veterinarian. Lack of appetite is often a symptom of a disorder. If your cat stops eating, he may have a mouth or tooth ailment.

A general rule of thumb regarding proper nutrition for the aging cat is to feed him smaller and more frequent meals, but less in total daily intake. Avoid fried, greasy, spicy, and salty foods, because older cats have less ability to assimilate them. Also, avoid any sudden changes in his diet.

Watch the weight of your cat after middle age. A cat that has been overweight all his life should be put on a reduced diet. Obesity can contribute to such disorders as heart and kidney disease. An overweight cat is also less likely to exercise (see Exercise).

Water is as important to a cat in old age as it is to younger cats. Make certain that you provide your elderly cat with plenty of liquids, as kidney function often declines in elderly cats. Warm water or milk are both quite suitable. Keep in mind that excessive thirst may be a symptom of such disorders as diabetes or kidney disease.

Constipation is another frequent complaint of the older cat. It some- times occurs when a cat does not take in enough liquids. Your veterinarian should be able to direct you to a simple laxative, such as milk of magnesia, to take care of occasional constipation.

For the underweight elderly cat, it might be a good idea to mix one teaspoon of lard into his food. This will help provide extra calories to an old, lean pet who can no longer absorb nutrients very well or who has lost his insulating layer of underskin fat.

EXERCISE

Because the musculoskeletal system in an older cat tends to stiffen, moderate exercise can help keep an aging cat's joints supple. Moderate exercise should be encouraged despite an elderly cat's propensity to sleep away the hours. Do not force an older cat to exert himself beyond normal levels of activity.

If your cat is suffering from some ailment such as heart disease, exercise should not be encouraged unless you first consult your veterinarian.

8

SAYING GOOD-BYE

No matter how much love or care you give an elderly or a sickly cat, the time may come when it is obvious that life is intolerably burdensome for your beloved pet. Your cat may be in terrible pain, or so diseased that she can no longer function. If and when that terrible day comes, you must make the difficult decision of whether or not to put your cat to sleep—a procedure known as euthanasia.

It may be best to let your veterinarian advise you about when it is best to say good-bye. His or her decision will be made based on the medical situation rather than on emotional factors.

Your immediate reaction may be grief or revulsion, but the welfare of your cat should be your first consideration. Do you want to prolong your cat's suffering, or would you rather let her die with dignity?

EUTHANASIA

Euthanasia is a painless procedure in which a veterinarian injects an overdose of an anesthetic into a cat's foreleg. Painful poisons are not used. The only pain your cat will feel is the prick of the needle. The anesthetic causes the cat to go to sleep in a few seconds. A cat anesthetized in this way will die peacefully within thirty seconds.

You may choose to be present. Many cat owners fear that the sight of their cat in her death throes will be more than they can bear. If you are present, you will see no death throes— only your cat going to sleep.

BURIAL AND CREMATION

Once your cat is dead, you may give your veterinarian permission to make arrangements for the disposal of her body. Of course, you can make your own arrangements, particularly if you happen to know of a pet cemetery where you would like to see your cat buried. Most veterinarians dispose of a cat's remains through public waste-disposal services or by cremation.

If you need more information about pet cemeteries, you should contact your local Humane Society. Pet cemeteries sell plots and can also provide headstones and monuments.

LOSS AND GRIEVING

Losing a pet can be as difficult as losing any other family member. Despite the emotional pain you may be feeling, you may find it difficult to discuss your feelings with friends, family, or neighbors, fearing that they will not understand all the fuss you are making over an animal.

This concern should not deter you from seeking companionship and sympathy. Do not ever be ashamed of expressing your grief. It is as healthy to mourn for a beloved pet as it is to mourn the loss of a human friend or relative. Talk about your grief; don't hold it in. Friends and counselors are available and more than willing to listen. If you want to find a grief counselor, call your local Humane Society and ask for a recommendation.

In 1969, Elisabeth Kübler-Ross wrote a ground-breaking book called *On Death and Dying.* In it she describes five stages of grief in the face of death: denial and isolation, anger, bargaining, depression, and acceptance. You may experience some or all of these emotions before or after the death of your longtime feline companion. Once you can begin to recall the happy moments you had with your cat without experiencing a great deal of emotional pain, your period of bereavement is over.

This does not mean that you have forgotten your feline friend. But perhaps it indicates a proper time to begin thinking about a new friendship with another cat in need of a loving owner.

You can soon learn to love another animal. You may not love a new pet in exactly the same way, but all animals are individuals, and you and your family will soon recognize that there is much to love about the new cat in your lives.

The death of a pet often has a particularly devastating impact on children and the elderly. For a child, death is a new experience. How you as a parent relate to your child's feelings can have a lasting influence. Be very sensitive. Discuss what happened to the cat honestly and openly. Not letting children know all the facts could leave them feeling guilty or somehow responsible for what has happened. You may even wish to plan a small memorial ceremony for your cat with your children. Getting them involved in the planning of this activity may help relieve their grief.

An elderly person who lives alone may have established a very special bond with the pet. When this close companion dies, the owner is often not only grief-stricken but may refuse to get another pet for fear of not outliving it and leaving it alone and in need of care. In such cases, a mature cat rather than a kitten may be the perfect choice. Such a cat already understands life in a human setting and is more than eager to settle right in. While the new cat may not replace the old one in the mind and heart of an elderly person, she will nonetheless bring numerous joys and pleasures and help her new owner live a longer and healthier life.

One effective way for an owner to cope with the prospect of dying before their pet is to make a will that specifies what they want done with the animal in the event of their death.

Bequests, memorial gifts, life insurance, and charitable trusts are ways in which many animal lovers prepare for their pets' futures after their own deaths. Surviving-pet maintenance programs are on the rise throughout the country. Your local Humane Society or veterinarian can provide you with information about such programs. If you die without a will, state law decides what happens to your money and property—and that includes pets.

For however long you own a cat, the important thing to remember is to enjoy the company of your feline companion and fulfill your obligation to see that she goes through life healthy and contented. A cat can't say it, but if she could she would probably express gratitude at being blessed with your affection and care.

PART III

THE ENCYCLOPEDIA OF CAT HEALTH

An At-a-Glance Guide
to Signs and Symptoms

THIS IS YOUR QUICK REFERENCE GUIDE to various symptoms your cat may experience. It helps you to identify the disorders with which a given symptom is associated and refers you immediately to the pages that discuss all the problems that may be indicated by that symptom.

For example: If you notice that your cat has suddenly begun to breathe noisily, consult this reference guide to find Breathing Problems. There you will see an entry for noisy breathing problems. Turn to the page indicated, and you will find information on that subject.

Remember that any given symptom has many possible causes. In addition, a severe symptom does not necessarily indicate that something serious is wrong with your cat. In fact, many minor disorders can provoke dramatic symptoms, while some far more seri-

ous ailments often have almost unidentifiable signs.

As with human beings, symptoms are the body's way of alerting you that something is wrong. Heed them, since early diagnosis and treatment of any ailment or disease increases the odds of a successful and speedy recovery.

It is especially vital that you pay close attention to your pet's health, because your pet cannot tell you that it is not feeling well. If you observe the slightest deviation from any of your cat's normal habits or any change in its appearance, contact your veterinarian immediately.

ABDOMEN
Exposed internal organs   214–215
Painful   114, 189, 193, 194, 229, 238, 250, 258, 259, 261, 262, 264, 265, 266
Swollen   186, 188, 215, 240

Abscesses, lesions   139, 154,
    163
Acne   149–150
Allergic reactions   155, 156,
    160
  Insects   349–350
  Poisons   255–267
Anal irritation
  Biting   181
  Bleeding   181
  Licking   181, 186
  Matted hair   150, 181
  Odor   181
  Pain   186
  Protrusions   182
  Rubs on ground (scooting)   181,
    182, 186
Anemia   117, 118, 123, 152, 153,
    172, 174, 184, 185, 194, 197
Anxiety   188, 239, 243, 249, 257,
    262
Appetite
  Loss of   114, 117, 121, 123, 139,
    140, 142, 145, 146, 162, 163,
    172, 173, 178, 186, 193, 194,
    196, 197, 212
  Increase of   183, 189
  Variability of   186
Back
  Hunched or arched   119, 194
  Rubs on ground (see Scooting)
Bad breath   138, 140, 142, 194
Balance impaired   121, 129, 131,
    176, 178, 251, 254, 255
Balding   149, 150, 153, 154, 156,
    248
Behavioral changes   120–121,
    176
Biting or chewing at itself   150
Blackheads   150
Bladder (obstructed)   194

Bleeding (see also Eyes, Ears,
    Nose, Mouth)
  In feces   123, 181, 183, 187, 259,
    262
  In urine   253, 262
  In vomit   253, 258
  Wounds   239, 253
Blindness (see Eyes)
Blisters   227, 240, 241
Bloat   240
Body (stiffening)   167
Bones (creaking, fragile)   169,
    170
Breasts
  Bloody   212
  Painful   213
  Swollen   212
Breath (see Bad Breath)
Breathing problems
  Labored   115, 117, 123, 160, 162,
    163, 173, 174, 197, 229, 238,
    239, 245, 248, 250, 251, 259,
    263, 264
  Noisy   122, 145, 173
  None   243
  Rapid   123, 172, 176, 213, 251,
    263
  Shortness of   115, 173, 213, 251
  Through mouth   145, 162
Brown stains in corners of eyes
    134
Bruises   151
Cataracts   132
Champing   244
Chewing (difficulty)   139, 140,
    142
Chiggers   151
Chills (see Shivering)
Choking   146
Collapse   120, 162, 172, 174, 188,
    213, 249, 254, 261, 262

COMA   120, 121, 176, 188, 254, 259, 261, 263, 266
CONJUNCTIVITIS (PINK EYE)   132
CONSTIPATION   181, 185, 188, 250
CONVULSIONS (SEE SEIZURES, SPASMS)
COORDINATION POOR (SEE BALANCE IMPAIRED)
COUGHING   115, 123, 146, 149, 160, 161, 162, 173, 174, 197
CRACKED PADS   167
CROUCHING   120, 129
CRYING   228, 229
CYSTS   214
DANDRUFF   158,
DEAFNESS   126, 129
DEHYDRATION   114, 117, 119, 123, 183, 186, 188, 194, 229, 250
DEPRESSION   114, 119, 162, 163, 188, 196, 215, 251, 261
DIARRHEA   114, 115, 117, 119, 123, 149, 180, 183, 184, 185, 186, 188, 189, 194, 197, 229, 250, 251, 261, 262, 264, 265, 266
DILATED PUPILS (SEE EYES; PUPILS, DILATED)
DISCHARGE (SEE EYES, EARS, NOSE, PENIS, VAGINAL DISCHARGE)
DISORIENTATION   177
DIZZINESS   177, 178
DRINKING, EXCESSIVE (SEE THIRST)
DROOLING (EXCESSIVE)   120, 121, 122, 139, 141, 188, 242, 245, 247, 249, 255, 261, 262, 263, 264
EARS
   Bald spots   129
   Dark material inside   127, 128
   Discharge   128
   Foul odor   128
   Infection   128
   Inflammation   128, 157
   Pain   128
   Reddening   128, 129
   Scaly Edges   154, 156
   Scratching   128, 129
   Swelling   128
EYEBALL (BULGING)   131, 135
EYES
   Cloudy   132, 133, 134, 135, 137
   Discharge   121, 132, 134, 135, 161
   Failing   131, 252
   Inflammation   121
   Loss of night vision   136
   Painful   132, 134
   Pawing at   133, 136
   Pink or red   132, 134, 136, 157
   Pupils dilated   135, 239, 248, 261
   Rapid jerking movements   129, 178, 254
   Sensitive to light   120, 134
   Sores   157
   Third eyelid   135, 136
   Turn yellowish   188
   Unevenly sized, bulging   131, 135, 243
EYELIDS (SWOLLEN, DISCOLORED)   132, 134, 149, 157, 238
FACE (SWOLLEN, PAWING AT)   139
FAINTING (SEE COLLAPSE)   142
FALLING   178
FANG MARKS   252
FALSE PREGNANCIES   213–214
FATIGUE   172, 173
FEET (SORE, SWOLLEN, TENDER)   169
FEVER   114, 115, 117, 119, 123, 146, 161, 162, 163, 167, 176, 186, 189, 194, 212, 215, 250
FITS (SEIZURES, CONVULSIONS)   177, 178, 244
FLATULENCE   182–183, 186

FLEAS   151–153
FLIES AROUND WOUND   154, 156
FOAMING AT MOUTH   161
FOLDED EYELID   134–135
FUR
  Clumps, comes out easily   241
  Dark specks   152
  Dull   186, 187
  Foul odor   150
  Wet with saliva   143
GAGGING   139, 146, 243
GROWTH, SLOW   228
GUMS (DISCOLORED)   114, 160, 162, 163
  Bleeding   142
  Painful   141
HAIR (LOSS, PATCHY) (SEE BALDNESS)
HEAD
  Drooping   119
  Shaking   178
HEARING (DIFFICULTY)   126, 129
HEAT (FREQUENT, PROLONGED)   214
HOARSENESS   146
INFERTILITY   214
INFLAMMATION OF MOUTH   141, 142
IRRITABILITY   186
JAUNDICE   188
JAWS (CHOMPING, HANGING OPEN)   121, 247
JERKY MOTIONS (GAIT)   194
JOINTS
  Enlarged   167, 169, 170
  Painful   167, 168, 169, 170, 194
  Rubbing and grating sounds   167
KITTENS
  Aggression toward   213
  Rejection, refusal to tend   213
LAMENESS   167, 168, 169
LARYNGITIS   146

LEGS
  Cold   172, 174, 251
  Paralyzed   168, 247, 258
  Rigid   115
  Swollen   148, 170, 250
  Weak   173, 189, 251
LETHARGY   114, 117, 119, 121, 122, 123, 146, 162, 173, 178, 185, 187, 189, 194, 196, 212, 215, 228, 249, 250, 251, 258
LICKING (EXCESSIVE)   150, 152, 156, 199, 200, 215
LIMPING   168, 246
LIPS (SEE ALSO MOUTH)
  Bumps   150, 157
  Burned   245
  Chapped   139
  Discolored   160, 162
  Retracted   115
  Ulcers   141
LUMPS AND BUMPS   157, 158, 195–196
MANGE   154, 157
MISCARRIAGE   214
MITES   127, 154
MOUTH
  Burned   242, 257, 258, 263, 266
  Difficulty opening   115
  Foaming   143, 244
  Irritated   157, 257, 263
  Pawing at   139, 142, 243
  Ulcers   141, 143, 150, 194
MUSCLE SPASMS   115, 244, 245, 261, 263
NOISY BREATHING (SEE BREATHING)
NOSE (DISCHARGE, NOSEBLEED)   115, 117, 121, 122, 144, 145, 161, 162, 247, 262
ODOR (FOUL)   154, 167, 181
PANTING   249, 260, 266
PARALYSIS   115, 121, 172, 213, 250, 254, 262

PATCHY BALDNESS (SEE BALDNESS)

PAWING (AT EYES, MOUTH, ETC.)   136, 139, 142

PENIS (DISCHARGE, EXTENDED)   199, 200

PERSONALITY CHANGE   120, 121, 176

POTBELLY (FILLED WITH FLUID)   173

PULSE (ABNORMAL)   172, 173, 248, 262

PUPILS (DILATED, CONSTRICTED)   135, 239, 261

PUS   142, 148, 150, 156, 167

RESTLESSNESS   120, 127, 188, 213, 228, 238, 262

ROLLS ON GROUND   178

RUBBING UP AGAINST (EXCESSIVE)   127

RUNNING (AIMLESS, IN CIRCLES)   129, 254

SALIVATION (EXCESS) (SEE DROOLING)

SCABS   156, 248

SCALINESS   135, 149, 156, 248

SCOOTING (RUBBING ON GROUND)   181, 182, 186

SCRATCHING (EXCESSIVE)   120, 127, 149, 150, 152, 153, 156, 157

SEIZURES   176, 177, 244, 245, 257, 259, 261, 262, 263, 266

SHIVERING   248, 250, 251, 255

SKIN (CHANGES)   122, 123, 135, 158, 169, 172, 174, 241, 242, 248

Inflammation   149, 150, 151, 154, 155, 241, 263

SNEEZING (EXCESSIVE)   115, 121, 122, 144, 145, 149, 161, 238

SOILING   40–42

SORES   129, 141, 142, 150, 156, 238

SPASMS (OF MUSCLES)   115, 213, 245, 257, 259, 261, 263, 266

SPUTUM (BLOOD IN)   174

STAGGERING   120, 129, 169, 177, 249, 251, 258, 261, 262

STIFFENING OF BODY   167, 248

STRAINING (STOOLS, URINATING)   181, 182, 186, 193, 194

SWALLOWING (REPEATEDLY, DIFFICULTIES)   115, 140

SWELLING (SEE LEGS, FACE, ETC.)

TAIL

Limp   248

Stiff   115

TARTAR   140, 141, 142

TEARING   133, 134, 135, 136, 137, 149, 238

TEETH (DAMAGED, LOOSE)   141, 142, 169

THIRST (EXCESSIVE)   183, 188, 189, 193, 194, 215, 251, 262

TONGUE

Bitten   253

Blue   160, 162, 163, 239, 243

Burned   257, 263, 266

Ulcers   121

TREMBLING   178

TREMORS (SEE SPASMS)

TURNING IN CIRCLES   129, 178, 254

UNCONTROLLABLE MOTIONS   127

UNKEMPT APPEARANCE   139, 140, 142, 143, 196

UPSET STOMACH (SEE ABDOMINAL PAIN)

URINATION

Discolored   117, 188

Urinating excessively   189, 193, 194, 215

Urinating, unusual places   193, 194

Urine (blood in)   193, 194

Urine (pus in)   194

VAGINAL DISCHARGE   214, 215

VOMITING   114, 115, 117, 119, 129, 146, 149, 185, 186, 187, 188, 189, 193, 194, 197, 229, 238, 250, 251, 252, 255, 259, 260, 261, 263, 264, 265, 266

WALKING DIFFICULTIES (SEE
    STAGGERING)   131
WEAKNESS   114, 172, 173, 184, 193,
    194, 196, 197
WEIGHT (LOSS, GAIN)   115, 117, 121
WHEEZING   115, 122, 123, 139, 140,
    160, 162, 172, 173, 174, 183,
    184, 185, 186, 187, 188, 189,
    194, 196, 197
WORMS   183–186
YAWNING (EXCESSIVE)   188

INFECTIOUS DISEASES

CATS ARE SUSCEPTIBLE to many infectious diseases caused by bacteria, viruses, protozoa, and fungi. These microorganisms can invade your cat's body and cause harm.

Cats usually catch infectious diseases when they come in contact with sick animals or their excreta. Infections in cats can also occur as a result of a bite from another animal, from puncture wounds, or, in the case of viral infections, from inhaling germ-laden droplets in the air. Diseases are also spread through the genital tract when cats mate, or through contact with spores in the soil or in the air.

Keep in mind that while there are germs everywhere, only a few cause infections, and even fewer are contagious. Most feline infectious diseases are not harmful to humans as long as you take some precautions and observe basic rules of hygiene. If your cat was wormed as a kitten and has been eating commercially prepared cat food or home-cooked meals, there is little risk that you will contract a feline infectious disease. Some infectious diseases that can in theory be passed on to humans include ringworm, rabies, toxoplasmosis, roundworm larvae, and fleas. Tuberculosis in cats, although rare, may also present a slight risk of contagion to people. The opposite is also true under certain conditions.

If your cat does not succumb to an infectious disease, he probably has chemical substances in his immune system to fight off the specific germs that can cause illness. Even if your cat contracts some infectious disease, the chances are good that his immune system will begin to produce these chemical antibodies to fight off the invading germ, usually resulting in full recovery.

When a cat does recover from such a disease, his body continues to produce chemicals to guard against future attack by the same germ. Cats also possess another type of immunity, called "passive immunity." This is usually passed on from mother to kitten. While in his mother's uterus and from his first milk, a kitten will actually receive antibodies against certain disease cells. These antibodies help guard against certain diseases in kittens for their first six to twelve weeks of life. Vaccinations are available to guard against various infectious diseases (see Vaccinations, p. 79).

In general, cats are by nature hardy creatures. With proper veterinary treatment and home care, most cats recover from whatever may ail them.

FELINE BACTERIAL DISEASES

Bacteria are minute, single-celled microbes or germs that can cause major infectious diseases in cats. They are ancient organisms whose ancestry can be traced back to the dawn of life on earth.

These invisible microorganisms surround us in our everyday lives. They are complex, metabolizing, self-reproducing, living organisms (as opposed to viruses, which are incapable of reproduction except within living cells).

FEVER

Fever is a symptom that appears in many illnesses. In cats, a body temperature above 103 degrees Fahrenheit is a fever. A fever is not *always* a symptom of illness, however.

The body temperature of many healthy cats will sometimes vary a degree or two depending upon the time of day. The cat's emotional state, his activity level, or the environment (such as riding in a heated car) also can affect his temperature.

The most common cause of persistent fever in cats, however, is viral and bacterial infections such as feline leukemia virus, panleukopenia, and respiratory infections.

How can you tell if your cat is running a fever? Take his temperature (see the section on taking a cat's temperature, p. 82). Some of the signs accompanying fever are depression, a sad expression, and lack of appetite. Your cat may also seem cold or shivery, or he may feel hot and pant, seeking relief in a cool place. A cat with fever may also have an increased heart or respiratory rate.

Not all bacteria are harmful. Many contribute toward the health of humans and animals by aiding digestion and performing other beneficial functions. Some bacteria, however, can invade the deep tissues of their hosts and produce disease. Bacteria can cause a wide array of infections in cats at different stages of life. Kittens are particularly vulnerable to harmful bacteria because their immune systems are not yet fully active.

The good news, however, is that many harmful forms of bacteria can be destroyed—or at least prevented from multiplying—by antibiotics. If your cat does fall ill with some bacterial infection, with early treatment the odds of recovery are quite good.

ACUTE RESPIRATORY INFECTION (see ASTHMA, p. 160)

CAT SCRATCH DISEASE

CAUSES: Cat scratch disease (CSD) has more effect on humans than on cats. If you are bitten or scratched by a cat, there is a good chance you may develop a skin rash or a painful enlargement of local lymph nodes. Children are most likely to experience CSD symptoms.

Most cases of CSD syndrome take place when contact is made with a newly acquired kitten or stray, rather than with a longterm pet.

SYMPTOMS: Humans will develop skin rash, fatigue, loss of appetite, fever, headache. There are no symptoms for cats.

TREATMENT: CSD is not dangerous or fatal for cats or humans, so treatment in most cases is not warranted. If your symptoms continue, consult your physician.

PREVENTION: Teach your child to treat your cat—or any cat—gently, and the child will probably not be scratched or bitten. Also teach your children not to let your cat lick any of their open wounds or chapped hands. If your child is scratched or bitten by a cat, clean the wound carefully and apply a topical disinfectant.

FELINE INFECTIOUS ANEMIA

CAUSES: The bacterium responsible for feline infectious anemia (FIA) is known as *Hemobartonella felis*. It may live for a long time in your cat's body by attaching itself to the surface of red blood cells—it does not cause any harm while it does so. If for some reason your cat's immune system becomes weakened, however, these bacteria may then begin to destroy the very cells they live on, and FIA is the resulting condition.

Researchers believe that this microorganism is responsible for most feline infectious anemia cases. Male cats one to three years of age are twice as likely to get FIA as are females.

There is still no conclusive evidence about how cats contract this disease. Researchers believe that the bite of a flea or an infected cat that has come into contact with the parasite may be the transmitting factor.

If a mother cat is infected with this microorganism, she is likely to infect her kittens. The bacterium has been found in some kittens within three hours of birth, as well as in stillborn kittens.

SYMPTOMS: High fever; rapid loss of appetite; weakness; depression; pale or whitish gums, tongue, or inner linings of the eyelids; jaundice sometimes occurs.

TREATMENT: Consult your veterinarian. Treatment may include the administration of drugs such as Chloromycetin and tetracycline, along with a program of nutritional support. In severe cases blood transfusions may be necessary. FIA often occurs in conjunction with leukemia, and the outlook for a cat suffering from both these conditions tends to be poor.

SALMONELLA

There are nearly 2,000 types of salmonella bacteria that play havoc with human as well as feline health. Whenever we read about an outbreak of food poisoning in the newspapers, salmonella is usually the culprit.

Salmonella causes gastrointestinal infection in those cats whose immune systems have been weakened by viral infection, malnutrition, or some other form of stress. Kittens housed in unsanitary conditions may contract a bacterial infection caused by salmonella. Otherwise, cats are highly resistant to the salmonella bacteria.

Eating contaminated food or coming in contact with other animals infected by the salmonella bacteria can infect your cat. Cats can also contract this bacteria from rodent or bird feces, from raw, undercooked, or contaminated meat, or from canned pet foods that have been tainted during processing.

Once a cat eats food that contains the salmonella bacterium, the microorganism skirts the acidity of the stomach juices and settles into the small intestine and lymph nodes. From there it can easily enter the bloodstream and spread throughout a cat's body.

SYMPTOMS: Poor appetite, high fever, vomiting, diarrhea, dehydration, abdominal pain. In severe cases cats suffer from depression and lethargy.

TREATMENT: Consult your veterinarian. Treatment may involve antibiotics such as Chloromycetin. If salmonella is left untreated, death can result.

PREVENTION: Make certain that your cat or cats are housed in sanitary conditions and are well fed and cared for so that their immune systems remain strong.

NOTE: If you have young children, or anyone in your family who is taking immunosuppressive drugs or antibiotics, keep those individuals away from a cat diagnosed as infected with salmonella.

TETANUS (LOCKJAW)

CAUSES: While tetanus is quite rare in cats, all warm-blooded animals—including humans—can be infected by this bacterium, known scientifically as *Clostridium tetani.*

Any cut, bite, or puncture, such as by a rusty nail, can give the tetanus bacterium entry into the body. Tetanus usually inhabits soil contaminated by horse or cow manure—something your cat is not likely to encounter if you live in the city, but may well encounter if he roams in rural areas. Most species of animals play host to this organism in their intestinal tracts, but it usually does not cause any disease.

SYMPTOMS: Spastic contractions, rigid extension of the legs, difficulty opening the mouth, difficulty swallowing, paralysis, retraction of the lips and eyeballs. Sometimes the tail sticks straight out; muscle spasms occur when the cat is stimulated.

TREATMENT: Tetanus is usually fatal if not treated early by a trained professional. Treatment may include use of antibiotics and antitoxins, sedatives, and intravenous fluids.

NOTE: Should you be bitten by a cat, clean the wound by soaking it with hot water containing an antiseptic. See your doctor if you have not been vaccinated against tetanus within the previous three years.

TUBERCULOSIS

CAUSES: Now relatively rare in the United States (although there has been a recent outbreak of cases) tuberculosis (TB) can infect cats just as it can humans and other animals.

Three strains of tubercle bacillus can affect humans. Cats, however, are most susceptible to the bovine strain of the disease, the form of TB that affects cows. In those parts of the world where milk is not pasteurized, the feline death rate from TB runs as high as 12 percent.

Once this organism is ingested, it enters the small intestine and becomes localized in lymph nodes. Cats can spread this disease to other cats and animals through their feces. TB can also be contracted from drinking infected milk or by eating contaminated, uncooked beef.

SYMPTOMS: *Respiratory form:* Sneezing, nasal discharge, wheezy coughing, labored breathing and shortness of breath, especially after exercising. *Gastrointestinal form:* Low-grade fever, chronic weight loss despite good care and feeding, lung infection, vomiting, diarrhea.

TREATMENT: Tuberculosis is difficult to cure and requires a veterinarian's care. Treatment is lengthy and may include antituberculosis drugs. Because there is a risk of human infection, any cat that has contracted tuberculosis may have to be euthanized.

FELINE VIRAL DISEASES

Unlike bacteria and fungi, viruses are not living organisms. They have no independent metabolism, do not process nutrients, and do not generate waste material. To survive and reproduce they rely on the living cells of their host. Yet many viruses kill their host cells. This results in disease and often provokes a severe response by the host's immune system as it tries to rid itself of these unwanted invaders.

Sometimes the response is so severe that it can cause more harm than the disease. Viruses do not always kill their hosts, however. Sometimes they live in their hosts for years and cause no damage.

Your cat's best protection against viral-causing disease—better than any antiviral therapy—is his own immune system. A good way to help prevent viral diseases is to have your cat vaccinated (see Vaccinations, p. 79).

Feline viral respiratory diseases are highly contagious among cats; serious viral infections are also the most common cause of death in cats. Resistant as they are to external injuries and falls, when it comes to viral diseases they are very susceptible.

If you own a kitten or an older cat or have adopted a stray who is in poor health, the risk of illness from feline respiratory diseases is high. If you have a multicat household, make certain that their living space is well ventilated and that your cats are not housed in crowded conditions. And all your cats, whatever their ages, should be vaccinated against possible viral respiratory infections. If you suspect that your cat is suffering from an infectious disease, make certain that you isolate the animal from any other cat in your household.

FELINE INFECTIOUS PERITONITIS

CAUSES: Feline infectious peritonitis (FIP) is a contagious and generally fatal viral disease of domestic cats and some wild cats as well. It is caused by a virus belonging to the *Corona* family of viruses.

FIP most often infects cats under three years of age. Older cats seem to have a natural immunity to this virus, which usually lodges in a cat's abdominal cavity. It can also attack other organs such as the liver, kidney, and brain. Some strains of this virus cause only mild respiratory infection—mostly in the form of a runny nose or eye discharge. Fortunately, less than 5 percent of the feline population develops FIP.

Researchers are not certain how this virus is spread or why only some infected cats develop chronic forms of it. It is believed that the virus, which spreads quickly and easily from cat to cat but does not infect humans, is transmitted by contact with an infected cat or his excrement.

The FIP virus is also suspected of causing the "kitten mortality complex" that often results in the death of unborn fetuses, newborn kittens (see Caring for Kittens, Chapter 21), and very young kittens.

Researchers have further discovered

that this virus cannot survive for long outside a cat's body, and that it is sensitive to ordinary disinfectants.

FIP is often fatal, but also relatively rare, especially in cats that are healthy and have strong immune systems. Even if your cat comes down with a mild form of the infection, he will nonetheless become a carrier of FIP for the rest of his life. Should he come into contact with a cat in a weakened condition, your cat may cause serious illness in the other.

If you have a cat who tests positive for FIP, keep her away from negative-antibody cats, but do not consider destroying her unless she is truly suffering. A cat can continue to lead a productive, happy life even if she has this virus.

SYMPTOMS: Can start with nasal congestion (mild FIP) and lead to emaciation, lack of appetite, lethargy, fever, dehydration, vomiting, diarrhea, jaundice, dark urine caused by liver failure, labored breathing caused by fluid accumulating in the chest and lungs.

TREATMENT: No effective therapy has yet been developed for FIP. Your veterinarian may prescribe medications to help ease your cat's suffering.

PREVENTION: There is a new vaccine available. You can make certain that your cat is well fed and not exposed to stressful situations that may lower his immunity. Keep your pet's bedding and eating bowls clean, especially if you own more than one cat.

FELINE IMMUNODEFICIENCY VIRUS

CAUSES: This usually fatal, AIDS-like infectious disease is more likely to be found in ill cats with weak immune systems than in healthy cats. Feline immunodeficiency virus (FIV) is also more common in older cats and in males. The virus is transmitted through saliva, bites, or scratches. FIV is similar to HIV (human immunodeficiency virus) but cannot be contracted by people.

SYMPTOMS: Anemia, fever, loss of appetite, pain while eating. Outward signs of this illness are uncommon. Cats diagnosed with FIV must be kept isolated.

TREATMENT: There is no specific therapy or vaccine available for FIV. AZT is sometimes used, as with humans who carry HIV.

PREVENTION: If you keep your cat indoors and do not allow him to have contact with other cats, the chances are unlikely that he will contract FIV.

FELINE LEUKEMIA VIRUS
(see also CIRCULATORY SYSTEM PROBLEMS, Chapter 14, and CANCER, Chapter 18)

CAUSES: Feline leukemia virus (FeLV) is caused by a virus that was discovered in 1964 and is still under study. This virus is one of the most important causes of feline cancer.

A cat infected by this virus does not

necessarily develop cancer. He does, however, become more susceptible to other infectious viral and bacterial diseases because the virus suppresses the cat's immune system.

FeLV is often transmitted between cats through infected saliva, urine, feces, and milk. Sharing water and food bowls, or even grooming or biting, may spread the virus if one of the cats is infected.

This virus can also be transmitted—especially to kittens—by cats with no visible symptoms of the disease. Sick and elderly cats are more susceptible to the FeLV virus than are healthy, adult ones.

A cat exposed to the FeLV virus may or may not become ill, but he will carry and transmit the virus for the rest of his life.

The good news is that many cats infected by FeLV recover from their illness. But cats who have been infected, yet not treated, are likely to die within three years.

SYMPTOMS: Two types of fatal feline cancers are caused by this virus. Lymphosarcoma is the more common. These painless tumors are found in the abdomen; in the most serious cases, there are swellings of the lymph nodes and anemia that ultimately leads to death. More than 80 percent of the tumors found in cats are caused by this type of cancer.

Leukemia is much less common than lymphosarcoma. It is the rapid and uncontrolled growth of white blood cells and may be accompanied by other changes in the blood composition.

TREATMENT: There is currently no cure for cancers produced by this virus. Upon diagnosis, your veterinarian will prescribe drugs that will attempt to extend your cat's life and make him more comfortable; some of these drugs can produce a temporary remission.

PREVENTION: A vaccine now exists against FeLV. Because this disease is so contagious to other cats (though, again, not to humans), any cat diagnosed as having leukemia should be isolated from other cats in the household or removed entirely. The premises should then be cleansed with a strong disinfectant. Wait at least thirty days before bringing any new cat onto the premises. If you bring a new cat home, have him tested for FeLV virus. If you know the previous owner of the cat, ask for certification that the cat is free of the virus.

While there is no evidence that cats infected by this virus can spread the disease to humans, it may be a sensible precaution to advise women of childbearing age, people with immunosuppressive illnesses, and young children to avoid close contact with virus-positive cats.

FELINE PANLEUKOPENIA

CAUSES: Also known as feline infectious enteritis, feline panleukopenia (FPL) is the most common viral disease afflicting cats. It probably claims more victims than any other disease.

There have been reports of feline

distemper sweeping through an entire neighborhood, leaving so many dying cats in its wake that it appears a poisoner has been at work. For this reason, the first vaccines developed for cats were to combat distemper.

Although not contagious to humans or dogs, FPL is one of the leading causes of infectious disease deaths in kittens who are not vaccinated.

The virus involved in feline distemper (not to be confused with the virus that causes distemper in dogs) is a very small one belonging to the *Parvovirus* group. This hardy strain of virus can live up to a year in the carpets, cracks, and furnishings of your home. It is also highly resistant to most disinfectants.

The FPL virus is spread between cats by direct contact with an infected cat or its secretions, such as saliva, vomit, urine, or feces. This virus can also be airborne or it can infect your cat by contact with contaminated utensils, such as food dishes, water bowls, or litter boxes.

A cat can contract the FPL virus if he is handled by someone who has touched or treated an infected cat. If a parasite bites a cat suffering from FPL, that parasite will continue to transmit the disease.

Once the virus gets into a cat's body, it damages cells, weakening the immune system and thus allowing bacteria to cause even further damage. Almost all the internal organs are affected by this virus—no part of the body is untouched. The lymph nodes are the first to be infected, the bone marrow the last.

The incubation period for the FPL virus is four to ten days, after which a cat is in grave danger. One of the characteristics of this viral disease is its sudden onset.

SYMPTOMS: Moderate to high fever, diarrhea, severe whitish or yellow vomiting, loss of appetite, lethargy, depression, dehydration, hunched appearance. The cat may hang his head over the water bowl.

TREATMENT: Early detection and treatment are important and may mean the difference between life and death for your cat. If you suspect FPL, call your veterinarian immediately. The main objective in treatment is to keep the ill cat alive and in fairly good health until his own immune system can deal with the virus. If antibiotics and other approaches can keep an infected cat alive for a week, the prognosis for recovery is good.

PREVENTION: Vaccination is the most effective way of preventing serious infection. Vaccines usually produce long-lasting immunity. Your kittens should be vaccinated between the ages of eight and ten weeks.

If you have a female cat that you expect to breed, she must be vaccinated to help ensure a healthy litter.

NOTE: Your female cat should not be vaccinated while pregnant because the vaccine can cause brain damage in unborn kittens.

Keep your cat's litter box and eating and drinking utensils clean. That also holds true for any other equipment or toys your cat touches. And before you allow a new cat into a household where a cat is already living, make certain the new cat is properly vaccinated.

PSEUDORABIES

CAUSES: Pseudorabies has no relationship to rabies, except that its symptoms resemble one form of that disease. Caused by a herpes virus that infects cats as well as dogs, it is not a common disease in the United States. Livestock appear to serve as a reservoir for the virus.

SYMPTOMS: Restlessness, intense pain, crouching in agony, excessive drooling, intense scratching, staggering, collapse, coma.

TREATMENT: Death usually occurs within twenty-four hours.

PREVENTION: There is no vaccine available. Do not allow your cat to roam

Abnormal salivation is a key indicator of pseudorabies.

and come in contact with infected livestock or eat raw meat.

RABIES

CAUSES: Rabies has been known to humankind since antiquity. It is a contagious and almost always fatal viral disease that affects both humans and animals. Rabies can strike nearly all warm-blooded animals. The rabies virus is bullet-shaped and belongs to the family *Rhabdoviridae*.

Rabies is most frequently transmitted when a rabid animal bites another warm-blooded animal or human being. The virus enters the body through the saliva at the site of the bite. The incubation period, between the time of infection and the occurrence of symptoms, is usually several months.

Rabies has always evoked fear in humans and rightly so, because it attacks the brain. Once the disease breaks out with its symptoms of altered behavior or paralysis, it is impossible to cure.

In recent years, many states have experienced rabies outbreaks. All cats—including those who spend the majority of their time indoors—should have rabies shots at least once a year.

SYMPTOMS: Severe changes in personality occurring in two stages: "furious" and "dumb." In the furious stage, a cat may suddenly show vicious, aggressive behavior. The animal will bite anything in his way. Loud noises or bright lights can provoke such biting attacks.

In the dumb stage, a cat with rabies

will become uncoordinated. Paralysis of the throat causes the voice to change. The lower jaw will become paralyzed and unable to close. The tongue and jaw will hang loose. General paralysis follows, along with coma and death.

Other symptoms might include unusual affectionateness; withdrawal or roaming long distances from home; unusual, subdued, hoarse cry; jaw hangs open and the cat drools saliva; dehydration.

TREATMENT: Consult your veterinarian. There is no effective treatment for cats.

PREVENTION: Make certain your cat is vaccinated at the age of three months and then revaccinated at least annually.

NOTE: Rabid cats are extremely dangerous because of their viciousness and quickness of action. You should exercise extreme caution in the presence of such an animal. Never try to handle a rabid cat.

If you are bitten by a rabid cat or other animal, consult your physician immediately. If your pet is bitten, thoroughly wash the wound with soap and detergent. A cat that has been vaccinated before being bitten should be revaccinated and confined inside the house—or walked on a leash—for at least thirty days after being bitten. Various types of rabies vaccine are derived from chemically killed viruses; there is also a form of vaccination that utilizes live viruses. The chemically killed virus type of vaccination offers protection against rabies for about a year, while the live virus variety gives protection for about two years.

If your cat has not been vaccinated and he is bitten by a cat or other animal known to have rabies, he will have to be euthanized. Again, consult with your veterinarian.

UPPER RESPIRATORY VIRAL DISEASES

CAUSES: At least three viruses can produce an infection of your cat's upper respiratory system, a condition that is commonly known as "cat flu." The upper respiratory system includes the sinuses, nose, and bronchia, all of which are discussed in further detail in later chapters.

The two major viral groups responsible for 80 to 90 percent of upper respiratory infections are the feline viral rhinotracheitis (FVR) and feline calici (FCV). A third type of virus, Reovirus, is much less serious than these others.

These viruses are spread from cat to cat by direct contact with infected saliva, nasal secretions, or eye discharge, through contaminated litter pans or water bowls, or by human hands.

SYMPTOMS: FVR: Inflammation of the eye, nose or windpipe, discharges from the eyes or nose, lethargy, fever, loss of appetite, continuous sneezing, sometimes painful ulcers on the tongue. FCV: Mild symptoms include a runny nose and moderate sneezing for a few days. Severe symptoms include tongue ulcers, excess salivation, loss of weight, poor physical appearance, refusal to eat.

TREATMENT: Consult your veterinarian, who will probably prescribe antibiotics and anti-inflammatory drugs. The worst danger is past when your cat begins to eat and drink on his own. Vaccines are available to guard against the most dangerous viruses, such as the herpes virus.

FELINE FUNGAL DISEASES

Most of us are familiar with fungi in the form of yeasts and molds. Some of the more recognizable fungi are mushrooms, bread molds, and baker's yeast. Some fungi, however, can produce disease in animals—especially if their immune system is in a run-down condition.

Disease-causing fungi can be divided into two groups. The first includes those that affect the skin or mucous membranes, such as Ringworm (see p. 156). The second causes more serious damage, but is less common in cats.

CRYPTOCOCCOSIS

CAUSES: This common yeast infection tends to occur in mature cats and generally affects the central nervous system. It is the most common systemic fungal infection in cats. The microorganism that causes cryptococcosis is usually found in pigeon and other bird droppings. Most cases of this infection result

from inhaling the microorganism rather than by ingesting it.

SYMPTOMS: Sneezing, sniffling, raspy breathing, a thick nasal discharge, chronic cough, weight loss, lethargy, a hard skin swelling on the head.

TREATMENT: Consult your veterinarian. If your veterinarian suspects cryptococcus, he or she will most likely prescribe antifungal drugs.

NOCARDIOSIS

CAUSES: Much like cryptococcosis, this disease is transmitted by contact with organic matter such as bird droppings. The fungi can also be spread in the air by spores and enter a cat's body through the respiratory system or through the skin if there is a puncture wound. Young cats are more prone to this disease than adults.

SYMPTOMS: In respiratory form, the symptoms resemble those of cryptococcosis. Large, tumorous masses are in evidence if the skin is affected.

TREATMENT: Consult your veterinarian. Antifungal medications will probably be prescribed.

PROTOZOAN DISEASES

Protozoa are minute organisms that are usually composed of a single cell. These parasites are not visible to the naked eye but may be seen under a microscope. They are usually found by examining stool specimens.

Infection usually results from the ingestion of the cyst form (oocysts) of the protozoa. The cysts then inhabit the lining of the bowel, where they grow into adult forms and are eliminated from the body through the feces.

COCCIDIOSIS

CAUSES: This intestinal disease most commonly affects young cats. It is not usually fatal and is transmitted among cats through feces containing oocysts. If the mother cat is a carrier, she can spread this disease to her young. Kittens can also reinfect themselves from their own feces.

SYMPTOMS: Diarrhea, weight loss, bloody feces, lesions on skin, bone, and eyes.

TREATMENT: Coccidiosis is usually treated with drug therapy including sulfamethazine.

TOXOPLASMOSIS

CAUSES: This infection, caused by parasitic protozoa, can invade most of the internal organs of a cat's body. The death rate from toxoplasmosis is very high. It is not known exactly how cats contract this infection; researchers believe the protozoa may be transmitted when cats eat infected birds or rodents. Humans may also contract this parasite from cats and from eating undercooked pork, beef, mutton, or veal.

SYMPTOMS: Fever, rapid or difficult breathing, coughing, loss of appetite, lethargy, weight loss, diarrhea.

TREATMENT: If toxoplasmosis is diagnosed early, a cat's life may be saved by treatment with various drugs such as sulfonamides and pyrimethamine.

NOTE: People with immune diseases and pregnant women may become exposed to toxoplasmosis through contact with cat feces found in litter boxes. If you fall into either category, arrange for someone else to clean your cat's box. Toxoplasmosis in humans can result in damage to the central nervous system and inflammation of the heart and lungs.

FELINE CYTAUXZOONOSIS

CAUSES: This disease, also caused by parasites, usually results in a cat's death, often in less than a week. It is still not known how this infectious parasite is transmitted, but the protozoan is known to attack red blood cells.

SYMPTOMS: High fever, anemia, jaundice, dehydration.

TREATMENT: Consult your veterinarian. There is no known treatment for this disease.

10

HEAD AND NECK PROBLEMS

MANY OF YOUR CAT'S chief sensory receptors, including the eyes, nose, tongue, and ears, are located in the head and neck. As you are about to discover, this region of the cat's body is highly developed. Certain organs are even more complex than those found in humans. By taking good care of the head and neck, you can help maintain and even sharpen your cat's already acute abilities to perceive the world.

THE EAR

Your cat's hearing is quite different from your own. Not only are cats' ears attuned to sounds too faint for humans to hear, but they are also sensitive to a multitude of ultrasonic sounds far higher in pitch than anything we can detect.

So sensitive are its ears that a cat can

distinguish between the sounds of several motors of the same make especially if one of them is in a car that belongs to his owner.

Highly developed hearing is not sur-

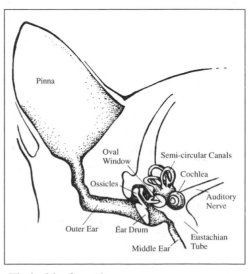

The inside of a cat's ear

125

prising in an animal born to hunt. Nor should it be surprising that creatures with such delicate hearing mechanisms tend to react with intense displeasure to shrill tones and loud noises that hardly even disturb our more muted auditory senses.

The cat's ears are also responsible for his remarkable sense of balance. Within a cat's inner ear are semicircular canals that allow him to handle his body with great speed and agility. This mechanism is also one reason why cats—unlike people and dogs—are highly resistant to motion sickness, a disturbance that is intimately associated with the sense of balance.

A cat's ear is divided into three main components. The external, or outer ear, consists of the earflap (or pinna) and the ear canal (or external auditory canal). The next component is the middle ear, composed of the eardrum (tympanic membrane) and the auditory ossicles (small bones). Last is the inner ear, which contains the cochlea, bony labyrinth, and auditory nerves. The inner ear is enclosed within the skull and contains the sensory structures of hearing and balance. Vibrations reach your cat's ear in the form of pressure waves in the air. These waves are channeled from the funnel-shaped outer ear down to the eardrum, whose membrane vibrates like a drum skin and moves a series of three tiny bones lying in the middle ear.

The waves are passed on to the inner ear's entrance, sometimes called the "oval window." From here, the waves move onward toward the cochlea, which are fluid-filled chambers. Within these chambers, the organ of Cort translates the sound waves into electrical impulses and sends them along the auditory nerve to the brain.

BACTERIAL INFECTIONS (see OTITIS)

DEAFNESS

CAUSES: There are various reasons for deafness in cats, ranging from heredity to old age. White male cats with blue eyes, for example, have a dominant gene that causes deafness. White cats with yellow eyes are least likely to suffer from deafness.

Hearing acuity can also sometimes diminish with age. Besides senility, deafness in cats can result from middle-ear infections, head injuries, blocked ear canals, and certain drugs and poisons.

SYMPTOMS: Lack of attentiveness to sounds. The cat does not awaken from her sleep when a loud noise occurs.

TREATMENT: No treatment is currently available.

NOTE: Your cat may begin to lose some hearing after age ten. Senile cats are still able to hear high-pitched sounds or stamping on the floor if you need to get their attention. Cats usually compensate quite well for their loss of hearing by using other senses, such as sight and smell.

EAR MITES

CAUSES: With their open, erect ears, cats have a predisposition toward ear problems. These include mite infestation, infection of the outer ear, tumors, and inflammatory polyps. Mites are a common nuisance and can cause fits in cats.

Ear mites are tiny, eight-legged parasites that live and breed on the surface of the ear canal. They penetrate into the deeper layers of the skin and burrow tunnels, feeding on skin, blood, and debris. They multiply by laying eggs inside the ear. They destroy skin tissue and cause infection.

These mites are so small that they can hardly be distinguished by the eye. If you apply a magnifying glass to the ear canal, these mites can be seen as small, whitish specks moving slowly over the lining of the canal.

Ear mites are relatively common in cats, and they can be spread from one cat to another. Flies, fleas, and lice may also transmit ear mites. Some cats may have small numbers of ear mites and not show any discomfort, while the same number of mites in another cat can produce inflammation and irritation of the outer ear and a great deal of discomfort.

SYMPTOMS: Constant shaking, rubbing, and scratching of ears; a large amount of dark brown wax in the ear canal; head-shaking and restless activity; rubbing of ears against furniture or along the floor.

TREATMENT: Clean your cat's ears daily with cotton balls lightly moistened with mineral oil (see p. 70). If the discharge is hard and caked, it must first be softened with a few drops of mineral oil. Then gently massage the base of the ear to loosen the caked material. Ear drops and droppers are usually available from your veterinarian.

NOTE: Even if only one ear appears to be affected, both ears should be treated, because mites can travel. If the condition or symptoms persist, consult with your veterinarian, who will prescribe an insecticide or special oil with which to treat your cat.

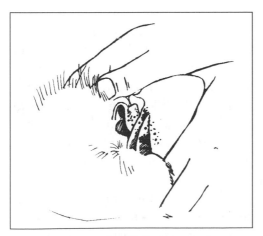

Ear mites lay eggs inside the ear, causing irritation and tissue destruction.

FOREIGN BODIES IN THE EAR

CAUSES: Sometimes foreign bodies such as grass seeds get into a cat's ears, although this is much more common in dogs than in cats.

SYMPTOMS: Ear scratching, head-shaking.

TREATMENT: If the foreign body can be seen, remove it with blunt-nosed tweezers or a cotton swab moistened in mineral oil. If the foreign body is deep inside the canal, your veterinarian will have to remove it.

FUNGAL INFECTIONS

CAUSES: Excess moisture and wax in the ear canal can lead to fungal infections. Dogs are more predisposed to such infections than cats.

SYMPTOMS: Dark and waxy ear discharge, rancid odor.

TREATMENT: Consult your veterinarian, who may prescribe antifungal medication.

HEMATOMA

CAUSES: A hematoma is a large or small but painful soft swelling caused by accumulated blood from a broken blood vessel. In cats, this most often occurs in the cartilage of the earflap, since blood vessels sometimes break as a result of head-shaking and ear scratching caused by otitis externa (see following entry) or by ear mites. The earflap can also become injured by bites and lacerations in catfights.

The ear flap is especially vulnerable to hematoma.

SYMPTOMS: A sudden swelling about the ear; taut, balloonlike bulge.

TREATMENT: Consult your veterinarian. Surgery may be required to drain the blood from the hematoma.

OTITIS EXTERNA

CAUSES: An inflammation of the external ear canal, otitis externa is usually caused by scratches and bites that become infected. The condition can also be brought on by ear mites or by accumulated wax and debris. This inflammation allows various bacteria to infect the area. If left untreated, it can lead to ulceration of parts of the ear canal.

SYMPTOMS: Foul odor and inflammation; head-shaking and constant scratching at the ears; discomfort or pain when the ear or earflap is touched; redness and swelling in the ear canal; pus may ooze from the inflammation.

TREATMENT: Consult your veterinarian. In severe cases, antibiotic preparations will be administered.

OTITIS INTERNA

CAUSES: If your cat is suffering from a middle-ear infection that goes untreated, the likelihood is that the infection will spread to the inner ear, a condition known as otitis interna.

SYMPTOMS: Vomiting, staggering, or falling toward the affected side, circling in the direction of the affected side, rapid eye movements. There may be some hearing impairment.

TREATMENT: Consult your veterinarian. Antibiotics or antifungal medications may be prescribed.

OTITIS MEDIA

CAUSES: The middle ear is susceptible to infection from bacteria, fungi, parasites, and other foreign bodies. These are not common feline infec-

tions, however, and affect dogs more often. These foreign bodies can gain entrance to the middle ear through a perforated eardrum; bacteria and other foreign agents may also infiltrate the middle ear through the Eustachian tube, which connects the back of the throat to the middle ear.

SYMPTOMS: Cat crouches low and tilts her head down on the affected side; displays an unsteady gait or other signs of lack of balance.

TREATMENT: Consult your veterinarian. Antibiotics or antifungal medications may be prescribed.

SUNBURNED EARS

CAUSES: Only white cats and cats with white ears suffer from sunburn.

SYMPTOMS: Hair falls out from tips and edges of the ears; skin becomes reddened; cat scratches at the ear; open sores may occur as a result of scratching.

PREVENTING SUNBURN

Cats—especially those whose coats are light colored or fine-textured—are prone to sunburned ears, just as fair-complexioned humans are. Cats fitting this description don't have to stay out of the sun, though. Try applying a hypoallergenic sunblock used by humans to the cat's ears. For maximum benefit, make sure it contains PABA (para-aminobenzoic acid).

TREATMENT: Do not allow your cat outside during the day. If sores do not heal, consult your veterinarian.

THE EYES

The eyes of a cat are very much like human eyes, with some minor differences. The nictitating membrane, or third eyelid, is one of these exceptions. Located in the lower part of the eye, it helps to protect the eye by conforming to the shape of the cornea. This membrane is also a diagnostic aid to veterinarians, since for as yet unknown reasons it will partially cover a cat's corneas if the animal is suffering from an intestinal disorder.

Another important difference is the iridescent layer of cells on the retina called the tapetum lucidum. These cells reflect light, which is why a cat's eyes shine at night.

A common myth about cats is that they can see in the dark. If by "dark" we mean total darkness, this simply is not true; cats cannot see any better than human beings in complete darkness. However, their eyes are better suited than our own to work in the dimmest light because of the elasticity with which their pupils expand and contract. The pupils control the amount of light allowed in to strike the retina. When the light is dim, your cat's irises become relaxed and the pupil significantly dilates; the opposite reaction occurs in bright light.

While cats do, indeed, have excellent night vision—to the extent of being able to see lightwaves invisible to us—humans have superior day vision. Cats see better at dusk than at noon on a bright, sunny day.

The eyes of a cat face forward. As their eyes are located at the front of the head, they have three-dimensional vision. This stereoscopic vision is the reason your cat is so accurate in judging distances for jumping, springing, or pouncing while hunting or playing.

Cats' eyes are comparatively large and set in deep pockets in the skull. They do not move freely, so in order to bring objects into sharp focus, a cat must sometimes turn his head and body.

Are cats color-blind? They are usually believed to be, but many a cat owner will tell you that his or her pet has a preference for certain colors of food dishes, bedding, and even furniture. Scientists have not yet resolved this issue.

The cat's eyes function very much like a camera. Light rays enter the eyes' fluid-filled anterior chamber and then pass through the vitreous body or

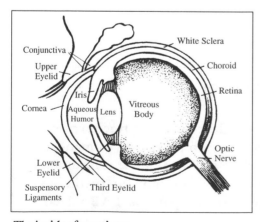

The inside of a cat's eye

aqueous humor, a transparent, jellylike substance that keeps the eyeballs firm. Next, the light rays hit the "heart" of the eye, the retina, which is located toward the back of the eye. This unique membrane contains more than a hundred million light-sensitive cells called "rods" and "cones."

The rods and cones set off a flurry of electrochemical activity that transmits an image to your cat's brain by way of the optic nerve in about two thousandths of a second.

Bulging eye (exophthalmos)

BLINDNESS

CAUSES: Various disorders to be discussed in this section—such as keratitis, cataracts, or uveitis—can lead to blindness, a generic term for any condition that prevents light from entering into the eye. It is not always easy to determine if your cat is blind or going blind, and the symptoms listed below are not conclusive.

If you own a blind cat, be aware that she can function quite well if she is kept in familiar surroundings. Under no circumstances should you allow a blind cat to roam about outdoors without supervision.

SYMPTOMS: Impaired body coordination, bumping into furniture, walking with nose close to the ground and feeling with whiskers.

TREATMENT: If you suspect blindness, consult your veterinarian for an exact diagnosis.

BULGING EYE

CAUSES: If tissue located behind the eye becomes swollen, it will push the eyeball forward. This condition can be caused by an infection spreading from the sinuses to the eyeballs or by a sudden blow to a cat's head. A growth behind the eyeball also can cause bulging eye, or exophthalmos.

SYMPTOMS: One eye seems larger than the other.

TREATMENT: Consult your veterinarian. Drugs and antibiotics will usually be prescribed. Surgery may be necessary to drain an accumulation of blood or pus.

CATARACTS

CAUSES: While cataracts are not as common in cats as they are in dogs, many cats are affected by this condition. A cataract is any opacity of the lens that blocks the light's passage

Cataracts prevent light from passing through the lens.

through the eye. Some contributing causes are conjunctivitis, an old eye injury, and eye infections. Cataracts are sometimes inherited and may also develop later in life in diabetic cats.

SYMPTOMS: The normally clear lens looks clouded. The pupil of the eye becomes a whitish-blue, then turns milky white and opaque as the disease progresses.

TREATMENT: Consult your veterinarian. Surgery may be recommended if the cataract is impairing vision. Your veterinarian must first make sure that the ailment is not due to an infectious disease or diabetes mellitus.

NOTE: After cataract surgery, your cat may have less than normal vision, although she should be able to function quite well. Make certain that there are no objects in your home that could harm your cat because she cannot see them. Supervise your cat when she is outside.

CONJUNCTIVITIS (PINKEYE)

CAUSES: Conjunctivitis is one of the most common eye problems in cats and is usually not painful. Contributing causes include bacterial infection, upper respiratory viruses, and allergic reactions.

Any of these factors can produce an inflammation of the lining of the membranes that cover the inner sides of the eyelids. The surface of the eyeball up to the cornea can also be affected. Should your cat display signs of pain such as squinting or tenderness to touch, a more serious eye ailment may be involved.

SYMPTOMS: Discharge from the eyes, accompanied by a red or inflamed eye; blinking; closure of the lids; soreness.

AGING CATS AND CATARACTS

Some older cats develop a condition known as senile cataracts; this is a normal part of aging in the eye. If you gaze into the eyes of your old pet, you may see a blue-white hue. Usually this haze does not in any way interfere with your cat's vision and does not require treatment.

Chlamydia conjunctivitis spreads from one eye to the other.

TREATMENT: There are several types of conjunctivitis, two of which require immediate veterinary attention. These are purulent conjunctivitis, in which bacterial infection has set in, and follicular conjunctivitis, usually caused by an allergy or infection. The mild, irritative form of this disorder—known as serious conjunctivitis—can usually be treated at home. You should nevertheless consult with your veterinarian before you apply any medication.

NOTE: Although not considered a significant human health hazard, a few cases of mild conjunctivitis have been reported in humans having contact with cats infected with *Chlamydia psittaci*. A veterinarian can determine the presence of the chlamydia microorganisms through conjunctival scrapings. Until you know the nature of the conjunctivitis, handle your cat carefully, and wash your hands with an antiseptic after touching him. Use gloves to apply all medications.

CORNEAL DISORDERS

The cornea is the transparent covering of a cat's eye. It has a protective layer of epithelial cells that can suffer injury as a result of a catfight or infection. Damage to these cells will eventually lead to some disorder of the cornea.

ABRASIONS

CAUSES: A scratch to the eye is the most common cause of corneal abrasion, which is extremely painful but will usually heal by itself.

SYMPTOMS: Squinting, watering of eyes, pawing at the eyes, swollen and cloudy look in the eye.

TREATMENT: In minor cases, none is required.

KERATITIS

CAUSES: Keratitis usually results from an inflammation of the cornea and may affect one or both eyes. Infectious diseases, injury, and direct irritation of the cornea can all produce keratitis.

There are various forms of keratitis. All should be considered serious, because if untreated keratitis can result in partial or complete blindness.

Superficial, or surface, keratitis most often results from a scratch. Infectious keratitis occurs when a corneal injury develops an infection. Chronic degenerative keratitis is believed to stem from an infection or injury to the cornea, although researchers are still not certain about its cause.

SYMPTOMS: Tearing, pain, squinting, sensitivity to light, cornea covered by whitish-blue film, exposure of the third eyelid, cornea may look dull or hazy, brown or black plaque on the surface of the cornea, swollen eyelids.

TREATMENT: Consult your veterinarian. Early treatment is important. Antibiotics and other drugs will probably be prescribed.

ULCERS

CAUSES: A dangerous condition usually brought on by an injury to the cornea or by viral, bacterial, or fungal infections. Other contributing factors include chronic irritation, foreign bodies under the eyelid, and chronic conjunctivitis.

If ulcers are not treated, they can result in blindness. In severe cases, the ulcers may actually invade the cornea and cause extreme damage that threatens the eyeball.

Untreated corneal ulcers can lead to blindness.

SYMPTOMS: Extreme pain in the eye, tearing, squinting, and sensitivity to light. Larger ulcers appear as dull spots or dished-out depressions on the surface of the cornea.

TREATMENT: Consult your veterinarian, who may prescribe corticosteroids and antibacterial and antiviral drugs. Surgery is sometimes required.

DARK STAINS IN THE CORNER OF THE EYE

CAUSES: Such dried pus or other eye discharge can signify bacterial infection.

TREATMENT: Consult your veterinarian.

EPIPHORA (WATERY EYE)

CAUSES: Excess tears may be caused by an irritation of the eye or an obstruction of the tear duct. These symptoms may also indicate a feline respiratory infection.

SYMPTOMS: Excessive tearing; a sticky, puslike discharge from the eyes and nose; red eyes.

TREATMENT: Consult your veterinarian, who must determine the underlying cause.

FOLDED EYELID

CAUSES: Some cats have eyelids that fold inward toward the eyeball. This is usually caused by a birth defect or can be caused by a laceration or scarring.

SYMPTOMS: Squinting, sensitivity to light, possible exposure of third eyelid.

TREATMENT: Consult your veterinarian.

FOREIGN OBJECT IN THE EYE

CAUSES: Anything from dust, dirt, and grass seed can become trapped behind the eyelids and nictitating membranes.

SYMPTOMS: Tearing, watering of eyes, blinking, squinting.

TREATMENT: Consult your veterinarian.

GLAUCOMA

CAUSES: Glaucoma is a general term that refers to an increase of fluid pressure within the eyeball. It can occur when the fluid, or aqueous humor, that is constantly manufactured and circulated through the eye, fails to drain due to scarring, inflammation, or some blockage in the drainage area.

Glaucoma usually develops slowly over a long period of time, but it can have a sudden onset. Some vision may be permanently lost before the disease is discovered. Glaucoma can affect one or both eyes.

Glaucoma may also be caused by a complication of diseases of the lens or the eye's anterior chamber. In such a case, the disorder is called secondary

glaucoma. This is the most common form of glaucoma in cats.

SYMPTOMS: Enlarged eyeball with or without red and enlarged surface blood vessels; dilation and clouding of the pupil; squinting; corneal haziness; blindness.

TREATMENT: Consult your veterinarian. Glaucoma may be managed for a while with drops and medications. Once vision is lost, elective surgery may be recommended to remove the eye's contents and replace it with a silicone prosthesis, mitigating disfigurement and discomfort.

IRRITATED EYELIDS

CAUSES. This condition, also known as blepharitis, frequently occurs when cats engage in combat with each other. Scratches and other surface wounds—in this case, to the eyelids—become infected. Irritation of the eyelids can also be caused by head mange and other types of mites as well as by ringworm infection.

SYMPTOMS: Itching, scratching, crust formation on the eyelids, accumulation of pus and debris on the eyelids. If a fungal skin irritation is the cause, the skin may look scaly or crusted.

TREATMENT: Consult your veterinarian. The course of treatment may include warm-water soakings of the eyelids to loosen scabs. Your veterinarian may also prescribe topical antifungal preparations along with oral anti-fungal medications.

RETINAL DISEASES

CAUSES: The retina is the thin, delicate membrane that lines the back of the eye. Various conditions can affect this membrane, all resulting in the eyes' inability to interpret the light that reaches it. Contributing factors to this impairment include infectious disease, congenital or metabolic defects, injury, or even improper diet. Some cats inherit a tendency toward retinal diseases; researchers still do not fully understand why.

SYMPTOMS: Progressive deterioration of vision, beginning with the loss of night vision.

TREATMENT: No effective treatment is available.

SUBJUNCTIVAL HEMORRHAGE

CAUSES: Any trauma to a cat's eye or severe straining can result in the rupture of small blood vessels in the eye.

SYMPTOMS: A diffuse, blood-red discoloration in the white of the eye.

TREATMENT: Consult your veterinarian.

SUNKEN EYE

CAUSES: A cat suffering from dehydration or rapid weight loss may develop a condition in which both eye-lids recede. In some cases, the eye may also be pulled back into its socket. This can result from an injury to the cornea or nerve trunk damage in the neck.

SYMPTOMS: The eye has a rolled-back look.

TREATMENT: Consult your veterinarian, who must discover the underlying causes for this condition.

THIRD EYELID

CAUSES: The third eyelid, or nictitating membrane, is believed to serve as a protection device for an injured eye. Normally the third eyelid is not seen unless your cat is suffering from an injured, inflamed, or irritated eye. It may also appear if your cat is depressed or in the throes of some upper respiratory illness, such as conjunctivitis. When both eyes show a third eyelid, your cat is almost certainly suffering from a viral respiratory infection.

SYMPTOMS: An opaque film rising from the lower corner of the eye nearest the nose. This film covers some portion of the eyeball. The eyeball appears to have moved upward out of its normal location. Excessive tearing, squinting, and pawing at the eye.

TREATMENT: Consult your veterinarian.

UVEITIS (SOFT EYE)

CAUSES: This common inner-eye disease can affect one or both eyes.

Uveitis can harm the iris and the blood supply to the retina. Unlike glaucoma, uveitis results in an increased softness in the eye and small pupil.

A major cause of uveitis is the inflammation of the inner, pigmented structure of the eye as a result of feline leukemia, feline infectious peritonitis, toxoplasmosis, or a penetrating eye injury.

SYMPTOMS: Squinting, watery eyes, clouding of the eye.

TREATMENT: Consult your veterinarian. Underlying causes will have to be determined.

THE MOUTH

A cat's digestive system is comprised of a number of parts, but none is more important than the oral cavity, or mouth, where food begins the process of being digested.

The cat's mouth is bounded on the front and sides by the lips and cheeks. On top of the mouth are the soft and hard palates. Below are the tongue and muscles of the lower mouth. Four pairs of salivary glands drain into the mouth. In close proximity is the throat, which is a space formed by the joining of the rear of the mouth with the nasal passageways.

If all this is not complex enough, the oral cavity also contains a flaplike valve, called the epiglottis, whose function is to keep food from going down the wrong way. When a cat swallows, this valve automatically shuts off the

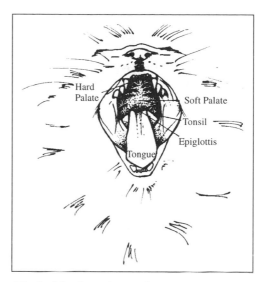

The inside of a cat's mouth

larynx and windpipe so that the animal does not choke.

Inside the mouth are the teeth, used not only to cut and tear food but also for attack or defense. The teeth are particularly designed for grasping, tearing, and shredding food, which is then swallowed and broken down by gastric juices.

While a kitten has twenty-six teeth, the average adult cat has thirty teeth. (Humans have thirty-two teeth, dogs forty-two.) The adult teeth should all be in place by six months. There are four kinds of teeth in a cat's mouth: incisors, canines, premolars, and molars. An adult cat's canine teeth incline inward slightly to trap food. In a healthy cat, the teeth are white and the gum line is pink, not red or swollen.

A cat's mouth produces alkaline saliva. This saliva contains antibacterial enzymes that fight harmful bacteria both in the food entering the mouth and on the cat's own body when she

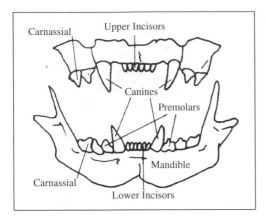

The average adult cat has 30 teeth.

licks a wound. However, cat wounds are more likely to become infected because cats—unlike dogs—are not very inclined to lick them; their tongues' rough surfaces irritate them.

Several symptoms may signal a mouth disorder; these include a failure to eat, unkempt appearance, bad breath, gagging, choking, excessive drooling, and difficulty in swallowing and opening the mouth.

If you recognize any of these symptoms in your cat, contact your veterinarian immediately.

BAD BREATH

CAUSES: Bad breath, or halitosis, is usually a sign of periodontal disease of some related mouth disorder such as gingivitis, or sore gums.

TREATMENT: Consult your veterinar-

PREVENTING TOOTH DECAY

In general, tooth decay is less common in cats than in people. Cats have thicker tooth enamel and their salivary juices are less damaging to their teeth. Also, the structure of feline teeth discourages the retention of food particles. Cats also generally have better diets than humans, consuming less sugar and junk food.

Nonetheless, tooth decay and other tooth problems do affect some cats. To help prevent dental problems in your cat, provide her with a good diet. Along with moist meals, give her dry food as well, which helps prevent tartar buildup. Dental checkups are another good idea. Paying attention to your cat's mouth will prevent many problems down the line.

To brush your cat's teeth, make a paste out of equal parts of salt and baking soda mixed in a little water. Moisten a rough cloth and wrap it around your finger. Dip the cloth in the paste. Rub the teeth from gum to tip. You may also use a child-sized toothbrush with soft bristles. Do

ian. The mouth must be examined, thoroughly cleansed, and restored to a normal condition.

BURNS IN THE MOUTH
(see BURNS, p. 240)

DENTAL ABSCESS

CAUSES: A rare condition in cats, usually affecting the root of the top premolar. It can lead to an abscessed frontal sinus.

SYMPTOMS: Difficulty eating, pain when chewing, weight loss, unkempt appearance.

TREATMENT: Consult your veterinarian.

PREVENTION: A program of good oral hygiene—including dental check-ups incorporated into regular visits to the veterinarian—will extend the life of your cat's teeth. You should brush your cat's teeth and gums at regular intervals (see p. 138) and make certain that your cat has a large knuckle bone or something to chew on at least once or twice a week (avoid long bones that splinter, such as rib or chicken bones).

FOREIGN OBJECT IN THE MOUTH

CAUSES: Bone splinters, gristle, slivers of wood, and fishhooks are among the many objects that can lodge in a cat's mouth.

SYMPTOMS: Pawing at the mouth, rubbing mouth along the floor, drooling, gagging, licking lips.

TREATMENT: Open your cat's mouth by pinching in at the cheeks with your thumb and forefinger. If the direct removal of the object is possible, do so using your fingers or a pair of blunt-nosed tweezers. Otherwise bring your cat to your veterinarian or nearest animal hospital.

INFLAMMATION OF THE LIPS

CAUSES: Infections in a cat's mouth can spread and infect the lips. If your cat is allowed to go outdoors, she may come in contact with weeds, brush, and other vegetation that can also irritate her lips.

SYMPTOMS: Crusty materials on the lips. As crust peels off, the smooth parts of the lip look raw and chapped.

TREATMENT: Consult your veterinarian. Treatment may include the use of antibiotics and steroid creams.

LACERATION OF THE LIPS AND MOUTH (see EMERGENCIES, p. 238)

LIP TUMORS
(SQUAMOUS CELL CARCINOMA)
(see also CANCER, Chapter 18)

CAUSES: Malignant tumors sometimes appear on the lips, gums, and the underside of the tongue.

SYMPTOMS: Lesions, difficulty and pain when eating, halitosis.

TREATMENT: Consult your veterinarian. Surgical removal or radiation therapy may be recommended.

MOLAR ABSCESS

CAUSES: While dental cavities are not common in cats, a broken tooth or cavity can, if left untreated, result in infection that will lead to an abscess in the molar or other teeth.

SYMPTOMS: See Dental Abscess, p. 139.

TREATMENT: Consult your veterinarian.

PERIODONTAL DISEASE

CAUSES: Hard drinking water can contribute to the development of tartar on the teeth. In felines, a diet of exclusively soft canned food can also contribute to tartar buildup.

Tartar is a mixture of calcium phosphate and calcium carbonate with organic material. It can accumulate and become mineralized. This mineralization forms hard, rough surfaces called plaque or calculus near the gum line.

These pockets of plaque, if not removed, can become breeding grounds for bacteria. They can also become infected. Once infection sets in, the gums become spongy and start to recede. This ultimately results in damage to the teeth because, in time, the tooth bone also starts to recede and the root is exposed, imperiling the stability of the tooth.

Older cats are more susceptible than younger ones to tartar formation. Sometimes this condition can become so serious that a grayish-white or brownish layer covers all the teeth. Halitosis and gingivitis result.

SYMPTOMS: Foul mouth odor, refusal to eat, weight loss, unkempt appearance.

TREATMENT: Consult your veterinarian. Treatment depends on how far the condition has progressed and whether the teeth are affected. In serious cases, antibiotics may be prescribed and teeth may have to be extracted. In such cases, a cat may have to be anesthetized in order for the plaque to be removed with an ultrasound device.

PREVENTION: Give your cat something hard to gnaw on at least once or twice a week. Avoid long bones such as rib or chicken bones because they can splinter. A large knuckle bone is an excellent chewing source. You should also feed your cat dry cat food in addition to moist meals; dry cat food helps to keep those dark-brown tartar stains from forming.

Your cat should also have regular dental checkups. An effective way to prevent periodontal disease is to brush your cat's teeth and gums at least twice a month. Older cats need to have their teeth brushed three or four times monthly (see p. 138).

PYORRHEA (TOOTH INFECTION)

CAUSES: Pyorrhea is caused by inflammation and infection of the gums around the teeth, usually as a result of tartar buildup and gingivitis.

SYMPTOMS: Inflammation, bleeding, lost or loose teeth, foul breath, loss of appetite, ulcers on the lining of the cheek near the affected teeth, gums sensitive to touch.

TREATMENT: Consult your veterinarian. It is important to get early treatment for this condition in order to prevent tooth loss and more serious infection.

RODENT ULCER (LIP GRANULOMA)

CAUSES: Researchers still are not exactly certain about the causes of this condition, which usually affects cats from nine months of age to nine years. These ulcers may be a result of a malfunction in the cat's immune system, or of a viral infection. They may also be caused by food allergies or irritation caused by the tongue.

Rodent ulcer tends to occur more in female cats than in males. More than one cat in a household may be affected by such granulomas. This ailment seems to cause cats little pain or discomfort; it simply looks unsightly. Granulomas should be treated or they can cause some partial damage to the lips.

SYMPTOMS: Thickened, red, and ulcerated sores on the lips, tongue, or inside the cheeks; excess salivation; refusal to eat.

TREATMENT: Consult your veterinarian. Treatment usually includes antibiotics, cortisone injections, and steroid creams. Surgery is sometimes required.

SORE GUMS (GINGIVITIS)

CAUSES: One of the commonest types of oral disease in cats is the inflammation of the mouth lining, known as stomatitis. There are various forms of stomatitis, the most prevalent being gingivitis, or gum infection.

Bacteria and viruses are believed to be responsible for gingivitis. Plaque and tartar accumulation may also contribute to this condition. The advent of gingivitis usually signals impending tooth decay.

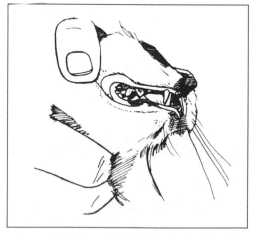

Plaque and tartar buildup are the most common causes of gingivitis.

SYMPTOMS: Bluish-red color and frequent bleeding of the gums; occasional pus-filled sores; loss of appetite; unkempt appearance; difficulty chewing; occasional drooling; unpleasant mouth odor; receding gums; lost or loose teeth.

TREATMENT: Consult your veterinarian, who may recommend that you brush and massage your cat's gums once a day. The veterinarian may also check for more serious illnesses of the liver and kidneys, which can contribute to chronic gingivitis and to bad odor in the mouth.

SORE MOUTH (STOMATITIS)

CAUSES: There are many possible causes for this condition, ranging from foreign objects in the mouth to feline leukemia.

SYMPTOMS: Drooling, refusal to eat, difficulty chewing, shaking of head, pawing at the mouth. The inside of the mouth looks inflamed or swollen.

TREATMENT: Consult your veterinarian, who must determine the cause.

TARTAR
(see PERIODONTAL DISEASE, p. 140)

TOOTH INFECTION
(see PYORRHEA, p. 141)

UPPER P4 SYNDROME

CAUSES: A cat's fourth premolars (P4) are the large upper teeth located directly under the sinuses. They can become infected.

SYMPTOMS: Protruding cheekbone under the eye; face looks distorted. In severe cases, the accumulation of pus causes a small opening under a cat's eye, and pus drains down the cheek.

TREATMENT: Consult your veterinarian.

THE TONGUE

Your cat's tongue is a very long, rough, and flexible organ that is used primarily as a grooming tool. It is covered with minute hooks of four different shapes that allow your cat to lick every trace of meat off a bone and to brush her coat spotlessly clean. Your cat also uses her tongue as a spoon to lap up liquids.

The tongue also has taste buds that are aided by a primitive gland (the vomeronasal gland) located behind the upper front teeth. If you carefully observe your cat, you may sometimes see her first "taste" her food by licking it and then flicking the tongue behind her upper front teeth. This distributes the taste to the sensitive vomeronasal gland.

One disadvantage of the tongue, however, is that hair clings to its sharp, backward-pointing tongue spikes (papillae), which are constructed virtually of the same substance as human fingernails. The only way your cat can get rid of this hair is to swallow it. This, of course, results in a major problem for cats—namely, hairballs (see p. 67).

BITTEN TONGUE
(see EMERGENCIES, p. 238)

FOREIGN OBJECTS IN THE TONGUE
(see FOREIGN OBJECTS IN THE MOUTH,
p. 139)

SORE TONGUE (GLOSSITIS)

CAUSES: There are various reasons—
including burns—why a cat may suffer
from a sore tongue. However, glossitis
is most often associated with feline
upper respiratory disease.

SYMPTOMS: The tip of the tongue
appears smooth and shiny; cat has
ungroomed appearance; fur on neck may
be dirty and wet with saliva; cat may froth
at mouth; mouth ulcers may be present.

TREATMENT: Consult your veterinarian. Mouthwashes and antibiotics may
be prescribed.

THE NOSE

Your cat's nose plays a vital role in protection, behavior, and reproduction.
This cold and moist organ is the smallest part of the cat's olfactory system,
but the internal organs of scent are
larger than one might expect of such a
small animal.

The nose is made up of the nostrils
and the nasal cavity, which are enclosed
by bone and cartilage and divided in
half by a vertical plate called the nasal
septum. The nasal septum is also made
up of bone and cartilage and has a
mucous membrane covering. Also

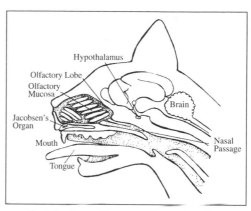

The inside of a cat's nose and nasal cavity

located inside the nose are large frontal
sinuses that are linked with the nasal
passages.

In addition, the cat's nose contains
numerous structures called conchae
and turbinates. These rolled structures
aid in filtering, warming, and humidi-
fying the air a cat inhales before it
enters the lungs. The turbinates are
also responsible for your cat's highly
developed sense of smell. Olfactory
nerves are located here as well as in the
nasal septum and sinuses.

Behind its hairless tip, your cat's
nose—much like our own—is lined
with mucous membranes, while, deep
in the nasal passageways, part of the
lining is filled with nerve endings.
When molecules are carried by the air
and deposited in the mucous membranes, the nerve endings are triggered
and send signals to the olfactory center
in the brain, identifying the odor.

Your cat's nose is especially sensitive
to odors that contain nitrogen compounds. This helps a cat avoid eating
rancid foods, since spoiled food releases
chemicals rich in nitrogen.

If there is one smell your cat will

never be able to resist, it's the odor of catnip. How this herb affects the cat internally is still a matter of conjecture. Researchers believe it contains a chemical called transneptalactone, which is closely related to a substance excreted by female cats—and yet catnip affects both male and female cats the same way.

Cats are quite susceptible to respiratory infections; nasal discharge and noisy breathing are two common symptoms. These symptoms are generally caused by an accumulation of phlegm in the air passages and usually signify the first stage of a respiratory infection.

If this infection also affects the trachea and larynx, the cat will probably cough and be short of breath. Have nasal infections treated quickly, because there is always the danger that pneumonia may set in if they are ignored. Pneumonia is usually accompanied by high fever and general apathy, and may lead to death.

FOREIGN OBJECTS IN THE NOSE
(see EMERGENCIES, p. 238)

NASAL ALLERGIES

CAUSES: Cats can suffer from a variety of allergies. Certain types of food, house dust, and other substances can set off a severe bout of sniffling and sneezing. Nasal allergies are usually a response to something in the air that stimulates a reaction by your cat's immune system.

SYMPTOMS: Short bouts of violent sneezing; a clear, watery discharge from the nose.

TREATMENT: Consult your veterinarian. Medications containing steroids or antihistamines will probably be prescribed. You should also try to identify the source of the allergen that is affecting your cat and remove it from the household.

NASAL DISCHARGE

CAUSES: A nasal discharge through both nostrils suggests a feline viral upper respiratory infection or an allergy. If just one nostril is involved, it may be the result of a foreign object in the nose, a nasal polyp, or tumor.

SYMPTOMS: Runny nose; a runny nose accompanied by sneezing suggests a cold, irritation or allergy; mucus in the discharge suggests a bacterial infection.

TREATMENT: Consult your veterinarian if symptoms persist for several hours.

NASAL INFECTIONS

CAUSES: Feline viral respiratory infections are the most common cause of nasal infections. Bacterial infections can also set in if your cat's nose lining has somehow been injured.

SYMPTOMS: Sneezing, nasal discharge, noisy breathing, mouth breathing, loss of appetite. In bacterial infections, the nasal discharge is thick with mucus or creamy-yellow in color.

TREATMENT: Keep the nose free of crusted secretions, and use baby oil to maintain a moist surface. Try administering children's strength nasal drops according to the package's directions. If the symptoms persist, consult your veterinarian. If bacterial infection already exists, antibiotics may be prescribed.

NOSEBLEED

CAUSES: Nosebleeds in cats are usually caused by an injury to the face. An infection, tumor, or parasites are sometimes secondary causes.

TREATMENT: Keep your cat quiet. Apply ice cubes wrapped in cloth or ice packs to the bridge of the nose; this will help reduce blood flow and aid in clotting. If bleeding continues, get prompt veterinary attention. If your cat bleeds from the nose with no known cause on several occasions, consult your veterinarian.

SNEEZING

CAUSES: Nasal irritation is the prime cause of sneezing in cats. This is a reflex action as a result of the nose lining being stimulated. If your cat sneezes persistently, it can indicate a viral upper respiratory illness.

TREATMENT: If sneezing continues throughout the day, consult your veterinarian. If the sneezing is accompanied by head shaking and pawing at the nose, it suggests that a foreign object may be lodged in the nose, requiring veterinary treatment.

SINUSITIS

CAUSES: If your cat has a respiratory infection that is left untreated, a secondary infection will probably affect the sinuses. Infection can also spread to the sinuses from an abscessed tooth or an allergy.

SYMPTOMS: A milky white or thick, yellowish nasal discharge; sometimes the discharge is streaked with blood. Frequent sneezing and sniffling.

TREATMENT: Consult your veterinarian. Antibiotics will probably be administered. In chronic cases, surgery may be recommended.

THE THROAT

The pharynx, or throat, extends from the back of the nasal cavity to the larynx, more commonly known as the voice box or Adam's apple. A flaplike valve, the epiglottis, closes off the larynx and the windpipe when food is swallowed, preventing food from going down the wrong way.

CHOKING (see EMERGENCIES, p.238)

LARYNGITIS

CAUSES: The larynx, which is located in the throat above the windpipe, is made up of cartilage and contains a cat's vocal chords. Laryngitis results when the mucous membranes of the voice box become inflamed. Although tonsilitis, throat infections, and even pneumonia can cause laryngitis, the condition is more often the result of excessive meowing and a persistent cough.

SYMPTOMS: Hoarseness, loss of voice.

TREATMENT: Consult your veterinarian. If excessive meowing is creating this condition, you should take steps to relieve the cause of your cat's anxiety or stress.

PHARYNGITIS (SORE THROAT)

CAUSES: Viral illnesses or mouth infections are primarily responsible for feline sore throats, although this condition is not common in cats.

SYMPTOMS: Coughing, fever, gagging, vomiting, grimaces caused by pain in the throat upon swallowing, loss of appetite.

TREATMENT: Consult your veterinarian, who will probably administer antibiotics.

SWALLOWING SHARP OBJECTS

CAUSES: Your cat may decide to gnaw at some discarded chicken bones or accidentally swallow some other sharp object, such as a safety pin. This could cause the cat to begin to choke.

SYMPTOMS: Choking, gagging.

TREATMENT: To best handle the cat, first wrap her in a heavy blanket. Pinch the cat's cheeks with thumb and forefinger to open the mouth. If you can see the object, remove it with your fingers. If you cannot find the problem or if the object is difficult to remove, get prompt veterinary assistance.

TONSILITIS

CAUSES: While tonsilitis is rare in cats, bacteria can sometimes affect the tonsils, which are located in the back of the throat.

SYMPTOMS: Similar to those of a sore throat, except that there is a high fever and significant lethargy.

TREATMENT: Consult your veterinarian. Antibiotics such as penicillin will probably be prescribed.

11

SKIN AND HAIR PROBLEMS

UNDER THE CLEAN, SLEEK, shiny coat of your healthy pet is a skin that is normally smooth and pale pink. The skin serves many functions, including the retention of water and body heat, and keeping out bacteria and other harmful foreign bodies. The skin also synthesizes vitamin D. Finally, in addition to guarding your cat from extremes in temperature, the skin provides sensory information about the outside world.

Skin has several basic components. First is the outer layer, called the epidermis. It can be thick or thin depending upon what part of the cat's body it covers. The next layer is called the dermis. Its primary function is to supply nourishment to the epidermis. The dermis is also responsible for such skin appendages as hair follicles, sebaceous glands, sweat glands, and toenails. The function of the sebaceous glands is to secrete an oily substance that coats the hair and gives it a healthy shine. These glands also waterproof your cat's coat.

The skin follicles produce three different types of hair in cats. The top coat is made up of long guard hair. The guard hair allows your cat to fluff out his coat in cold weather and helps

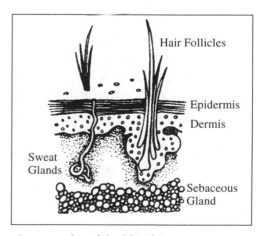

A cross section of the skin of a cat

147

to insulate him by trapping warm air close to his body.

The underfur is much more plentiful. Its purpose is to provide warmth and protection. Other types of hair on your cat are whiskers, eyelashes, and the carpal hair that you will see if you examine the back of your cat's front legs.

Whiskers are one of the best-known characteristics of cats. These long, stiff hairs can be fanned out and are used by your cat to make contact with his environment. Whiskers serve to supplement a cat's sharp sense of smell and hearing.

Your cat also has sweat glands throughout his body. These glands, which are located at the base of the tail and on the sides of your cat's face, produce a milky fluid. It is believed that these fluids are involved in sexual attraction.

If you notice moisture at the tip of your cat's nose, the animal is not sweating. This is evaporating water; your overheated cat is cooling himself off.

Now look at your cat's feet. You will see the claws and pads, which are specialized structures of the epidermis. Your cat's front paws contain five toe-pads and five claws, plus two metacarpal pads that usually do not make contact with the ground. On your cat's back feet you will find four toe-pads and four claws, plus a large metatarsal pad. All of a cat's claws can be retracted. The skin of the pads is tough and contains sensory nerves that allow your cat to feel unfamiliar objects. The toenails are made of keratin, a solid, proteinlike substance encased in a cuticle or hard sheath. Beneath the cuticle are blood vessels, nerves, and the cells responsible for nail growth.

Together, the skin and hair provide an excellent window onto your cat's health. Any disruption in the smoothness of the skin or significant changes in coat color are sure signs that something is amiss.

The signs of skin disease in cats are not specific to any one disorder. Loss of hair, changes in skin condition or coat color, inflammation, and irritation are common to a variety of skin diseases. Remember that some skin problems are not caused by disease or infestation. They may simply be scars or some other damage from a recent scrap with another cat.

While cats suffer from skin disorders much less frequently than dogs do, any prolonged abnormality of the skin is cause to have your cat looked at by your veterinarian. In addition, if you adopt a stray cat or acquire a new pet, it would be prudent for you to have your veterinarian check the animal for any possible skin disorders.

ABSCESSES

CAUSES: Abscesses are common results of animal bites, fights, and untreated injuries.

SYMPTOMS: Soft swellings on the limbs or elsewhere on the body; affected areas are tender and painful to the touch; pus forms under the skin.

TREATMENT: Consult your veterinarian.

PREVENTION: Treat all skin wounds promptly.

ALLERGIES

CAUSES: Allergies in a cat can be triggered by anything from certain foods to substances in the air, such as pollens and powders. The cat's immune system reacts to these and other irritating substances. For an allergy to develop, the cat must be exposed to the allergen at least twice.

SYMPTOMS: Itching, sneezing, coughing, tearing, swelling of the eyelids, vomiting, diarrhea. The main sign of skin allergies is severe scratching.

TREATMENT: Consult your veterinarian, who must determine the cause of the allergic reaction.

ALLERGIC CONTACT DERMATITIS

CAUSES: Repeated contact with chemicals such as soaps, detergents, or solvents may cause a skin reaction in some cats. The reaction generally affects those parts of a cat's body where the hair is thin or absent, such as the feet, chin, nose, abdomen, and groin.

SYMPTOMS: Red, itchy bumps, inflammation of the skin, scaliness, hair loss.

TREATMENT: Consult your veterinarian.

Future bouts of allergic contact dermatitis can be prevented by eliminating the irritating substance from your cat's environment.

BACTERIAL SKIN INFECTIONS

The skin of a healthy cat is normally highly resistant to invasion by harmful bacteria. However, sometimes a small number of disease-producing bacteria can make their way through these defenses and cause various infections.

ACNE

CAUSES: Some cats tend to develop bacterial infections on their chins because there are numerous oil glands located in this area. When oil and dirt accumulate, blackheads form, along with inflammation around the hair follicles and oil glands. If this condition is not treated, it may develop into a more serious skin disorder.

What causes some cats to develop acne while others do not? Researchers suspect that cats who are lazy about cleaning their chins are most likely to develop this type of infection. Feline acne may also be transmitted genetically, because kittens of mothers who suffer from this condition often tend to develop similar problems.

SYMPTOMS: Blackheads or pimple-like bumps that come to a head and drain pus. In severe cases, the entire chin and lower lip may swell.

TREATMENT: Consult your veterinarian, who will most likely tell you to clean your cat's infected skin twice daily with a hydrogen peroxide solution or surgical soap. Topical antibiotics may also be prescribed.

LICK GRANULOMA

CAUSES: Excessive licking or biting at one area of the skin for reasons still not exactly clear to researchers can result in damage to the skin and accompanying bacterial infection. Insect bites or some other form of irritation may be the cause. As this condition progresses, the skin gets red and shiny-looking and may eventually ulcerate.

SYMPTOMS: Excessive licking or biting, red and angry-looking skin condition, loss of hair around bitten area, sores, ulceration of sores, oozing of pus.

TREATMENT: Consult your veterinarian. Early treatment is important to prevent the spread of this infection.

PYODERMA

CAUSES: When bacteria that live on the surface of a cat's skin cause an infec-tion, the condition is known as pyoderma. This disorder generally stems from untreated cases of flea allergy dermatitis (see Flea Allergy Dermatitis, p. 155) or from a skin irritation due to injury or other causes. Pyoderma often occurs in cats who are run-down or suffering from malnutrition.

SYMPTOMS: Small pustules that may rupture; licking or scratching at a reddened, infected area. If the infection spreads to the deeper layers of the skin, oozing ulcers may result.

TREATMENT: Consult your veterinarian. Treatment will involve preventing the further spread of this infection.

STUD TAIL

CAUSES: An oversecretion by the oil glands may result in an accumulation of waxy brown material near the base of your cat's tail. In severe cases, infection can set in. Tomcats are most prone to this disorder, but females also sometimes suffer from it.

SYMPTOMS: Accumulation of waxy brown materials in the tail area, greasy and matted hair, sharp odor, loss of hair.

TREATMENT: Consult your veterinarian. Special shampoos with which to wash the tail area may be prescribed.

BITES
(see EMERGENCIES, p. 238)

BRUISES

CAUSES: Bruises can be caused by a blow to a cat, such as if it is struck by a car but not otherwise seriously injured.

SYMPTOMS: Discoloration, collection of blood beneath the skin, areas that are tender to the touch.

TREATMENT: Small bruises usually heal by themselves. If not, consult your veterinarian.

BURNS (see EMERGENCIES, p. 238)

CUTS (see WOUNDS, p. 242)

DERMATITIS (see ALLERGIES, p. 238)

EXTERNAL PARASITES

When grooming your cat (see p. 67), you may find, and should be looking for any signs of, external parasites. Fleas, ticks, and mites are the most common of these culprits. These pesky creatures can not only cause your cat discomfort, but if not attended to may result in conditions leading to suffering and even death.

Parasites are living organisms residing on or within other living organisms. Insect parasites are responsible for the majority of skin ailments in cats.

If you groom your cat at regular intervals, external parasites should not be a problem. If fleas, mites, and other insects are on your cat's skin despite such grooming, ask your veterinarian about the best way to get rid of them.

CHIGGERS

CAUSES: These harvest mites are of concern mainly to cats who are allowed to roam outdoors. Adult chiggers live on vegetation; only the larval forms are parasitic. If you live in the country and your cat happens to encounter an area where chiggers are busy reproducing, it may become infested.

SYMPTOMS: Scratching, irritated skin Red, yellow, or orange specks in areas where your cat's skin is thin, such as around the ears and mouth. Chiggers are barely visible to the naked eye but may be seen with a magnifying glass.

TREATMENT: Consult your veterinarian, who will probably prescribe antiparasitic medication, usually in the form of dips, ointments, and shampoos.

FLEAS

CAUSES: There is no more common external parasite found on a cat's skin than these small, dark-brown, blood-sucking insects. Some cats never get fleas while others do—a mystery that researchers are still trying to unravel.

The flea family is divided into several different species, and some of them can infect humans even if there are no household cats around. Dogs, too, are a favorite target of fleas. The cat flea is called *Ctenocephalides felis,*

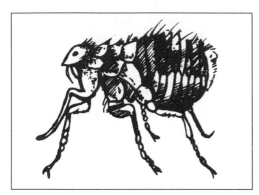

Enlarged depiction of a flea. A single flea can bite twenty times an hour.

while its dog-bugging cousin is known as *Ctenocephalides canis.* The cat flea is much more common.

Fleas are small wingless parasites that hop when they want to get about. A single flea can bite twenty times an hour, so the potential for misery is great. Because fleas have powerful, jointed legs, they can hop, spring, and jump for considerable distances. They move through the hair rapidly and are difficult to catch. Ticks and lice, on the other hand, are slow-moving insects and are easy to pick off.

Fleas lay their eggs on the ground, in a cat's bedding, or in floor crevices, which means that ridding your cat's skin of fleas does not necessarily resolve the problem. That is why many pet owners prefer flea powders to flea sprays or baths. The powder can be spread around areas where cats like to spend time, eliminating new flea generations.

Cats with simple flea infestation may harbor an incredible number of fleas, yet show few or no clinical signs. In most cases, the fleas may cause only a mild itch. Such heavy infestation, however, is dangerous to a cat's health despite minimal signs of discomfort. Because fleas feed on a cat's blood, any large infestation of fleas can result in severe anemia and may cause the death of a cat.

Fleas are also dangerous because they act as intermediate hosts, which means that they are carriers of other parasitic infectious diseases such as tapeworms. Such diseases can cause serious illness in cats and other animals.

Fleas thrive in warm climates and humid environments. They are most common in summer, although they may inhabit a household year-round. On cats, fleas are most often found around the head, the ears, the back of the neck, the rump, and the tail.

If your cat is scratching himself, study these areas. Part the hair and explore the skin surface. Fleas are dark brown and flat. If you observe white specks about the size of sand grains on your cat's coat, these particles are flea droppings.

If you suspect that fleas are the cause of your cat's discomfort, consult your veterinarian about what to do. Your vet should take a look at your pet because cats often suffer serious skin irritation as a result of flea bites.

SYMPTOMS: Scratching, twitching, frenzied licking, salt-and-pepper-like grains about the size of grains of sand found on the coat.

TREATMENT: Consult your veterinarian, who will recommend the most effective products on the market for destroying fleas. These may include insecticides, sprays, shampoos, or powder, which is helpful in exterminating fleas in the surrounding environment.

NOTE: When exterminating your household, remove your cat from the premises. If you have children at home, explicitly inform them of the areas affected by the process, warning them to stay away from all surfaces touched by insecticides. Follow manufacturers' directions. If you plan to use a flea collar, remember that they work best on cats who live indoors. Make certain that your cat does not chew on the collar. Also be aware that some veterinarians do not recommend such collars because they contain insecticides that can be absorbed directly into an animal's bloodstream.

A flea may jump from cat to human but will not remain on the person's body. Rather, the flea will probably bite the human and then leap off. To help stop the spread of fleas, you may want to consider confining your cat to one area at the beginning of treatment, and to keep your cat out of close contact with people and other pets.

LICE

CAUSES: There are two types of lice—biters and bloodsuckers. The biters most often attack cats. Fortunately, lice are not very common in cats and usually affect animals who are malnourished and run-down. Such cats generally have lost interest in keeping their coats well groomed, so are easily subjected to lice infestation.

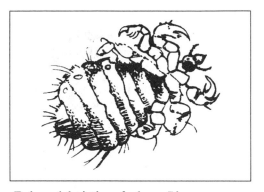

Enlarged depiction of a louse. Lice are uncommon in cats, but they are capable of causing severe damage by acting as intermediary hosts.

Lice are wingless, slow-moving, pale-colored parasites who like to lodge beneath matted hair and around the ears, head, neck, and shoulders of cats. They can often be detected by the naked eye as they move around in a cat's fur.

These parasites are capable of eventually causing the death of a cat, because they act as an intermediate host for tapeworms and other dangerous organisms. Should you find that your cat has lice, be sure to get it prompt veterinary attention.

SYMPTOMS: Scratching; bald spots where the hair has been rubbed off; run-down and anemic condition.

TREATMENT: Consult your veterinarian. Baths and insecticide dips are commonly recommended. Because of their weakened condition, malnourished cats who are seriously infected may require gentler treatment, such as insecticide powders. Feline lice are host-specific and will not affect humans.

MAGGOTS

CAUSES: Cats who have neglected wounds, matted coats, or other skin problems may be infested with maggots in warm weather. Blowflies are attracted to such conditions and lay clusters of light-yellow eggs in open wounds or soiled hair coats. These eggs hatch within ten to twelve hours, and the larvae grow into large-sized maggots. Maggot saliva produces an enzyme that can damage a cat's skin; the maggots then penetrate the skin and introduce harmful bacteria.

SYMPTOMS: Lesions that have a "punched out" appearance and nauseating odor; large sections of skin may literally "crawl" with maggots.

TREATMENT: Consult your veterinarian. Insecticides and topical antibiotics will most likely be prescribed.

MITES

CAUSES: Cats frequently fall victim to attacks by various kinds of mites, which cause a skin condition known as mange. Mites are minute, spiderlike creatures that penetrate into the deeper layers of the skin, burrow tunnels, and breed by laying eggs. They destroy skin tissues and cause infections.

The areas of mite infestation often become itchy and encrusted. In the case of head mange, the hair falls out. Head mange, also known as feline scabies, is caused by a mite called *Notoedres cati*. It is a highly contagious form of mange and is primarily transmitted

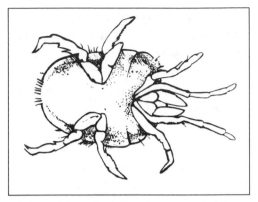
Enlarged depiction of a mite, a parasite that is in the same taxonomic class as the spider

by direct contact between cats. It can cause itchy eruptions on humans, as can walking mange, which is caused by a mite called Cheyletiella.

SYMPTOMS: Itching, inflammation, crusty area on the edge of the ear or face, hair loss, and the appearance of bald spots.

TREATMENT: Consult your veterinarian. Insecticide shampoos and dips to kill the mites are the likely course of treatment.

TICKS

CAUSES: Country-dwelling cats are more likely to come into contact with these insects than their city-dwelling cousins. Until recently, ticks were most often found in the Midwestern, Western, and Southern states, but now they can be found almost anywhere in the United States.

There are many varieties of ticks, which are bloodsucking creatures. They are more often found on dogs

REMOVING A TICK

Should you spot a tick on your cat's body, avoid the temptation of simply trying to pull it out. All you will get is the body, while the head and jaws remain buried in the cat. The remaining parts can cause irritation and inflammation.

The most effective way to remove a tick is to dab it with alcohol or fingernail polish. This will not harm your cat and will kill the tick. Then pull it out of your cat's body with tweezers. Place the tweezers as close as you can to the skin, so that the head is removed.

than cats because of the fastidious care cats take of their coats, but owners whose cats go outdoors should be alert to tick infestation.

Ticks are tenacious and persistent pests. Their fearsome mouth and jaws enable them to bite into the skin and hold on tight while they are sucking blood. They are shiny gray in color and can swell to the size of a pea. Ticks are often found on the head of a cat, but they may also attach themselves to other parts of the body. A male tick is always small and flat; a female tick puffs up after feeding on a cat. If you see a puffed-up female tick on your cat, look for a male somewhere nearby.

SYMPTOMS: Swollen, pea-sized insects in the hair or between the cat's toes. Ticks often resemble tumors or cysts.

FLEA ALLERGY DERMATITIS

CAUSES: An allergic reaction to the saliva of fleas may result in this skin condition, which affects some cats but not others.

SYMPTOMS: Hair loss, extremely reddened skin, usually around the back and the base of the tail; possible scabs or infection.

TREATMENT: Consult your veterinarian. Insecticide powders are the usual course of treatment.

Flea allergy dermatitis causes skin irritation and infection. Another flea-related dermatitis can be caused by flea collars.

FLIES

CAUSES: Cats are normally not afflicted by flies, but occasionally a fly may deposit its eggs on raw or infected wounds.

SYMPTOMS: Lumps beneath the skin that may become infected.

TREATMENT: Consult your veterinarian. Treatment usually involves the careful removal of maggots and eggs, as well as the administration of an antibacterial agent.

FUNGAL SKIN INFECTIONS

Fungal diseases can affect either the skin or the mucous membranes. They may be local or widespread throughout a cat's body. Systemic, or widespread, fungal infections are rather rare in cats. Some fungi that cause infection in cats may also cause illnesses in humans.

RINGWORM

CAUSES: Ringworm has nothing to do with worms; a fungal disease—the most common one occurring in cats—it is a plantlike growth that invades the outer layers of the skin, nails, and hair.

This condition gets its name from its typical appearance—a rapidly spreading circle with hair loss and scaly skin at the center and an advancing red edge. There are several species of ringworm. The fungus that most often affects cats is called *Microsporum canis.*

The fungus is usually contracted from the soil or from the infected hair of other animals. It is a highly contagious disease. Cats can spread the disease to other cats, dogs, and even to humans. If your cat is suspected of having ringworm, your children should avoid handling the cat until he is treated. Be sure to wash your hands thoroughly after handling your cat.

SYMPTOMS: Scabs, crust, scaly patches, hair loss, moderate itching, draining sores that provoke licking and scratching. Patchy baldness with or without redness. Small scabby circles on any part of the skin, most often on the ears, face, neck, and tail.

Although these are the most typical symptoms of ringworm, the disease can be present in their absence. Ringworm used to be one of the worst banes of a cat's life, but an antibiotic discovered in 1939 has made this fungus disorder less difficult to cure.

TREATMENT: Consult your veterinarian. Internal as well as external treatments are involved. Oral and topical medications usually are prescribed, along with environmental cleansing. Long-haired cats may have to be shaved.

HIVES

CAUSES: Hives are an allergic reaction to the saliva of fleas, and they occur whenever fleas are prevalent. This allergic reaction affects some cats but not others, for reasons as yet unknown.

SYMPTOMS: Sudden swelling of the head, usually around the eyes and mouth; welts and itching.

TREATMENT: In mild cases, cats usually recover without treatment. If distress continues for more than a few hours, consult your veterinarian.

HORMONAL SKIN DISORDERS

Hormonal skin disorders are rare in cats. If they do occur, however, they may result in feline endocrine alopecia, balding, or a thyroid deficiency.

FELINE ENDOCRINE ALOPECIA

CAUSES: If your cat appears to be balding, he is suffering from feline endocrine alopecia, which most often affects neutered males. Unneutered males and females, however, also are sometimes affected. The loss of sex hormones in older cats may cause this condition.

TREATMENT: Consult your veterinarian. An estrogen/testosterone combination injection may be administered.

MANGE (see MITES, pp. 127, 154)

PORCUPINE QUILLS

CAUSES: Porcupine quills are a painful reality to cats in some parts of the country. Cats tend to attack porcupines and pay for it.

SYMPTOMS: Porcupine quills in the muzzle and head area.

TREATMENT: Removal of porcupine quills is painful, so it is best to bring your pet to the veterinarian's office, where a general anesthetic will be administered.

SEBACEOUS CYST

CAUSES: Less common in cats than in dogs, these are benign tumors that erupt from skin glands.

SYMPTOMS: A lump that feels like cheesy material; it may grow to an inch or more in size.

TREATMENT: Sebaceous cysts may become infected. If the cyst doesn't drain by itself, consult your veterinarian, who will lance it.

SKUNK ODOR

CAUSES: Kittens are most likely to have a run-in with skunks because most older cats know better than to mess with them.

TREATMENT: Wash your cat with water and a baby shampoo. Try to gently flush out her eyes with water (be careful not to rub soap in the eyes). If the cat's eyes are badly inflamed, characterized by dark redness, swelling of the lids, and irritation, consult your veterinarian.

TUMORS
(see SEBACEOUS CYSTS, p. 157)

WARTS

CAUSES: Warts are far less common in cats than in people. Older cats tend to get these skin growths.

SYMPTOMS: Warts resemble pieces of chewing gum stuck to the skin.

TREATMENT: If warts begin to bleed or become irritated, consult your veterinarian, who will remove them.

THE HAIR

A cat's skin follicles produce three different types of hair: long guard hair, which makes up the top coat; underfur, which provides added warmth and protection; and carpal hair, which consists of the whiskers and eyelashes.

DANDRUFF

CAUSES: Dandruff, or flakiness of a cat's skin, can be caused by a diet deficient in oils or fats, by too much bathing (which dries the skin), or by worms. Dandruff is also common in housecats who stay inside most of the time; the skin dries out from lack of fresh air. Skin infections caused by mites can sometimes produce dandruff.

SYMPTOMS: Skin flaking.

TREATMENT: Consult your veterinarian, who will determine the cause of your cat's dandruff.

SHEDDING

CAUSES: Shedding is a normal process. Some cats shed year-round while others do so only in the spring. Shedding allows new hair to replace the old.

SYMPTOMS: Dead hairs fall out.

TREATMENT: To prevent excessive shedding, keep your cat well brushed; the more you brush his hair and skin, the healthier he will be. Bathing your cat once a month with a mild soap may also help prevent excessive shedding (see Grooming, p. 67).

12

RESPIRATORY SYSTEM PROBLEMS

JUST LIKE A HUMAN, a cat depends upon her respiratory system to provide oxygen to her body—oxygen that is crucial in metabolizing nutrients. The feline respiratory system consists of the upper respiratory tract—the nose, sinuses, bronchi, and larynx (voice box)—and the lower respiratory tract,

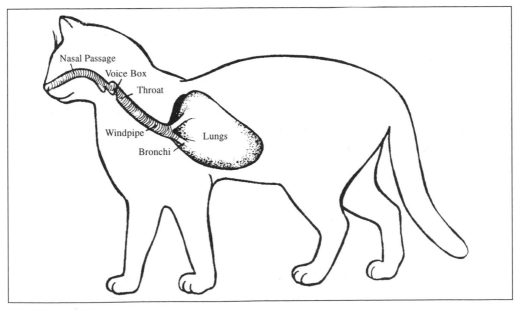

The feline respiratory system

HOW TO RECOGNIZE ABNORMAL BREATHING

Cats normally breathe about 25 to 30 times per minute when they are at rest. After exercise, this rate rises to 60 to 90 breaths per minute. It also takes a cat almost twice as long to exhale as it does to inhale. The breathing process in a healthy cat is smooth and unrestrained.

A cat who is suffering from a respiratory infection may show signs of illness in shortness of breath, noisy and forced breathing, and coughing.

Rapid breathing also can be caused by pain, emotional stress, fever, and even overeating. Shallow breathing is frequently a symptom of respiratory infection but may also signify pleurisy, fluid or air in the chest cavity, or narcotic poisoning.

If your cat begins to wheeze, her airway may be obstructed at some point between the larynx and bronchial tubes. Wheezing is also often a symptom of asthma, lungworms, congestive heart failure, or tumors in the airway passages.

---

which includes the trachea, bronchial tubes, and lungs.

The trachea is more commonly known as the windpipe; it conducts air from the larynx to the lungs. The trachea divides at its lower end into two main air passages—the bronchi—that lead to the right and left lungs.

The lungs consist of the trachea and bronchi—breathing tubes—along with air sacs and blood vessels. The ribs and muscles of the chest, along with the diaphragm, serve as bellows to move air into and out of the lungs.

ASTHMA (ALLERGIC BRONCHITIS)

CAUSES: This asthmalike bronchial disease resembles bronchial asthma in humans. It is believed to be caused by an allergic reaction to pollens, grasses, dust, or other irritants. It usually develops at certain times of the year, most often in the spring. Feline asthma tends to be recurrent but is usually not very severe.

SYMPTOMS: Heavy, distressed breathing; wheezing; dry, hacking cough; blue tinge to the tongue, gums, and lips.

TREATMENT: Consult your veterinarian. Medication to open the bronchial tubes and allow normal breathing is usually prescribed.

BRONCHITIS

CAUSES: The inflammation or infection of the air tubes—the bronchi—that link the windpipe to the lungs is known as bronchitis. The most fre-

Labored breathing is a key indicator of acute bronchitis.

quent cause of bronchitis is an acute viral upper respiratory illness. Other causes of this disorder include irritants, such as gases or smoke, and foreign bodies such as grass seeds or pollen to which a cat may be allergic.

SYMPTOMS: Dry, hacking cough; in more severe cases moist or bubbling cough; foamy saliva; retching.

TREATMENT: Consult your veterinarian. If left untreated, bronchitis may develop into a more chronic form and cause serious damage to the breathing tubes.

CHEST WOUNDS (see EMERGENCIES, p. 238)

CHRONIC BRONCHITIS

CAUSES: If a case of bronchitis persists for several weeks, it is referred to as chronic. Bacterial infection usually sets in; if not treated, this can cause severe damage to the breathing tubes.

SYMPTOMS: Moist or bubbling cough, retching, expectoration of foamy saliva.

TREATMENT: Consult your veterinarian. Rest and proper humidification of your environment probably will be recommended. Antihistamines will be prescribed to treat the cough.

COLDS

CAUSES: Like people, cats are subject to catching colds. There is no conclusive evidence that the human head cold and the feline cold are the same, nor is there any evidence that people can transmit their colds to a cat or dog or vice versa. Colds in cats are caused by viruses that produce symptoms resembling the human cold.

SYMPTOMS: Discharge from the eyes; a runny nose; coughs; sneezes and slight fever.

TREATMENT: If the cold lasts for more than two days, or if the symptoms worsen, consult your veterinarian.

COUGHS

CAUSES: Coughing typically indicates an irritation of the air passages, usually brought about by infectious agents such as viruses, bacteria, or fungi. A cough accompanied by fever, sneezing, noisy breathing, and discharge from the nose and eyes suggests a viral respiratory disease.

TREATMENT: Consult your veterinarian. Treatment will depend upon the root cause of the cough.

HAY FEVER
(see ALLERGIES, p. 149)

LUNGWORMS

CAUSES: These slender, hairlike parasites mostly affect cats in rural areas. The larvae of these parasites are eliminated through the feces, which are eaten by snails and slugs. These snails and slugs in turn are eaten by birds, who then become infected. If a cat eats one of these infected birds, she becomes infected.

SYMPTOMS: Most cats show none. Others may develop a chronic cough. Fever, weight loss, wheezing, and nasal discharge are sometimes symptoms of lungworm.

TREATMENT: If you suspect lungworm, take your cat to a veterinarian, who will be able to see larvae or eggs in your cat's stool.

PLEURISY

CAUSES: Two feline infectious diseases—peritonitis and leukemia—can cause fluid to accumulate in the chest cavity. When this happens, a condition known as pleurisy, or pleural effusion, results, making it difficult for a cat to breathe. Pleurisy may also develop as the result of a puncture wound to the chest produced in a catfight. The resulting bacterial infection can lead to pus formation. A heart condition may also cause pleuritis symptoms, since it may affect circulation just as pleurisy would.

SYMPTOMS: Difficulty in breathing; open-mouthed breathing; any effort produces sudden distress or collapse; lips, gums, and tongue may look pale, gray, or blue (resulting from insufficient oxygen in the blood).

TREATMENT: Consult your veterinarian. Any fluid buildup in a cat's chest requires immediate attention. Treatment usually involves the draining of fluids.

PNEUMONIA

CAUSES: While not very common in cats, when it does occur pneumonia is usually a complication of severe flu. Pneumonia is also caused by an infection of the lung tissue brought on by viral, bacterial, or fungal parasites such as cryptococcus. An irritation of the lungs from chemicals in the air can also cause this disorder.

SYMPTOMS: Labored, rapid breathing; loss of appetite; fever; severe depression; extreme lethargy; deep, moist cough.

TREATMENT: Consult your veterinarian. Antibiotics will probably be administered.

PNEUMOTHORAX

CAUSES: A ruptured lung or a puncture or laceration in the chest can cause air to enter it. The air then surrounds and presses against the lungs, keeping them from expanding normally when the cat tries to breathe. This can be an emergency situation requiring immediate action, since lack of oxygen can lead rapidly to unconsciousness.

SYMPTOMS: Difficulty in breathing; gums, tongue, and inner lining of the eyelids begin to turn blue; the cat's stomach may rise and fall as she tries to breathe.

TREATMENT: Consult your veterinarian, who will attempt to prevent air from leaking into the chest cavity.

PULMONARY EDEMA

CAUSES: Pulmonary edema is usually caused by an abnormal accumulation of fluid in the lungs, often as a result of complications in disorders such as congestive heart failure, heart muscle disease, or a brain tumor. Pulmonary edema also can have a sudden onset, such as in the case of an allergic reaction, electric shock, or insect or spider bites.

SYMPTOMS: Difficult breathing, wheezing.

TREATMENT: Consult your veterinarian. Early treatment is important. Treatment will attempt to rid the lungs of fluid using diuretics and bronchodilator drugs.

PYOTHORAX

CAUSES: An untreated bite wound to the chest can result in pyothorax, in which a bacterial infection leads to an accumulation of pus around the lungs, preventing them from functioning properly.

SYMPTOMS: Difficulty in breathing, high temperature, loss of appetite, depression.

TREATMENT: If your cat suffers such a wound, make certain that your veterinarian examines it and any resulting abscesses around the chest and neck.

13

MUSCULOSKELETAL SYSTEM PROBLEMS

HUMANS MAY BE ROUGHLY fifteen times the size of the cat, but they have fewer bones. The cat has 244 bones in his skeleton—about forty more than humans do. Their distribution is different, too.

However, if you stood the skeleton of a cat on its back legs so that it was erect, you'd find almost a bone-for-bone similarity to a human's. Your cat's skeletal system has essentially the same parts as humans, but many of the bones have been modified to meet the cat's special needs. As in humans, tendons connect muscle to bone and ligaments strengthen the structure of joints.

The structure of the skeleton permits muscles and tendons to move the individual bones in their joints in such a manner that all of a cat's necessary movements can be performed with a minimum expenditure of energy. The hind legs are an effective lever system—helped along by strong muscles in the back—that give a cat his great jumping power and tremendous speed.

When bones join together to form a joint, a protective layer of cartilage on each bone edge prevents friction. Most of your cat's joints are hinged, with the exception of the shoulders and hip joints, which fit together like a ball and socket.

The outside of the bone is called the cortex. It is made up of minerals and proteins. If your cat is not getting a well-balanced diet, nutritional deficiencies can cause poor bone development. This can cause bones to fracture easily.

Within the bones is the marrow cavity. Bone marrow serves the important function of producing red blood cells. Two essential minerals, calcium and

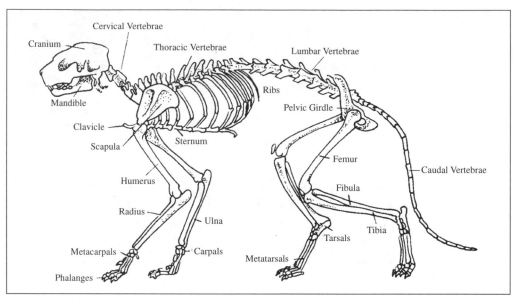

The feline skeleton contains 244 bones.

phosphorus, are also stored in bones and distributed when needed from there. Calcium is vital to your cat's health because it contributes to a regu-lar heartbeat and assists the nerves in conducting messages.

Cats are highly flexible because of their extremely articulate backbones.

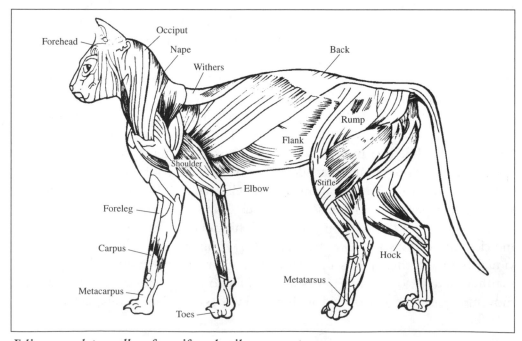

Feline musculature allows for swift and agile movement.

In fact, the joints connecting the cervical, or neck, bones are so flexible that your cat can lick himself everywhere but the back of his head.

Diseases and other disorders can occur in any part of the cat's musculoskeletal system for a number of reasons. Such disorders run the gamut from trauma or injury to the bones to bacterial infections.

There are many symptoms of musculoskeletal disease; most common are lameness, stiffness, swelling, joint grating or grinding, and hesitation to move or walk.

AMPUTATION
(see EMERGENCIES, p. 239)

ARTHRITIS

CAUSES: Arthritis is a common chronic disease that can affect one or more of the movable joints in a cat's body. This degenerative joint disease involves the deterioration of the cartilage. To protect itself, the joint undergoes structural changes, such as developing excess bone.

There are various forms of arthritis. The most common variety is called osteoarthritis, which most often affects older cats as a normal process of aging. It can also result from injury, a poor fit in the joint, or misuse of the joint. Osteoarthritis is less common in cats than dogs and produces milder symptoms.

SYMPTOMS: Tenderness and pain, limping, enlargement of the joint, rubbing or grating sound heard when the joint is moved, stiffness, lameness upon rising that improves as the day wears on.

TREATMENT: Consult your veterinarian. Treatment involves the carefully monitored use of non-aspirin painkillers. The aim of the treatment is to relieve discomfort, restore the function of the joint, and prevent further degeneration.

BONE INFECTION (OSTEOMYELITIS)

CAUSES: Osteomyelitis is a bacterial bone infection that is usually more common in cats than in dogs. It can result from a bite or other puncture wound, open fractures, or bone surgery—virtually any condition in which bacteria have entry to the bone and blood circulation in the area has been disturbed.

SYMPTOMS: Lameness, fever, pain, swelling, wound that does not heal, fluid and pus discharging from a wound, foul odor from the wound.

TREATMENT: Consult your veterinarian. Antibiotics usually are utilized. Treatment is often lengthy, because bone infections are difficult to eliminate.

CRACKED PADS

CAUSES: While cat's pads are tough protective coverings, they nonetheless are sometimes vulnerable to penetration by such objects as glass, tacks, and nails.

SYMPTOMS: Limping.

TREATMENT: Check to see if any foreign object or debris has lodged in the pad (see Foreign Objects in Foot, below). Wash thoroughly with warm water and soap, and apply an antiseptic. Keep the wound bandaged so dirt and debris do not get in (see Foot Wound, p. 86).

DISLOCATED JOINT

CAUSES: A cat who is in an accident can fracture or dislocate a leg or a paw. The hip is the most commonly dislocated joint in a cat. Sometimes a joint can be displaced as a result of a fall or cat fight.

SYMPTOMS: Pain, inability to use the limb.

TREATMENT: Consult your veterinarian immediately. He or she needs to make certain that there is not an accompanying fracture. Dislocated joints treated within twenty-four hours can usually be reset without surgery and with minimal healing time.

FOREIGN OBJECTS IN THE FOOT

CAUSES: Sometimes a splinter or piece of glass can lodge itself in your cat's foot pad.

SYMPTOMS: Limping, pain.

TREATMENT: Carefully examine the pad. If the foreign object is visible, try to remove it by hand or with tweezers. Make certain to wash the wound with warm water and a disinfectant soap. If you cannot see the object or if it is difficult to remove, consult your veterinarian.

HIP DYSPLASIA

CAUSES: This congenital bone disorder rarely affects cats. Other common bone disorders include extra toes or kinked tails.

TREATMENT: Consult your veterinarian.

LAMENESS

CAUSES: When a cat limps there can be several possible causes ranging from bone or joint disease to muscle damage. A common cause is simply an injury to the pad. Dislocations, sprains, and fractures are also common causes of lameness in a cat.

TREATMENT: Examine your cat for the most obvious causes, such as a foreign body in the pads. Consult your veterinarian.

METABOLIC BONE DISORDERS (see NUTRITIONAL SECONDARY HYPERPARATHYROIDISM, p. 169).

MUSCLE STRAIN

CAUSES: Muscle strains come on suddenly as the result of overexertion.

SYMPTOMS: Local swelling, discoloration of skin under fur, mild pain.

TREATMENT: Strains gradually heal on their own.

NUTRITIONAL SECONDARY HYPERPARATHYROIDISM (PAPER BONE DISEASE)

CAUSES: Paper bone disease is a metabolic disorder that affects cats and is a major disease of kittens. It is caused by an imbalance of calcium and phosphorus, usually the result of an all-meat diet. Meat contains an abundance of phosphorus and little calcium. The body compensates for the resulting lack of circulating calcium by taking it directly from the bones themselves.

SYMPTOMS: Painful, swollen elbows and front wrist joints; toes are spread wide and splayed outward; bones fracture for little or no reason; loose and lost teeth. In kittens: reluctance to move; staggering, uncoordinated gait; thin, paper-like bones that are easily fractured; sometimes lameness in the back legs; front stance is often bowed.

TREATMENT: Consult your veterinarian, who may prescribe calcium supplements and recommend a diet that meets all the nutritional requirements for growing kittens and adult cats. A good prognosis depends upon the extent of skeletal damage. In severe cases, little can be done. If the disorder is caught at an early stage, calcium supplements, dietary changes, and a few weeks of rest and immobilization will often restore your cat's health.

OSTEOCHONDRITIS DISSECANS (SEPARATION OF JOINT CARTILAGE) (see DISLOCATED JOINT, p. 168)

PAINFUL, SWOLLEN JOINTS AND FEET

CAUSES: Bursitis, arthritis, and rheumatism are among the various causes of painful, swollen joints and feet.

TREATMENT: Consult your veterinarian. Do not give your cat human pain relievers such as aspirin, which are toxic to cats. Try to keep your cat relatively still and as comfortable as possible.

PATELLAR DISLOCATION (SLIPPED KNEECAP)

CAUSES: While very unlikely, once in a while a cat's kneecap will be injured after a fall or other accident. The internal ligaments can be ruptured or separated.

SYMPTOMS: Pain on flexing and extending the knee, looseness of the joint, clicking sound in the joint.

TREATMENT: Consult your veterinarian. Your cat will probably need to be X-rayed to determine the extent of damage. The best way to transport him to the veterinarian is to gently place your cat in his carrier or anything that will limit his mobility and hold him snugly.

RICKETS

CAUSES: Called osteomalacia in adult cats, rickets is a rare disease caused by a vitamin D deficiency. Researchers believe that the development of rickets in cats also suggests other vitamin and mineral deficiencies.

SYMPTOMS: Bowing of legs and other growth deformities in kittens. Enlargement of the joints where the ribs meet the cartilages of the sternum. In severe cases, bones fracture easily.

TREATMENT: Consult your veterinarian. Treatment involves dietary corrections and supplements. The speed and degree of recovery depend upon the extent of damage.

SPRAIN

CAUSES: Sprains can be caused by joints that are suddenly stretched or by the tearing of the joint capsule (the covering of a joint) or ligaments.

SYMPTOMS: Pain in the joint, swelling of tissue, lameness.

TREATMENT: Consult your veterinarian. Treatment consists of getting the cat to rest the sprained area. Keep your cat inside. You may need to confine your cat to one room if he is particularly active.

TENDON INJURIES

CAUSES: A sudden wrenching or twisting injury can result in a tendon that is stretched, partly torn, or completely ruptured.

SYMPTOMS: Temporary lameness, pain, and swelling.

TREATMENT: Consult your veterinarian. Treatment consists of resting the injured tendon. Surgery may be necessary to repair the tendon, especially if it has ruptured.

14

CIRCULATORY SYSTEM PROBLEMS

TWO IMPORTANT TASKS are performed by the feline circulatory system: transporting oxygen and other vital materials to all corners of a cat's body, and combating infection. The system comprises the heart, blood, blood vessels, and spleen.

The feline heart is a muscular pump about the size of a small plum. It has four chambers: the right and left auricles, and the right and left ventricles.

Blood is pumped from the left ventricle through the arteries to reach the network of capillaries that permeate all the body's tissues. Blood returns to the heart through the veins, then is pumped through the right auricle and ventricle into the lungs through the pulmonary arteries. There the blood is infused with fresh oxygen, and carbon dioxide is eliminated. The oxygenated blood then returns to the heart through the pul-

monary veins, passes through the left auricle and left ventricle, and again begins its journey through the tissues.

Blood is composed of red blood cells, white blood cells, platelets, and plasma. Each of these components plays an integral role in the body's well-being and health. Red blood cells carry oxygen and food to the cells.

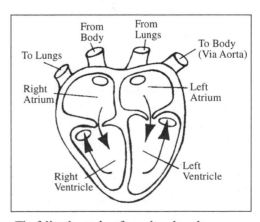

The feline heart is a four-chambered organ.

171

White blood cells fight disease. Platelets aid in clotting, while plasma holds all of the blood's components in suspension. The blood vessels transport blood through the body. The spleen, located in the abdomen, filters and removes old, damaged blood cells from the bloodstream. It also maintains a storage of extra red blood cells.

Heart disease is much less common in cats than in people. Blood disorders are the major health threat to the feline circulatory system.

AORTIC THROMBOSIS

CAUSES: An embolus, or blood clot, may break off from the left side of the heart and become lodged in the blood vessels going to the hind legs. This cuts off blood supply. Other parts of the body can also be affected by such a clot, which commonly occurs as a result of heart muscle disease. Such a blockage is called a thrombosis.

SYMPTOMS: Sudden paralysis of the muscles in the hind legs, legs cold to the touch, bluish skin, calf muscles contract and become very hard, pain when legs are squeezed.

TREATMENT: Consult your veterinarian immediately. Medications may be administered to try to dissolve the clot. Surgery may be required.

ANEMIA

CAUSES: Any condition that results in an inadequate circulation of red blood cells is called anemia. Anemia is common in cats, and can be the result of leukemia, bacteria-like parasites in the blood cells, serious internal disease, or blood poisoning. Diseases like feline infectious anemia, and any trauma that results in hemorrhaging, also can result in anemia.

SYMPTOMS: Pale eye and mouth membranes; lack of appetite; weight loss; excessive lethargy; generalized weakness. In severe cases, the pulse and breathing rate increase. Overexertion may cause a cat to collapse.

TREATMENT: Consult your veterinarian. Treatment depends on the causes, which can range from nutritional deficiencies to more complicated ailments.

HEART FAILURE

CAUSES: Weakened heart muscles may reduce the heart's ability to pump blood. These muscles can be affected by disease, old age, or other causes, all of which result in the inability of the heart to provide the kind of circulation the body requires.

When the heart weakens, the left ventricle starts to fail. This often results in a buildup of fluids in the lungs' air sacs—a condition known as pulmonary edema (see Respiratory System Problems, p. 163). This is usually accompanied by lung congestion.

As the pulmonary edema progresses, the cat cannot get enough oxygen. Any stress on the heart, from excitement to exercise, is likely to cause collapse. Additional breathing difficulties occur because fluid can accumulate around the lungs.

SYMPTOMS: Shortness of breath, labored breathing, noisy breathing, coughing after moderate exercise, fatigue, wheezing.

TREATMENT: Consult your veterinarian. Immediate treatment could involve administering oxygen and diuretics, and possibly removing fluid from the lungs. Long-term therapy often consists of drugs to regulate blood pressure and heartbeat.

LEFT-SIDE HEART FAILURE

CAUSES: When the left ventricle begins to fail, the result is lung congestion and accumulation of fluid in the air sacs, or pulmonary edema (see Respiratory System Problems, p. 163).

SYMPTOMS: Shortness of breath, fatigue, coughing, labored breathing.

TREATMENT: Consult your veterinarian.

RIGHT-SIDE HEART FAILURE

CAUSES: Much less common than left-side heart failure, this condition is brought about by the weakening of the right heart muscle, creating excessive pressure in the veins.

SYMPTOMS: Lethargy, loss of appetite, shortness of breath, rapid pulse.

TREATMENT: Consult your veterinarian.

HEART MURMUR

CAUSES: Not all murmurs, or disturbances in the flow of blood through the heart, are serious. Anemia is often a common cause of heart murmurs in cats. A murmur can indicate more serious problems in heart function; some cannot ultimately be attributable to any known cause.

SYMPTOMS: Some murmurs can be heard at home as a "shh" sound in the middle of a normal heartbeat.

TREATMENT: Consult your veterinarian, who will determine whether the cause of the murmur is serious enough to warrant treatment.

HEART MUSCLE DISEASE

CAUSES: The origins of heart muscle disease are not well known, although the problem is common. It is characterized by the heart muscle failing to function properly. In the early stages of this disease, the heart becomes enlarged and inflamed. The heart muscle itself will sometimes bleed. Cats two to three years of age are most often affected by this disease, which can produce acute heart failure and may result in death.

As heart muscle disease progresses, the heart is less and less able to pump blood. The muscle has difficulty contracting, often the result of a deficiency in the amino acid taurine. Ultimately, the heart muscle begins to deteriorate and symptoms of congestive heart failure appear.

SYMPTOMS: Signs are vague. They may include a fluid-filled "potbelly," labored breathing even at rest, a sitting position with head and neck extended in an effort to get more air, below-normal body temperature, feet that seem cool to the touch.

TREATMENT: Consult your veterinarian. The condition may be managed through medication and through a nutritional approach, including supplementation of taurine, unless permanent damage has already occurred.

HEARTWORM

CAUSES: These round parasites are more common in dogs than in cats, but sometimes felines are affected. The technical name for heartworms is *Dirofilaria immitis,* and they are generally transmitted by mosquitoes, which transmit the worm embryos once they suck blood from an infected dog or cat.

The larvae burrow into a cat's tissues and develop into small adult worms. These circulate in the blood, heading for the muscle and fatty tissues. They grow until they are ready to make their way through the blood system to the heart, where they reach maturity.

SYMPTOMS: Coughing, labored breathing, collapse upon exercising, anemia, loss of weight, bloody sputum (material coughed up from the lungs).

TREATMENT: Consult your veterinarian. Drugs are available to kill these parasites, although different ones are used to kill the adult worm and the embryos.

THROMBOSIS
(see also AORTIC THROMBOSIS, p. 172)

CAUSES: The clotting of an artery due to the obstruction to the flow of blood is called a thrombosis. The most common site of blockage is the point at which the abdominal aorta branches into the main arteries to the legs. Two possible causes are blood clots and the buildup of arterial plaque.

SYMPTOMS: Sudden onset of weakness in the rear legs; cold legs; bluish skin.

TREATMENT: Consult your veterinarian. Medications may be given to try to dissolve the clot. Surgery is sometimes required.

15

NERVOUS SYSTEM PROBLEMS

THE JOB OF COORDINATING your cat's various body systems so that they function in harmony is actually performed on two levels—by the nervous system and by the endocrine, or hormonal, system. The cat's elaborate nervous system makes it one of the most alert and perceptive animals on earth.

A cat's central nervous system is composed of the cerebrum—the front part of the brain—the cerebellum, or midbrain, and the spinal cord. The brain and central nervous system of the cat closely resembles that of the dog, but are quite different from that of the human.

Sensory receptors detect events in the outside world and within the cat's body. The brain and the spinal cord—the major thoroughfare for the transmission of motor nerve impulses from the brain—process this information. Nerve messages are then sent out to initiate and control the body's responses.

The largest part of the brain is the cerebrum, which is involved with the functions of learning, memory, reasoning, and judgment. This seat of conscious, deliberate, and rational action is smaller than the equivalent organ in dogs or humans. The smaller-sized cerebrum, however, does not diminish feline intelligence (see Intelligence and Awareness, p. 22).

The cerebellum is an extremely large and well-developed brain organ that is mostly involved with body motions; it is also the seat of instinct, unconscious memory, and reflex actions. The cat's is as highly developed as the dog's.

Located in the midbrain are centers that control respiration, heart rate, blood pressure, and other essential activities. At the base of the brain are the hypothalmus and the pituitary gland, which regulate the cat's body temperature and hormonal system. Responses such as hunger, thirst, or rage are also initiated by the hypothalmus and pituitary gland.

Disorders of this complex system are fairly rare in cats. Most injuries to the nervous system result from cats being involved in accidents or falling from great heights. Other sources of harm include poisons, drug toxicities, and brain infections.

BRAIN INFECTIONS
(see ENCEPHALITIS)

COMA

CAUSES: A coma, or a depressed state of consciousness, usually follows a trauma such as a blow to the head. Comatose cats are not responsive to pain. Coma may also be brought on by various brain diseases and central nervous system disorders.

SYMPTOMS: Stupor; cat is difficult to arouse; legs are rigid; breathing is rapid, shallow, and irregular.

TREATMENT: If cat is unconscious, make sure the airway isn't blocked. If it is, draw out the cat's tongue and clear the airway with your fingers. Wrap the cat in a blanket and get veterinary help.

CONVULSIONS
(see EMERGENCIES, p. 238)

ENCEPHALITIS
(BRAIN INFECTIONS)

CAUSES: If the brain becomes infected or inflamed, a condition known as encephalitis develops. Brain infections are not common in cats. When encephalitis does occur, it is usually caused by viruses or bacteria that gain entrance to the brain through the bloodstream or through a sinus infection or an infection of the nasal passage, eye, head, or neck region.

SYMPTOMS: Fever, lack of coordination, unstable gait, changes in behavior or personality, seizures, coma.

TREATMENT: Consult your veterinarian. The aim of treatment is to determine the underlying causes of the condition. Steroids are sometimes used to reduce the swelling of the brain.

EPILEPSY (see CONVULSIONS, EMERGENCIES, p. 244)

A seizure occurs when a cat appears to lose control of his body due to a malfunction of the brain. The most common cause of seizures is epilepsy, a recurrent condition brought about by the sudden discharge of electrical impulses anywhere inside the brain. The size and location of the affected area determine the kinds of symptoms and their severity.

CAUSES: Researchers are still not exactly certain what causes animal epilepsy. The disease is more common in dogs than cats. There is some evidence that it may be a hereditary disorder. Any type of excitement can cause an epileptic fit; it can also be brought on by infections, stroke, tumors, poisoning, or hyperthyroidism.

SYMPTOMS: Recurrent seizures.

TREATMENT: For immediate care, see Emergency Procedures, p. 232. Consult your veterinarian. Treatment generally includes anticonvulsive medications. If your veterinarian does prescribe medication, make certain that you administer it regularly to avoid additional seizures.

HEAD INJURIES

CAUSES: Many cats hit by cars suffer head injuries. If the blow is of sufficient magnitude, the skull can be fractured and the brain injured.

A cat suffering from a head injury, if not unconscious, may be dazed and disoriented, and may have unevenly dilated pupils.

SYMPTOMS: If not unconscious, the cat is dazed, staggers, and is disoriented. Its pupils may be unevenly dilated.

TREATMENT: Get veterinary help.

HERNIATED DISC

CAUSES: Herniated or ruptured discs are very rare in cats. The few occurences of this condition usually appear in older cats who have suffered some kind of accident. A form of spinal arthritis can also lead to a herniated disc.

SYMPTOMS: Rarely cause clinical signs.

TREATMENT: Consult your veterinarian. The condition usually improves with rest and the administration of corticosteroids.

HYDROCEPHALUS

CAUSES: A blockage in the flow of cerebrospinal fluid can cause the enlargement or malfunction of the head, a condition known as hydrocephalus. Fluid builds up, resulting in damage to the brain. A rare condition in cats.

TREATMENT: Consult your veterinarian. To date, there is no effective treatment for hydrocephalus. Recovery depends upon the amount of damage caused by the fluid buildup.

MENINGITIS

CAUSES: An uncommon disease in cats, meningitis is usually caused by the spread of infection from other parts of a cat's body. This infection eventually affects the membranes covering the brain and spinal cord.

SYMPTOMS: Extreme pain, lethargy, fever, loss of appetite, convulsions (see First-Aid Guide, Chapter 22).

TREATMENT: Consult your veterinarian immediately. Recovery depends upon stopping the spread of infection before damage is done to the nervous system.

PARALYSIS (see FIRST-AID GUIDE, Chapter 22)

TREMBLING

CAUSES: Trembling or shivering usually indicates fever. Almost any type of ailment can cause trembling, including poisons that affect the central nervous system.

TREATMENT: Consult your veterinarian, who will determine the cause of the fever and prescribe proper treatment.

VESTIBULAR DISEASE

CAUSES: Often mistaken for a stroke, this condition results from an infection of the nerves, inner ear, or parts of the brain that control body motion. Other causes include cerebrovascular disease, encephalitis (see p. 176), or drug toxicity.

SYMPTOMS: Severe twisting of head and neck to one side; loss of balance; dizziness; rapid, jerky eye motions; wobbling, circling, falling, and rolling over.

TREATMENT: Consult your veterinarian. Cats usually recover from idiopathic (i.e., of unknown cause) vestibular disease without medication within three weeks. When the disease is the result of a chronic ailment, treatment and recovery depend upon the veterinarian's ability to treat it.

16

DIGESTIVE SYSTEM PROBLEMS

THE CAT'S DIGESTIVE ORGANS very much resemble those of humans. They include the mouth, esophagus, stomach, duodenum, small intestine, large intestine, and rectum.

The primary role of this complex system is to break food down into nutrients to be absorbed by the body, while also guarding against many varieties of harmful bacteria and disease-producing agents that your cat may accidentally ingest.

One difference between the feline and human digestive systems is in the mouth. Although digestion for both humans and cats begins here, food remains in the human mouth much longer than it does in the feline's. Watch your cat eat. You will see that he tears off a piece of meat, chews it rather quickly, and swallows it.

Moreover, the salivary juices in your cat's mouth function differently from the way yours do. Human salivary juices contain an enzyme called ptyalin, which helps convert starches into blood sugar. Cats' salivary juices contain hardly any ptyalin; instead, starches in a cat's body are only really acted upon when they reach the small intestine.

The gastric juices of cats not only digest unchewed pieces of food, but also destroy any bacteria contained in the food. This is why cats have a high immunity to diseases passed on in food.

In the small intestine, food that has been broken down by gastric acid and enzymes is reabsorbed. It then enters the bloodstream. When food reaches the large intestine, most of the fluid is extracted from the waste matter, which is then formed into feces.

Cats have surprisingly sensitive stom-

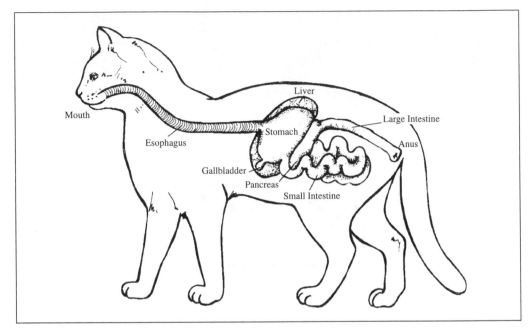

The feline digestive system

achs. If your cat eats a mouse, for example, she will retain the nutritive parts of the rodent and regurgitate its hair, bones, and nails. Your cat will also regurgitate most foods that she cannot digest.

Diarrhea, or the passage of loose, unformed stools, is a common symptom for many digestive ailments; though it is associated with many abdominal and intestinal problems, it is not in itself a disease. If diarrhea persists in your cat for more than twenty-four hours, consult your veterinarian.

Other common problems affecting the feline digestive system are weight loss and bloating. If your cat is eating a balanced diet, nutritional problems should be rare. If they do occur, they are probably caused by an allergic reaction to some foods.

ANAL OR RECTAL PROBLEMS

The digestive tract begins at the mouth and ends at the anus, or rectum, where waste material is defecated. Symptoms of disease in the anal and rectal areas include bright red blood on the outside of the stool (rather than mixed in with it, which could indicate the presence of poison, internal parasites, and other more serious internal disorders), pain on defecation, and severe straining.

If your cat attempts to defecate from a standing position, this may be an indication of rectal pain. If she scoots along the floor on her rear end and is not in heat, this may suggest anal itching, possibly caused by an anal sac disorder, inflammation of the anus, or intestinal parasites.

ANAL PLUG

CAUSES: Cats are sometimes unable to defecate because of accumulated stool and matted hair around the anus. This is a condition most commonly occurring among long-haired cats.

SYMPTOMS: Swellings on the side of the anus or just below it. Scooting or rubbing of the rear end on the ground. Straining to defecate and unable to do so. Foul odor. Skin under matted hair is irritated and inflamed.

TREATMENT: Pointing the scissors away from the anus, gently clip away the hair that is holding the plug against the skin. Wearing a pair of gloves, hold the hair between your fingers and cut it. This method allows you to use your hand as a buffer between the scissors and your cat's anus. Once you remove the accumulated stool and matted hair around the anus, clean the area with mild soap and warm water. Try to keep this area free of long hair to prevent recurrence.

ANAL SAC ABSCESS

CAUSES: Anal sac abscesses are caused by an infection of the anal glands, or sacs, located near the anus. These pea-sized glands are sometimes referred to as "scent" glands because they secrete a malodorous, light gray to brown liquid that marks the cat's stool with an individual smell that helps the cat to establish her territory.

SYMPTOMS: Inflammation, abscesses; the cat may rub, bite, or lick at the area.

TREATMENT: Consult your veterinarian. Surgery may be required.

ANAL SAC INFECTIONS (see ANAL SAC ABSCESS)

ANAL SAC TUMORS

CAUSES: Rectal tumors and polyps—grapelike growths—are usually not malignant and can be removed surgically. They are not common in cats, but should be removed if they occur. If not removed, they may obstruct the passageway and cause severe impactions (material packed too tightly in a narrow space) and chronic constipation. They may also become malignant.

SYMPTOMS: Constipation. Ulcerated, bleeding growths in the rectal area.

TREATMENT: Consult your veterinarian.

BLOOD IN THE STOOL

CAUSES: The passage of bright red blood in the stool is often a symptom of anal or rectal disease. Other possible causes include internal parasites and the ingestion of poison.

TREATMENT: Consult your veterinarian.

CONSTIPATION

CAUSES: Hairballs (see Grooming, p. 67) are the most common cause of constipation in cats, although improper diet, overfeeding, and lack of exercise can also bring it on. Impacted anal glands are another cause of constipation.

SYMPTOMS: Frequent trips to the litter box without being able to defecate. Straining to pass a stool.

TREATMENT: If constipation lasts for more than two days, consult your veterinarian.

DIARRHEA (see INTRODUCTION TO THIS SECTION)

INFLAMMATION (see PROCTITIS, below)

OBSTRUCTION OF RECTUM (see ANAL PLUG, p. 181)

PROCTITIS

CAUSES: The rectal canal can become irritated by the passage of hard, dry stools, straining, elimination of bone chips and other foreign objects, and repeated bouts of diarrhea. The resulting discomfort is called proctitis.

SYMPTOMS: Straining, scooting, licking at the anal area.

TREATMENT: Consult your veterinarian, who may recommend soothing ointments, such as petroleum jelly or topical antibiotic ointments.

RECTAL PROLAPSE

CAUSES: Chronic constipation, diarrhea, urinary obstruction, or infections—in short, any condition that results in a long period of straining to defecate—can cause rectal prolapse in your cat. In rectal prolapse, a short length of the bowel turns inside out and protrudes from the anus.

Once this happens, the prolapse acts as an irritant and causes more straining. Some cat owners may confuse this condition with hemorrhoids, but hemorrhoids rarely, if ever, occur in cats.

SYMPTOMS: A small or large cylindrical red mass near the rectum, usually very inflamed or even bloody.

TREATMENT: Consult your veterinarian. Treatment usually involves lubricating the rectal tissue with petroleum jelly, gently pushing the prolapse back into place, and, in extreme cases, making a temporary pursestring suture around the anus to hold it in place while it heals.

SORE BOTTOM (see CONSTIPATION, p. 181)

FLATULENCE (FLATUS)

CAUSES: Flatus, or the passing of gas, is caused by undigested carbohydrates producing gas when fermented by bacteria in the colon. Flatus is usually caused by highly fermentable foods such as onions, beans, cauliflower, and cabbage.

TREATMENT: A change in your cat's diet may correct the problem. If not, consult your veterinarian.

INCREASED APPETITE
(see DIABETES, p. 188)

INCREASED THIRST
(see DIABETES, p. 188)

INTESTINAL PARASITES

Intestinal parasites, usually worms, can be found in virtually any of your cat's tissues, including the eyes, lungs, and heart. The most common worms that infest the digestive system are roundworms, tapeworms, and hookworms. These parasites are most often transmitted to a cat at birth, through ingesting an infected mother's milk, from eating uncooked meat or raw fish, from contact with infected fleas, lice, and mosquitoes, and from contact with infected soil or feces.

If you discover that your cat is infested with worms, she is not necessarily suffering from some serious disease. Many cats can have worms in their body without developing disease.

However, if there is a change in the appearance of your cat's stools, or if other symptoms develop—such as decreased appetite, loss of weight, diarrhea, or the passage of mucus or blood—there may be cause for concern and you should immediately consult your veterinarian.

It is also important to note that your cat's stools may not show any worm infestation, yet she may still harbor them. This is a good reason to have your veterinarian conduct a yearly stool sample evaluation as part of your cat's annual checkup.

A number of over-the-counter deworming preparations are available at drugstores, though most of them are not very effective. However, should you decide to use one of these preparations, ask your veterinarian first.

You can take some steps to prevent worm infestation. Clean your cat's litter box frequently. Wear gloves when you do so to prevent becoming infected by worms or by other parasites yourself. Discourage your cat from eating raw meat and fish, mice, rats, or birds; immediately dispose of any freshly killed prey your cat brings home. Have stool samples tested annually for an indoor cat, and biannually for an outdoor cat.

COCCIDIA AND GIARDIA

CAUSES: Both of these tiny parasites live in the intestinal tract. They are microscopic and cannot be seen by the naked eye. They are transmitted by ingestion of fecal-contaminated material. Coccidia are usually found in kittens. Mother cats with these parasites usually pass them on to their litters.

SYMPTOMS: Diarrhea, some blood in diarrhea, weight loss, dehydration.

TREATMENT: Consult your veterinarian. Deworming drugs are the usual course of treatment.

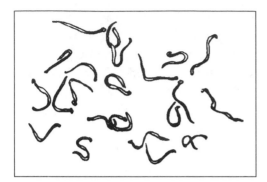

Enlarged depiction of hookworms, which look like tiny fishing hooks and are rarely longer than one-half inch.

HOOKWORMS

CAUSES: Hookworms, or ancylostoma, come in four types and are more common in dogs than in cats. They are bloodsucking parasites about one-fourth to one-half of an inch long and are shaped like hooks. They nourish themselves on blood drawn from the walls of the small intestine. Hookworms are mainly found in the southern United States, where it is warm and wet—conditions they thrive in.

These small, thin worms enter their hosts by burrowing through the skin rather than migrating to the small intestine as other varieties of worms do. Cats contract hookworm by ingesting their larvae in soil or feces. The parasites are frequently transmitted to kittens through the mother's milk if she is infected.

SYMPTOMS: Diarrhea, anemia, weakness, weight loss, spaghettilike particles in vomit or feces, ricelike particles around the anus.

TREATMENT: Consult your veterinarian. A number of drugs are effective against this parasite, including pyrantel pamoate and disophenol, which is given by injection.

ROUNDWORM

CAUSES: Roundworms, also called ascarids, can be transmitted to kittens in their mother's milk. They look like small spaghetti and are the most common worm parasite in kittens. Adult cats contract these worms from contact with the worms' eggs, which are eliminated in the feces of infected cats, or they may eat an insect or a rodent that has feasted on them.

Once ingested by a cat, the larvae hatch in the stomach and make their way through the stomach wall. From there they move on to the liver. The larvae continue to grow as the blood transports them to the lungs, trachea, and eventually back to the intestinal tract. In the intestinal tract they can grow into adulthood—sometimes becoming three to four inches long within three weeks.

These sexually mature ascarids then lay eggs, which are eliminated with the

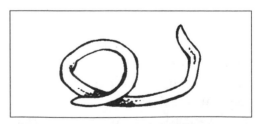

Roundworms lack the sharp hooklike curve of the hookworm and can grow up to four inches long.

ROUNDWORM PREVENTION

If you own several cats and one has contracted roundworms, there are several important steps you should take in order to prevent the spread of this intestinal parasite:

- Clean the litter box frequently. Try to remove fecal matter as soon as possible.
- Deworm all cats at the same time, not just the one known to be infested.
- A second deworming is necessary two to four weeks later.
- Make sure a fecal exam is performed after the second deworming.

---

feces. The host cat may reinfect itself if it comes in contact with these eggs, or it may pass the infection on to another animal.

If a cat is heavily infested, these worms can be seen in vomit or stools. They may be spread to humans through ingestion of soiled material and contact with feces.

SYMPTOMS: Vomiting of worms, loss of weight, diarrhea, constipation, anemia, swollen body, lethargy.

TREATMENT: Consult your veterinarian. A number of new dewormers in both tablet and liquid forms are quite effective against roundworms. During treatment, keep your cat indoors.

TAPEWORMS

CAUSES: Also known as cestodes, tapeworms are dangerous bloodsucking parasites that can grow up to three feet in length. These worms are made up of seg-ments that are thickly covered with eggs and are eliminated in the cat's stool.

At least eight different types of tapeworm can infect cats. The most common variety is absorbed by a cat when she eats mice infected with tapeworm larvae. Another form of tapeworm is transmitted to cats through flea bites.

Tapeworms are the most common internal parasite in the adult cat but are not as dangerous as roundworms. Tapeworms generally live in the small intestine and share the cat's digested food. They often attach themselves to a cat's anal area, where they look like rice grains.

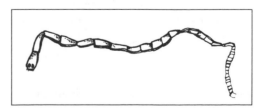

Tapeworms are composed of segments and can grow to three feet in length inside a cat's body.

SYMPTOMS: The presence of tapeworm segments on the hair or skin around the anus or in a fresh stool. Excessive licking of the rectum, scooting, variable appetite, mild diarrhea, coat changes, irritability.

TREATMENT: Consult your veterinarian. Effective medication is available to treat tapeworm infestation, but the major problem is reinfestation. The best way to prevent this is to rid the cat's environment of fleas. You may also have to repeat the deworming procedure.

INTESTINAL TRACT DISORDERS

As we've already discussed in the introduction to this section, all nutrients in your cat's digestive system are absorbed by the small intestine. These nutrients are then sent into the bloodstream and lymphatic system. When they reach the large intestine, water is extracted and the feces become firm.

If intestinal tract disorders develop in a cat, two common symptoms are diarrhea—sometimes mixed with blood and mucus—and constipation.

BLOCKED BOWEL

CAUSES: There are many ways a bowel can become blocked, ranging from the swallowing of foreign objects to tumors. An intestinal blockage can be complete or partial. Either is extremely dangerous and requires immediate veterinary attention. A blocked bowel can lead to death if there is any hesitation in treating it.

SYMPTOMS: **Complete blockage**: vomiting, dehydration, swelling of the abdomen, no gas or stools passed. **Partial blockage**: weight loss, vomiting, diarrhea.

TREATMENT: Since this condition is serious, consult your veterinarian immediately. In many cases surgery may be required. Gently place your cat in a carrier that will immobilize her and prevent worsening her pain.

NOTE: There are many causes of intestinal obstructions but one of the most common is hair balls. Cats who frequently groom themselves tend to accumulate a soggy, dark-colored mass in the stomach. If your cat can't regurgitate or eliminate that mass, his bowel may end up blocked. (See Chapter 4 on grooming tips that will help eliminate the problem.)

ENTERITIS AND COLITIS

CAUSES: Enteritis is an acute inflammation of the lining of the small intestine due to bacterial or viral infections, toxic chemicals, or other foreign material. If untreated, it can lead to dehydration. Although the exact cause is still unknown, bacterial infection is also thought to be responsible for colitis, an inflammatory disease of the large intestine.

SYMPTOMS: Fever, vomiting, diarrhea, loss of appetite. **Colitis**: In addition to symptoms above: straining, pain upon defecation, flatulence, passage of many small stools sometimes mixed with mucus and blood.

TREATMENT: Consult your veterinarian. If necessary, treatment may include fluid and nutritional support. Specific therapy depends upon the cause of the problem; it might consist of dietary control (long- or short-term), parasite control, and/or antidiarrhea medication. Some cases may require the use of antibiotics or steroids.

GASTRITIS (UPSET STOMACH)

CAUSES: A cat who accidentally ingests poison or an irritant such as grass, bones, or toxic plants is likely to have a bout of acute gastritis, an inflammation of the lining of the stomach. Acute gastritis usually comes on suddenly. In chronic gastritis, the condition develops more slowly and may be caused by poor diet or food. Hair balls and persistent grass-eating can also cause chronic gastritis.

SYMPTOMS: **Acute gastritis**: Sudden onset of severe and continuous vomiting. **Chronic gastritis**: Sporadic vomiting, lethargy, dull coat, weight loss, and other signs of nutritional deficiency.

TREATMENT: Consult your veterinarian. Diagnostic tests such as biochemical analysis of the blood, blood count, X rays of the abdomen, and tissue removal are available to determine the cause of gastritis. If your cat's gastritis is being caused by certain foods or brands of commercially prepared cat-food, your veterinarian may prescribe a special diet.

GASTROENTERITIS (see ENTERITIS, p. 186)

VOMITING

CAUSES: Vomiting is a common occurrence in cats and is caused by many types of ailments and diseases, including digestive and intestinal disorders. It is most commonly caused by overeating, eating too quickly, food allergies, and hair balls. Cats also vomit regularly because they can regurgitate at will; it is their way of relieving indigestion.

TREATMENT: If the vomiting is persistent, contains blood, or is forcefully ejected and the cat is weak, shows abdominal pain, or has a fever, immediately consult your veterinarian. The veterinarian may examine the cat's blood or perform X rays to determine the cause of the vomiting. The causes may range from the presence of foreign objects in the digestive tract to kidney failure.

LIVER PROBLEMS

CAUSES: The liver is the largest organ in the cat's body. It is divided into six sections, or lobes, each of which is made up of thousands of tiny structural and functional components, or lobules. No organ plays a more important role in the digestive process than the liver. Its primary functions are to synthesize proteins and sugars, extract wastes from the bloodstream, manufacture enzymes, and detoxify the cat's system of many drugs and poisons.

There are many symptoms of liver disease, but the most specific are jaundice and ascites. Jaundice develops when bile—an alkaline fluid secreted by the liver that aids in digestion—accumulates in the bloodstream; the skin and the whites of the eyes turn yellow, and the urine becomes tea-colored. Ascites is the accumulation of fluid in the abdomen. If your cat's abdomen looks swollen or bloated, it may be the result of a dysfunction of the portal veins that drain into the liver.

The liver is a vulnerable organ. It can suffer harm from poisons, parasites, direct and indirect infections, malnutrition, and tumors.

SYMPTOMS: Increased thirst, vomiting, diarrhea, fever, depression, changes in stool color, constipation, dehydration, weight loss, swollen abdomen, jaundice, collapse, coma.

TREATMENT: Consult your veterinarian. Special laboratory work may be required to determine the exact cause of the liver dysfunction.

MOTION SICKNESS

CAUSES: Motion sickness is due to a disruption in the cat's balance center, which is located in her inner ear. Most cats get over motion sickness once they get used to traveling.

SYMPTOMS: Anxiety, restlessness, excess salivation, frequent yawning, vomiting.

TREATMENT: Cats travel best on empty stomachs, so do not feed your cat before taking a trip. Dramamine (12.5 mg one hour before you plan to travel) often helps cats with persistent motion sickness problems. Ask your veterinarian if this drug is compatible with your cat's system.

PANCREATIC PROBLEMS

The pancreas, which is located next to the liver, has two main functions. It is responsible for producing digestive enzymes; it also produces insulin, which circulates through the body, acting upon cell membranes and allowing blood sugar to enter the cells, where it can be metabolized to form energy.

The most common pancreatic disorders are sugar diabetes and chronic pancreatitis, both of which often afflict elderly cats.

DIABETES

CAUSES: Diabetes mellitus, or sugar diabetes, is the most common form of diabetes in middle-aged and elderly cats. This metabolic disease is caused by the inability of the body to utilize sugar in the blood because the pancreas is not producing enough insulin.

As a result of insulin deficiency, glucose derived from the diet and from

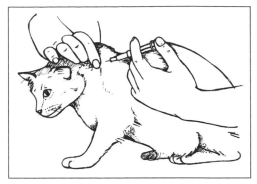

Daily injections of insulin can control diabetes in cats.

metabolism within the body cannot be stored for future use. Much of it is simply excreted in the urine.

A cat with diabetes often tries to compensate for his inability to metabolize sugar by eating more food. The cat appears insatiably hungry but nonetheless continues to lose weight. In the later stages of this disease, loss of appetite and malnutrition set in.

SYMPTOMS: Excessive appetite, excessive thirst, frequent urination, weight loss, lethargy, dehydration, diarrhea, vomiting, occasionally rear legs weaken.

TREATMENT: Consult your veterinarian. Feeding your cat a balanced, high-quality food and giving her daily injections of insulin may be necessary. Home treatment of a diabetic cat demands an attentive owner who will be committed to caring for the cat for the rest of her life.

PANCREATITIS

CAUSES: Pancreatitis is a rare ailment in cats. It causes the release of pancreatic enzymes that break down nearby tissues, resulting in bleeding, shock, and possibly death. Pancreatitis can be diagnosed as acute, traumatic, or chronic.

SYMPTOMS: As the symptoms of pancreatitis often do not appear, it is usually diagnosed after death, when an autopsy is performed. **Acute form**: High fever, abdominal pains, persistent vomiting. **Chronic and traumatic forms**: Intermittent vomiting.

TREATMENT: Consult your veterinarian. Dietary control is an essential part of the treatment. Acute pancreatitis requires hospitalization, since intravenous fluids and antibiotics must be administered. The veterinarian will try to find out if any other organs are involved, such as the liver, and act accordingly. Some cats with chronic pancreatitis develop diabetes and have to be treated for this condition as well (see p. 188).

WEIGHT LOSS
(see DIABETES, ENTERITIS, COLITIS, INTESTINAL PARASITES, LIVER PROBLEMS, BLOCKED BOWEL, GASTRITIS)

17

URINARY SYSTEM PROBLEMS

THE URINARY SYSTEM is designed to remove various toxic wastes from a cat's body. It consists of the kidneys, ureters, bladder, and urethra. These are the routes that nonfecal wastes follow on their way to the outside world.

There are two kidneys, located behind the rib cage on either side of the spine. These act as filters for the blood by removing waste products. They also maintain water and mineral balance in the cat's body.

Waste products are passed from the kidneys as urine down along the ureters to the bladder, which is located in the abdominal cavity. When your cat's bladder fills with urine, it sends a signal to the brain and your pet trots off to the litter box.

In female cats, the urine passes from the bladder through the urethra to the vagina, where it is expelled through the vulva. In the male, the urine passes down the tiny urethra tube and is expelled through the penis. Urine normally has a clear yellow appearance; infections, however, can affect its color.

The urinary tract is subject to various diseases, which fall into two categories: those that affect the kidneys and ureters and those that afflict the bladder and the urethra, known as the lower urinary tract. The common term for diseases of the lower urinary tract is feline urological syndrome (FUS). The exact cause of FUS is unknown, but whatever the culprit, it often results in obstructions that can prevent the passing of urine from the bladder.

Your cat may be suffering from bladder or urethra problems if it is in pain while urinating, or if it passes a weak or splattering stream of urine. Other related symptoms include bloody urine,

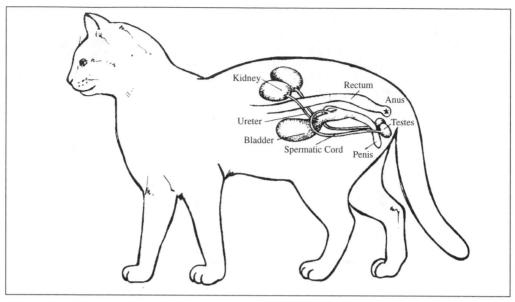

The male urogenital tract

pain and swelling of the abdomen, and loss of bladder control.

Should you suspect a urinary tract problem in your cat, it is important to get immediate veterinary attention.

Any inflammation can damage the cat's defense mechanisms and establish the basis for bacterial invasion, repeated infections, and more serious urinary tract problems.

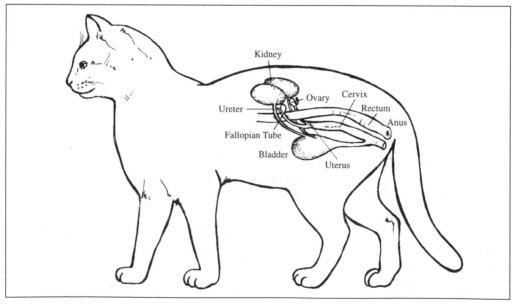

The female urogenital tract

BLADDER INFECTION (CYSTITIS)

CAUSES: One of the most common health problems in the cat is cystitis, an acute or chronic infection of the urinary bladder. It affects both male and female cats. The condition is usually the result of bacteria traveling upward from the urethra to the bladder.

Cystitis is frequently complicated by stones composed of minerals that block the urethra. If the blockage is not quickly unplugged, a fatal condition known as uremia can develop. Levels of toxic materials build, and the cat's inability to eliminate these poisons from his system can result in death.

If you suspect that your cat is suffering from cystitis, a quick visit to the veterinarian is in order. Cats have died as soon as forty-eight hours after the onset of symptoms.

SYMPTOMS: Frequent but scanty urination; straining to urinate; traces of blood in the urine; frequent licking of penis or vulva to ease the pain; urination in unusual places; uncharacteristic crouching without the release of urine; pressure on sides causes pain. **If uremia is developing**: loss of appetite, vomiting, weakness, increased thirst.

TREATMENT: Consult your veterinarian. Antibiotics will probably be prescribed. Stones may be destroyed with drugs or removed surgically. Antispasmodics may be administered to enable the bladder to relax, thereby preventing obstruction from occurring again.

PREVENTION: Always make sure your cat gets enough water to prevent the buildup of stones (see Liquids, p. 63). Also, stay away from dry foods, which are very low in moisture. Make sure your cat gets plenty of exercise.

BLADDER STONES
(see URINARY CALCULI, p. 194)

KIDNEY FAILURE

CAUSES: Acute kidney disease and kidney failure usually are caused by the obstruction of the urethra in the male cat. The ingestion of certain poisons, or damage to a urinary organ, can also result in this condition. Infections also are responsible for some cases of kidney failure, as is heredity.

When the kidneys are unable to eliminate waste products from the blood, toxins build and cause uremic poisoning. This condition may develop slowly as the result of aging, or because of chronic or repeated kidney illness. It can also come on suddenly as the result of serious

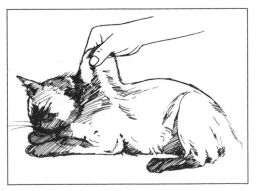

Weakness and dehydration are characteristic of acute kidney failure.

kidney damage. Symptoms often appear when a cat finds himself in a stressful situation, such as being challenged to fight or being placed in a kennel.

SYMPTOMS: Decreased appetite, lethargy, vomiting, diarrhea, weakness, foul breath, increased thirst and urine output, joint pain, tendency to bleed easily, dehydration.

TREATMENT: There is no cure for kidney failure. Your veterinarian will try to control the progress of the disease. If only one kidney is affected, treatment will aim at keeping the other kidney functioning. The veterinarian will strive to keep your cat properly hydrated, with a solid acid-base balance and a steady electrolyte supply.

KIDNEY INFECTION

CAUSES: A bacterial infection of the bladder (cystitis) can migrate up to the kidneys and affect one or both. Any infection in the lower system can also result in a kidney infection. Some kidney infections occur when bacteria reach the kidneys through the bloodstream. There are both acute and chronic forms of kidney infection.

SYMPTOMS: **Acute form**: Fever, pain in kidney area, stiff-legged gait, hunched-up posture, pus in urine, bloody urine. **Chronic form**: Excessive thirst, increased urinary output, loss of weight, vomiting, bad breath, sore, ulcerated mouth, anemia, dehydration.

TREATMENT: Consult your veterinarian. Antibiotics will probably be prescribed.

URINARY CALCULI

CAUSES: This is a chronic condition that can result in partial urinary obstruction. It is caused by sandlike matter that accumulates in the bladder and obstructs passage of urine out of the body. Urolithiasis, as the condition is also called, is most common in males but also affects female cats.

SYMPTOMS: Straining to urinate. Small amounts of urine, pain, urination in inappropriate places, blood or sandlike matter in the urine.

TREATMENT: Consult your veterinarian. Treatment may involve manual application of pressure on the bladder, catheterization, or a suction procedure to relieve the obstruction. Prompt attention should be given to this condition to prevent total urinary obstruction, which can lead to death.

18

CANCER

WHETHER APPLIED TO human beings or animals, cancer is a frightening word. This often fatal disease can strike a human being or an animal at virtually any age.

Cancer in all its forms is found in the cat; in fact, it is one of the most common feline diseases, and its frequency increases with age. Up to 6 percent of all cats suffer from cancer of the skin, mammary glands, and bones, and as many as 10 percent suffer from leukemia and other cancerous conditions in blood-forming tissues.

Why do normal cells transform into malignant ones and cause cancer? Although much has been learned about it, the exact reason for this phenomenon is still unknown. Some researchers suggest that long-standing contact with harmful environmental agents, such as ultraviolet rays or cigarettes, can induce cancer. Others point to viruslike agents called "oncogenes," or to some mysterious failure of the immune system, or simply to hereditary factors.

Whatever the case, as in humans, cancer in cats often can be brought under control—or even cured—if it is detected in time. Cats who are stricken with cancer usually do not cry or moan in pain. If you pay close attention to your cat, however, you will become aware of other symptoms.

Any sort of unusual lump or bump under the skin may be one symptom of cancer. These growths, or tumors, can be benign (harmless), or malignant, which means the cells in this growth can spread throughout the body and become potentially life-threatening.

Malignant tumors invade or infiltrate adjacent tissue, and after a period

---

RECOGNIZABLE SYMPTOMS OF CANCER

- any unusual lumps or bumps that were not previously detected
- loss of appetite
- gradual weight loss
- weakness
- ugly skin growths
- lethargy
- depression
- unkempt coat
- wounds that do not heal

---

of growth they can break off and be carried to other parts of the body by the bloodstream or lymphatic circulation. They then lodge and proliferate in these other parts of the body—particularly the lungs.

Cats tend to develop tumors of the skin, lymphatic system, respiratory tract, gastrointestinal tract, muscle, bone, cartilage, liver, kidney, mammary glands, reproductive tract, thyroid glands, adrenal glands, pituitary glands, and central nervous system—exactly as people do.

The most commonly occurring tumors in cats are lymphosarcomas (malignant tumors), which mostly affect the thymus, kidneys, and the intestines. Mouth and skin tumors are also extremely common in cats. When such tumors spread they frequently affect the lungs, resulting in coughing and difficulty in breathing.

If your cat develops cancer, all is not hopeless. Modern veterinary science has made great strides in dealing with this disease. Surgery, radiation, chemotherapy, and immunotherapy are some of the ways veterinary medicine treats malignancy.

The prognosis for recovery from a cancerous disease varies with the type and location of the cancer, the overall health of your pet, and the animal's response to surgery.

CANCER TREATMENT

If you suspect that your cat has cancer, it is important to consult your veterinarian immediately. Recovery is often dependent upon when the cancer is first sighted. Treatment options include surgery, in which the entire tumor is removed; chemotherapy, which utilizes drugs or chemical agents; radiation therapy; cryosurgery, a technique in which certain tumors, especially those of the skin and mouth, are subjected to freezing-and-thawing techniques; and immunotherapy, which involves the strengthening of a cat's immune system so that it can fight cancerous cells.

LEUKEMIA

CAUSES: A cancer of the blood-forming tissues, leukemia is a common disease in cats. Feline leukemia virus (FeLV) (see p. 117) has been identified as one major cause of leukemia in cats. FeLV targets white blood cells, causing them to multiply rapidly and attack normal cells and tissues.

SYMPTOMS: Anemia, weight loss, poor appetite, weakness, chronic diarrhea, chronic vomiting, coughing, difficulty breathing.

TREATMENT: There is currently no cure for leukemia. Treatment consists of trying to prolong a cat's life.

19

FOR MALES ONLY

THE MALE GENITAL TRACT consists of the penis, the testes—which produce sperm necessary for reproduction—and the scrotum, the fur-covered sacs located under the anus that contain the testes.

The penis is located within a fold of protective skin called the prepuce, or sheath. It is located just below the scrotum. The penis may protrude from the prepuce during licking and grooming and during stimulating play. It also protrudes during sexual intercourse.

Several disorders of the male genital tract can interfere with mating and even cause infertility. Two common problems are balanoposthitis, or the infection of the sheath and head of the penis, and paraphimosis, a condition in which a male cat cannot retract his penis.

DISCHARGE FROM THE PENIS

CAUSES: If your cat's penis drips blood, it could indicate an infection or stones in the bladder or kidney.

SYMPTOMS: Cat licks himself excessively; a bloody or foul-smelling discharge from the prepuce.

TREATMENT: Consult your veterinarian.

INFECTION OF THE PENIS SHEATH AND HEAD

CAUSES: During mating, the foreskin and head of the penis can become irritated by female hairs caught in the spines or barbed tip of the penis. Other sources of irritation include excess sexual activity and foreign bodies caught beneath the sheath. Such irritation may lead to infection of the sheath or penis head.

SYMPTOMS: Excessive licking of the penis area, foul-smelling discharge from the prepuce.

TREATMENT: Consult your veterinarian. Treatment generally includes application of ointments and other solutions.

INFERTILITY

CAUSES: Infertility can affect both male and female cats. In males, infertility can be caused by excessive sexual activity that results in a low sperm count.

TREATMENT: If you are interested in breeding your cat and are not meeting with success, consult your veterinarian. Diagnosis for male infertility usually involves a semen analysis to determine the sperm count.

NEUTERING

Neutering a male cat entails the surgical removal of his testicles. This sim-ple procedure is usually performed after puberty (which occurs at about age six months). Neutering greatly reduces the roaming, howling, and fighting associated with mating (see Sexual Behavior, p. 33) and makes male cats less aggressive and more affectionate.

This surgery also lessens your cat's urge to spray strong-smelling urine to mark his territory. A neutered cat may gain weight, so exercise and attention to his diet are important.

PENIS UNABLE TO RETRACT

CAUSES: This disorder is known as paraphimosis. It occurs when a ring of long hair around the sheath of the penis prevents it from retracting back into the sheath. This condition can be prevented by trimming long hair around the prepuce before the cat mates.

TREATMENT: You may be able to force the penis to retract. Gently push the skin (prepuce) back along the penis shaft, taking care to remove any stray hairs. Carefully pull the penis's head, now exposed, forward (olive oil dabbed on the penis will help you accomplish this). Then replace the prepuce around the head. If this doesn't work, call your veterinarian.

20

FOR FEMALES ONLY

IN THIS SECTION we will examine specific issues, needs, and problems affecting the female cat, from pregnancy to birth to postlabor complications.

BIRTH CONTROL

If you are one of the millions of cat owners in this country and you own a female cat, the time may come when you must decide whether or not to allow her to have kittens. Unless you own a pedigreed cat, this is a decision that requires lots of consideration.

Unplanned or unrestricted breeding, in which a cat owner simply allows "nature to take its course," may not only help spread feline diseases, but may also aggravate the already serious problem of homeless cats. Each year, thousands of unwanted strays are put

to death by humane societies, and the numbers continue to grow.

While keeping your female cat indoors may prevent indiscriminate mating, it can also pose problems for you. Females in heat can be noisy and disruptive. During a cat's mating season she may be in heat as much as once a month, each bout lasting ten to fourteen days if she is not mated. So what is a cat owner to do?

The answer may be to have your cat spayed. Many cat owners find this a responsible way to prevent unwanted kittens and improve their cat's disposition as well. Spaying is generally recommended for any female cat you do not wish to breed. In no way will it diminish your cat's enjoyment of life.

Spaying is the surgical removal of the female cat's ovaries and uterus. It is usually done after she is six months old, or between heats or litters of kittens.

Spaying stops the howling, rolling, roaming, and pacing associated with mating behavior (see Sexual Behavior, p. 33). It can also prevent pyometra—a severe uterine infection that occurs frequently in older, unspayed females—and greatly reduce your cat's risk of breast cancer.

Many people believe that spaying will cause a female cat to gain weight. While there may be a tendency to put on more weight, obesity will not be the result. Obesity is the result of overeating, lack of exercise, and, sometimes, metabolic problems. A spayed cat who eats a well-balanced diet, isn't overfed, and gets regular exercise should not be prone to obesity.

PREREQUISITES FOR BREEDING

If you own a pedigreed cat, you may want to breed her. Purebred kittens rarely go unwanted; your only concern is whether you have the necessary time, money, and knowledge to properly breed your cat and care for her litter. Additionally, owners usually charge for the services of their purebred studs.

Whatever you decide, take some time to read this chapter before you mate your cat. Even if you are thinking about breeding your ordinary housecat, you will find the information contained here useful. Whatever type of cat you own, it is important, for example, to understand the principles and practices of feline sex and reproduction—this will

help make your endeavor much more successful.

Female cats reach sexual maturity between seven and twelve months; males become sexually mature between ten and fourteen months (see Sexual Behavior, p. 33). During this period females begin coming into heat. You will become quite aware of this once your cat begins to emit vocal "calls" while rubbing herself against objects, rolling on the ground, and otherwise acting peculiarly. Males show their readiness to mate by becoming highly territorial, spraying objects with their urine, becoming much more aggressive with other males, and displaying a tendency to roam.

If you decide you want to breed your female, it is wise to wait until her second heat cycle—when she is one year old—before attempting a mating. At this age she is physically and emotionally mature and able to adjust well to motherhood. If her first heat cycle occurs at twelve months of age or later, she is ready to be bred. Females can be bred only when in heat; males can mate at any time.

Before mating your cat, be sure that she is properly vaccinated. A thorough examination is in order to make certain that she is in optimum health. When you visit your veterinarian, take a stool sample from your cat so that it can be analyzed for internal parasites. Many harmful parasites can be passed on to kittens by their mothers; this can kill kittens, who are too weak to tolerate medication.

Make certain that your female cat has a special, quiet place where she can give birth and nurse her kittens. Her own bed will work well; a maternity box (see p. 206) is also effective. You can expect up to eight new feline additions to your household, so be sure to provide ample space for your cat's new family.

Make sure that other pets and children are kept away once the litter arrives. If disturbed, the mother is apt to leap up to protect her kittens and might possibly hurt one of them. Also remove any valuable objects that the kittens may damage as they grow and explore.

An important prerequisite in breeding cats is to select your cat's partner well in advance. You should try to meet with your cat's mate-to-be and his owners, and learn all you can about his characteristics and qualities. Get a clean bill of health from the cat's owners, making sure he has no inheritable diseases or parasites.

ESTRUS

Heat, or estrus, is nature's signal that the female cat is ready to mate. Queens, as female cats in heat are also called, experience several heats over the course of a year; the number and frequency depend upon the time of the year as well as the nature of each cat.

Heat cycles are seasonal. They usually start in January and peak in March or April, in June, and in September.

The beginning of estrus is characterized by frantic rubbing and vocalization.

Female cats ordinarily have no estrus cycles between October and December—but of course there are always exceptions.

If you do not allow your female to breed, the number of heats she experiences will increase. These heats may recur at intervals of about two or three weeks and continue until she copulates. A heat period lasts about four to seven days if the queen has been bred; if she hasn't, the heats last at least ten days.

Estrus occurs when conditions are right, including the length of daylight, temperature, and the availability of partners. The queen's hormonal system becomes activated and she starts her reproductive cycle. Before estrus even begins, the ovaries secrete hormones that prepare the cat to become pregnant. The inner walls of the uterus grow rich with blood, and eggs, or ova, begin to be produced in the ovaries.

Then the queen enters the estrus period, during which she will permit mating. She will begin her frantic rubbing activity and issue either quiet and repetitive cries or even yowls (this is especially true of Siamese cats in heat). During this cycle your female will also begin spraying. The spray consists of hormonal products that earn the rapid attention of any nearby stud or tom—two terms for unaltered males.

Copulation (see Sexual Behavior, p. 33) begins with the insertion of the tom's penis, which has barblike spines that stimulate the vagina, into the vulva. Female cats are unique in that they require copulation to stimulate ovulation, and often they require more than one mate to do so. Once stimulated, the ovarian follicles release progesterone, a female hormone that prepares the uterus for fertilized eggs and regulates the pregnancy. A queen that has copulated with different males in the same estrus may carry kittens by different fathers.

Once ovulation begins, the queen loses interest in any further mating. Now the eggs leave the ovaries and move into the fallopian tubes, where spermatozoa swim up to meet them and the eggs become fertilized. The fertilized eggs next pass through the uterus into its two long horns, where they grow while attached to the nutrient-rich lining.

ARRANGING THE BREEDING

Much mating among cats takes place outdoors, hidden from human eyes. For owners who wish to breed their cats, the process requires a great deal of study and preparation. Choosing the right cat is important—and complicated—if your cat is a purebred. Most towns and cities have cat clubs that will be more than willing to provide you with information on all aspects of breeding. (If you plan to breed your nonpedigreed cat and are looking for a suitable mate, talk to your veterinarian or local humane society.)

You will first want to make certain that your cat's potential mate is in excellent health. Do not hesitate to ask for a veterinary certificate, record of vaccinations, or other proof that the mate is free of infectious diseases such as Feline Leukemia Virus.

If you own a purebred and plan to register the kittens, you will want to know all about your cat's mate. His owner, in turn, will want to know all about your cat's pedigree credentials.

If you are mating a female for the first time, try to choose a stud with experience. The goal of breeding pedigreed cats—or any cat, for that matter—is to produce physically and psychologically healthy animals. Through such selective breeding you will also be trying to produce offspring that improve the strain of their parents.

Owners of purebred studs who are asked to provide their cats' services often charge a fee for the mating. The rate depends upon the cat's past performance as both a sire and show winner. Fees often start as low as $100 but can go much higher.

When you and your cat are ready for the mating to begin, you must make arrangements to have your pet transported to meet her partner. The arrangements must be made as soon as your cat goes into heat. (The queen goes to the stud because male cats feel much more comfortable and relaxed on their own territory.)

One common procedure is to keep both cats in separate but close quarters so that they can become acquainted with each other. Once the female begins to make advances to the male, she will be allowed to enter his quarters. When mating is completed—and this may take place three or four times over several hours—the female is returned to her own quarters and is ready to be taken home.

Remember that your female may still be in heat, so do not allow her out of the house. If she continues to yowl, cry, or otherwise exhibit the behaviors of being in heat, the mating was probably not successful and you will have to try again. If she did conceive, you can expect a litter of kittens within nine weeks.

PREGNANCY AND BIRTH

The interval between mating and the birth of the kittens is approximately sixty-three days. During the first three to four weeks of this gestation period, little in the cat's behavior suggests that she is pregnant, and nothing much needs to be done for her. Keep her surroundings comfortable and give her lots of affection. There is no need to change her normal diet during this period. If you notice fleas or parasites, ask your veterinarian what measures you should take to get rid of them. Not all pesticides may be appropriate to use on a pregnant cat.

By the thirty-fifth day, your queen's nipples will begin to enlarge and turn pinkish. By about the fortieth day, her abdomen will be noticeably swollen; X-rays will show the presence of kittens. As the time of birth approaches you may notice a milky white fluid being excreted from the enlarged breasts. The cat will also begin to gain weight, since just prior to delivery she will be eating about twice the amount of food she normally does.

EXERCISE DURING PREGNANCY

Moderate exercise is very good for a pregnant female and will help make delivery easier. The fetuses are well cushioned and will not be harmed by normal activity. Avoid violent, aggressive play, however; your pregnant cat should not be allowed to jump from high places, and children should not lift her. Any fall could result in a miscarriage.

MEDICATIONS DURING PREGNANCY

Avoid medications, vaccinations, and worming during your cat's pregnancy, unless your veterinarian advises you otherwise.

A NOTE ON GROOMING

Because of her increased size, your cat may not be able to groom herself properly. She will enjoy it if you brush and comb her every day to remove loose or dead hair and keep her skin in good condition (see Grooming, p. 67).

PREPARING FOR DELIVERY

During the last weeks of pregnancy your cat may become quiet and sedentary, perhaps lounging in a favorite spot for long periods of time. Do not be concerned. This "favorite" place is probably where your cat will give birth.

When the actual moment of birth arrives, however, your female may decide to change locations—moving to an open drawer, laundry bin, or some other place of privacy such as a maternity box. Many veterinarians recommend that you provide your pregnant cat with such a box: a large container (an ordinary cardboard box will do nicely) with a lid, lined with rags, cotton sheeting, or newspapers.

This maternity box, which is best introduced to your cat a week or two before the kittens are due, should be twice as large as the cat's usual bed so that there is room for her and her litter. The sides of the box should be high enough to keep the kittens from climbing or falling out.

The box should be placed in a private and quiet corner of your household. If your cat prefers another location, move the box there. Your cat may be happy with the area, but eschew the actual box. If this is the case, put newspapers or towels on the floor, keeping the box nearby (in case she decides she likes the box after all). Keep the area warm.

The location you establish as a birthplace should not only be kept warm, but clean and dry as well. Cold, damp quarters are one of the leading causes of early kitten mortality. The floor temperature should be between eighty-five and ninety degrees Fahrenheit for the first week of the kittens' lives. If your heating system cannot supply such heat, you might try placing a heating pad wrapped in a blanket beneath the maternity box. Infrared lamps no lower than three feet above the box are another option. After the first week, the temperature can be reduced to seventy degrees.

At the end of the eighth week of pregnancy, let your veterinarian know that delivery is imminent. Most births are routine, but you will feel better knowing that veterinary assistance is available should you need it.

DELIVERY

Delivery commonly takes place at night and often begins with your cat going through a sudden bout of anxiety and restlessness. She may salivate and lick herself a lot, or squat in her litter box trying to relieve herself of the unaccustomed pressure. She may also chew or claw some favorite item.

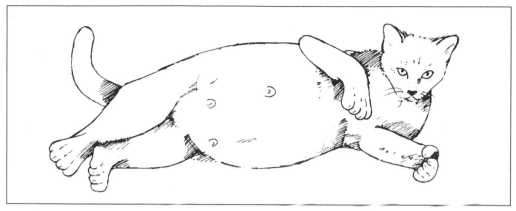

The first stage of labor: The cat's body begins to stretch as involuntary contractions of the uterine muscles begin to push the kittens out.

Other signs of labor include digging in the maternity box or trying to hide in a closet or dark corner. This phase normally lasts twenty-four hours.

The length of labor and delivery varies from two to six hours overall. During the first stage of labor, your cat's body will begin to stretch and strain as involuntary contractions of the uterine muscles begin to push the kittens out.

This is not a good time to disturb your cat. She will probably go to her maternity bed and may start rhythmic breathing and purring, which increase as the moment of birth approaches. As this stage concludes, she may also release clear or slightly cloudy water and/or a little blood.

The second stage of labor usually lasts from ten minutes to half an hour and involves more involuntary uterine contractions, with voluntary abdominal muscle contractions, or straining. This "bearing down" takes place once every fifteen to thirty minutes. Eventually there will be a protrusion of fetal membrane and other materials at the vulval opening. Part of a kitten may be seen within it.

More contractions generally follow; a kitten will emerge momentarily. The kitten may come out head first or tail first—both eventualities are perfectly normal. The kitten may be born bullet-shaped and enclosed in a sac of membranes filled with fluid. The mother's instinctive response is to chew the

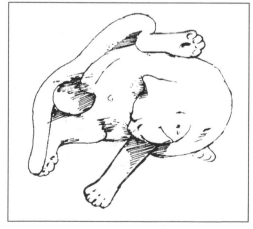

The second stage of labor: The increase in involuntary uterine contractions results in the protrusion of fetal membrane.

The third stage of labor: The kitten may be born bullet-shaped and enclosed in a sac of membranes filled with fluid.

branes, which then come right behind them, along with the umbilical cord. After she licks the kitten the mother eats these membranes. Do not allow your cat to eat more than one or two afterbirths; too many may cause diarrhea. Also, try to make certain that all the afterbirth for each kitten has been expelled, since retained membraneous matter can cause infection.

The licking is quite important. The mother will lick her kitten rather roughly to dry it and remove obstructive material from its nose and eyes. This apparent roughness is necessary because the mother cat is trying to stimulate breathing and blood circulation.

By the time the mother cat finishes this routine, the kitten's fur is beginning to dry and its breathing is normal. Minutes later, this regimen is repeated all over again as the next kitten appears.

Births can be separated by periods of thirty minutes to two hours. This

membranes open and lick the kitten to stimulate its breathing. Once the kitten begins to move, the mother will probably chew the umbilical cord and eat the membranes, or afterbirth.

Some kittens are born free of mem-

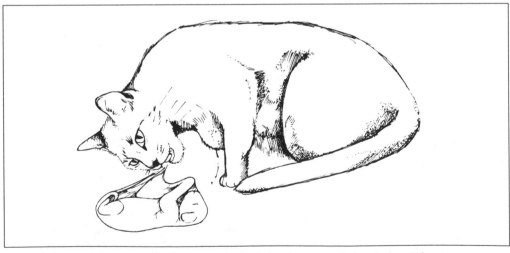

After delivery, the mother will eliminate the fetal membranes and detach the cord.

DANGER SIGNS DURING DELIVERY

1. Contractions continue for several hours without a kitten being born. This may indicate two kittens blocking the birth canal or a kitten too large to pass through the canal. Sometimes a cesarean section is necessary.
2. Contractions stop after one or two kittens are delivered, yet there appear to be more kittens in the mother's body. This may signal uterine inertia (see Uterine Inertia, p. 215).
3. Painful screams as the cat tries to deliver a kitten.
4. There is no "bearing down" for six hours after blood or any colored discharge appears from the vulva.
5. A dark-green fluid is passed before delivery of the first kitten. (The appearance of green or bloody fluid *after* birth is normal.) The placenta may have become detached from the uterine wall, cutting off the kitten's oxygen supply before birth.
6. A kitten emerges only partially from the birth canal and the mother is unable to complete delivery.

time lapse is one of the mysteries of cat birth. Once the interval is established, the mother usually repeats it with each kitten. It is very important to allow labor to progress without disturbance. The only time you should step in is if a problem arises (see below).

It is often difficult to determine when all the kittens have been born. The average litter numbers four kittens. If your cat has stopped straining and seems calm and relaxed, the birth process has probably been completed. If all the births do not appear to have taken place (see next section), veterinary assistance will be required.

When all the births are complete, the new litter should be ready to suckle. The peaceful nursing period, guaranteed to provide pleasure for you and your family, is beginning.

Although delivery is usually routine and presents little danger to the mother, complications sometimes do occur. You should be aware of some of the danger signs. If any of the problems listed above develop, call your veterinarian. If your vet does not make house calls, a trip to the animal hospital may be necessary.

LABOR PROBLEMS

A kitten can become stuck in the birth canal. Other problems can also develop, such as a sac bursting prematurely before delivery.

If the kitten emerges only partially from the birth canal, you should first restrain your cat (see Restraining Your Cat, p. 85). Next, grasp the kitten with a clean, dry towel and pull it gently in a downward direction toward the mother's feet.

Respond to the cat's contractions with a gentle pull—don't jerk or pull hard on the kitten. As the mother strains during contractions, pull a little harder. As she relaxes, simply keep your hold on the kitten so that it is not retracted back into her body.

Once the kitten is out, use a soft towel to clean off the face, especially around the mouth and nostrils. If necessary, use presterilized surgical scissors to cut the umbilical cord about one inch from the kitten's body. Squeeze the cut end for a minute or so to prevent bleeding. Tie it off with a piece of thread.

POSTNATAL CARE

Once your cat has delivered her kittens, she will be both exhausted and relieved. Gently guide her to the litter box, and then change the bedding in her quarters. Place a bowl of water near her quarters.

If your female has had her litter elsewhere than in the maternity box, carefully cup each kitten in your hand and transfer it to the box. Let your cat settle down in it to take care of her kittens. For the first couple of days after delivery, new mothers are often reluctant to budge from their families. You may not only have to encourage your female to go to the litter box, but to get a little exercise as well. Try to accomplish this with a calm, soothing voice and gentle gestures. You need to reassure her that it is okay to leave her kittens for a while and that they won't be disturbed.

Feed your cat as much soft and bland food as she desires for the first day or two, plus plenty of fresh water. After this period, she can return to her regular diet. Include the same high-protein food that she ate during her pregnancy.

Your cat will be going through a

A mother cat may refuse to leave her litter for the first few days after delivery.

SIGNS OF POSTPARTUM PROBLEMS

1. Your cat refuses food and water.
2. She runs a fever.
3. She persistently expels a foul-smelling or greenish vulvar discharge.
4. She suffers from profuse vaginal bleeding.
5. The kittens cry continuously, indicating that the mother may not be able to supply enough milk.
6. The mother's breasts are distended and discolored.

---

period of lactation: the production of milk. During this period her caloric requirements will increase sharply—up to 300 percent of normal. If your cat is not getting enough to eat, she will fail to produce enough milk to satisfy her kittens.

Do not worry about overfeeding your cat during this period; she has several hungry mouths to feed, and suckling puts a tremendous drain on her body, so keep her well fed. You should be able to tell if she isn't getting enough food by her appearance—an inadequate diet will result in a cat who appears thin and tired.

Try not to let too many people disturb the kittens. The fewer people who see or handle them before weaning, the more secure the new mother will feel. Don't let your children play with the kittens until they are weaned.

You may observe your cat vomiting her food for her kittens to eat. This is perfectly normal. Queens partially digest their food and then regurgitate it as a step between breast-feeding and teaching their kittens to eat solid food.

Various postpartum problems can affect the mother during this period. If you notice any of the following danger signs, consult your veterinarian.

Problems after delivery are rare. However, if you have any reason to suspect something may have gone awry, it is crucial to contact your veterinarian within the first twenty-four hours after delivery.

POSTPARTUM PROBLEMS

HEMORRHAGE

CAUSES: Sometimes bleeding occurs after a difficult delivery, but this problem does not occur often. Hemorrhaging may be caused by a tear in the vaginal wall. As in all cases of excessive bleeding, this problem must be treated quickly in order to avoid shock (and, possibly, death).

TREATMENT: Consult your veterinarian. It will be very difficult to control this kind of bleeding on your own, so it is essential that your cat get immediate treatment. The damage incurred during pregnancy may require surgery. On the way to the veterinarian, you might try elevating your cat's hind legs, if this doesn't cause her too much distress.

INADEQUATE MILK SUPPLY

CAUSES: A first-time mother may be too upset by the strain of giving birth to allow her kittens to suckle. When kittens do not suckle for twenty-four hours, her milk supply begins to dry up.

SYMPTOMS: Kittens are hungry, noisy, and unkempt-looking.

TREATMENT: Consult your veterinarian. Pituitary injections and other hormones can help stimulate the flow of milk.

MASTITIS

CAUSES: Too much milk in a mammary gland can result in the inflammation of the breasts. This happens when the mother's milk is not being suckled in sufficient quantity by her kittens. A deformity of the nipples or disease can also cause mastitis. Another possible cause is infection, which is very serious and could result in the production of toxic milk.

SYMPTOMS: Breasts are feverish and swollen; scant milk production; milk is brownish in color or blood-tinged; skin of breasts becomes shiny and purplish.

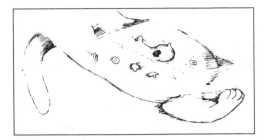

Mastitis may be a simple breast inflammation, or it may be caused by an infection that can lead to the production of toxic milk.

TREATMENT: Remove all kittens from the affected nipple and consult your veterinarian, who will show you how to coax the milk out of the nipple if it is not infected. A warm pack wrapped in a soft towel will ease your cat's pain. If the nipple is actually infected, your veterinarian will administer antibiotics.

METRITIS

CAUSES: Metritis is a bacterial infection of the lining of the uterus that has spread upward through the birth canal. It can be caused by unsanitary conditions in the birth area or after an extremely difficult labor.

SYMPTOMS: Lethargy, refusal to eat, fever, refusal to clean the kittening area or take care of her litter.

TREATMENT: Consult your veterinarian. Acute metritis is a life-threatening illness. Kittens may have to be separated from their mother and raised by hand.

MILK FEVER (ECLAMPSIA)

CAUSES: Milk fever is caused by a lowering of blood calcium levels after delivery. It is called milk fever because it usually occurs during the first three weeks of lactation, when there is a sudden and dramatic drain on a mother cat's calcium stores.

SYMPTOMS: Restlessness, short and rapid breathing, pale mucous membranes, body spasms, fever, paralysis, and collapse.

TREATMENT: Immediate veterinary assistance is required to save the cat from this life-threatening condition. An intravenous calcium solution will be administered, and kittens will be prevented from nursing. After the danger has passed, the mother will be given vitamin and mineral supplements.

MOTHER CATS WHO IGNORE THEIR LITTER

CAUSES: There are many reasons why a mother cat may ignore her kittens. Sometimes the maternal instinct simply fails and she becomes indifferent to her new family. Poor diet, lack of exercise, illness, or injury can also contribute to such neglect. A mother may not have enough milk to feed her brood, or her nipples may not be fully formed. After a difficult delivery, a mother may be too exhausted to display any interest in her kittens.

TREATMENT: If such a situation develops, consult your veterinarian. If the mother is displaying outright aggressiveness toward her kittens, remove the kittens until she calms down.

PYOMETRA (see METRITIS, p. 212)

SORE NIPPLES

CAUSES: Sore nipples are most often caused by too many kittens, or kittens who bite too hard while suckling. Breast infection (see Mastitis, p. 212) can also cause this condition.

SYMPTOMS: Rejection of kittens.

TREATMENT: Consult your veterinarian, who must determine the cause of the sore nipples. If it is simply the result of the kittens' teeth, the veterinarian may recommend that you switch to bottle feeding and begin to wean the litter (see Weaning, p. 220).

REPRODUCTIVE PROBLEMS

FALSE PREGNANCY

False pregnancy is less common in cats than it is in dogs. During a false pregnancy, the female exhibits all the physical and behavioral signs of a true pregnancy. Many queens actually go through labor pains at the time they are supposed to be delivering.

CAUSES: This disorder seems to be the result of a malfunction of the ovaries in which progesterone—the pregnancy hormone—is released, producing symptoms of pregnancy in the absence of fertilized eggs. Such so-called false pregnancies usually disappear after five weeks.

SYMPTOMS: The signs of pregnancy (see Pregnancy and Birth, p. 205).

TREATMENT: Consult your veterinarian. Most cases generally require no treatment. If several false pregnancies occur, the female should be spayed, unless you are sure you want to try to breed her.

INFERTILITY

CAUSES: If a female fails to conceive after several matings, the infertility problem may rest in either of the two partners. In the female cat, an infection in the reproductive tract is the most frequent cause of infertility.

TREATMENT: Consult your veterinarian. Diagnosis for male infertility usually involves a semen analysis to determine sperm count. Treatment in the female depends on diagnosis of whatever condition may underly her inability to conceive.

MISCARRIAGE

CAUSES: If your female cat is pregnant, and she begins straining but does not give birth, she may be about to miscarry. This is fairly common in cats and may be caused by poor health, uterine infection, many types of disease, or improper development of the fetuses inside the womb. Accidents, injuries, or rough handling can also bring about a miscarriage.

SYMPTOMS: Blood or other discharge from the vulva; after the fourth or fifth week of gestation, her enlarged abdomen looks small again.

TREATMENT: If you think your cat may be in the process of miscarrying, get immediate veterinary assistance. You'll want to help her avoid infection and excessive bleeding, which requires expert consultation.

OVARIAN CYSTS

CAUSES: Cysts are growths that vary from pimple-sized to plum-sized. Ovarian cysts are those that grow on the ovaries of pregnant female cats. They are believed to be caused by excess output of estrogen, the female hormone, from the ovaries.

SYMPTOMS: Frequent and prolonged heat periods; irritation; refusal to mate.

TREATMENT: Consult your veterinarian. Treatment involves removing the ovaries or the cysts.

PROLAPSE OF THE UTERUS

CAUSES: A breakdown of the muscles of the vagina and uterus causes the uterus to protrude from the vagina. Severe straining during delivery of kittens or tumors can cause such a prolapse.

TREATMENT: Consult your veterinarian. In some cases the uterus can be pushed back into the pelvic area. Otherwise a partial hysterectomy may be necessary.

PYOMETRA (see also METRITIS, p. 212)

CAUSES: Uterine infections are often the result of an overproduction of progesterone. This hormone can be produced in excess when ovulation fails to result in pregnancy. The lining of the uterus thickens, and fills with fluid and cyst-like material. Bacteria begin to breed on this surface.

Uterine infection may sometimes develop to the point where abscesses form in the uterus—the life-threatening disorder known as pyometra.

SYMPTOMS: Lethargy, loss of appetite, depression, fever, excessive thirst, excessive urination. Uncharacteristic firmness and distension of the abdomen.

TREATMENT: Consult your veterinarian. If abscesses in the uterus are present, a hysterectomy may be necessary.

UTERINE INERTIA

Uterine inertia, a common cause of kitten death, is an absence of contrac-

tions in the uterus. Researchers are not exactly sure what causes this condition.

CAUSES: One body of evidence indicates that uterine inertia is a hereditary disorder and that the anxious queen is especially susceptible to it. Such a cat releases adrenaline into her bloodstream, which may inhibit the hormone production responsible for contractions. Low calcium levels are also believed to contribute to this disorder.

SYMPTOMS: Contractions occur in a highly irregular, sparse fashion, or don't occur at all.

TREATMENT: Consult your veterinarian immediately. In most cases, treatment will involve getting the mother to relax and feel as comfortable as possible.

UTERINE INFECTION (see METRITIS, p. 212)

VAGINAL INFECTION

CAUSES: In female cats, vaginal infection can lead to uterine infection. Bacteria can enter through the vagina and spread to other areas of the female genital tract.

SYMPTOMS: Excessive licking at the vulva; discharge.

TREATMENT: Consult your veterinarian. Vaginal douches and oral antibiotics may be prescribed.

21

CARING FOR KITTENS

NEWBORN KITTENS REQUIRE tremendous amounts of care and attention. Your objective will be to monitor the relationship between the mother and her litter, to be certain that all of the kittens' many needs are met.

THE NEWBORN

Kittens are born blind and deaf—their eyelids are closed and their ears are folded back. Even so, within minutes they begin moving in search of their mother, upon whom they are totally dependent for survival. It is believed that newborn kittens locate their mother by smelling her scent and feeling the heat from her body. They may even feel the vibrations from her purr.

Once they make contact with their mother, the kittens begin to suckle within an hour or two after birth. It is extremely important that your cat's new family nurse for at least the first forty-eight hours after birth. Newborn kittens weigh approximately three to four ounces. That weight will double in a week, triple in two weeks, and quadruple in three weeks!

Early nursing is important because kittens require an adequate supply of

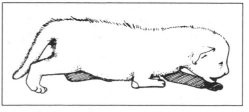

A newborn kitten will immediately crawl toward its mother in search of food and protection.

colostrum, the milk that females produce after giving birth. Colostrum is rich in antibodies that for a few weeks protect kittens from various diseases. Kittens cannot fend off these diseases because they have not yet developed immunities of their own.

Even if your cat is not feeling well, you should make every effort to have the kittens nurse for at least two days. If this is not possible, remove the kittens to an area where they will remain isolated from all other household pets. Then talk to your veterinarian about an early immunization schedule.

Examine the mother cat every day to make certain that her abdomen, vulva, and rectum are clean. Also check to make sure that her breasts are not caked with milk. Kittens are born utterly helpless, and they rely on their mother's milk to gain strength. If they cannot suckle milk from their mother's breasts because of caking, serious development problems—even death—can follow.

Occasionally, a newborn kitten is abandoned by his mother. She will remove him from other members of the litter. The mother probably feels that something is wrong with him, and she probably is right.

You should try to replace the kitten in the litter. If the mother cat still shuns him, be prepared to raise him as an orphan. (Foster care of new kittens is discussed later in this chapter.) The first thing you should do, however, is place the newborn in a box of his own and keep the temperature between eighty-five and ninety degrees Fahren-

heit. If the kitten becomes cold or chilled, he will probably die.

Within the next eight weeks, the kittens become much more independent. Their eyes start to open at five to ten days and become fully open in eight to twenty days. The eye color of newborn kittens is usually gray-blue, but they begin to change color at about twelve weeks.

Newborn kittens start crawling when they are between sixteen and twenty days old, and usually start eating solid foods at three to four weeks. Somewhere around the third or fourth week, the kittens cut their baby teeth. (The permanent teeth come in at about six months.)

The weaning process must begin at six weeks. After the kittens have their teeth, they start to bite while nursing, and this can cause pain to the mother (see Weaning, p. 220).

The first three weeks after delivery should be a tranquil and happy time both for you and your cat, who you should nevertheless keep an eye on. If she has a healthy appetite and uses her litter box regularly and normally, things are going well. Be alert to such symptoms as lethargy, loss of appetite, or diarrhea. Also keep a careful watch on the behavior of the kittens. If you notice anything out of the ordinary, consult your veterinarian.

Do not be surprised if your cat suddenly decides to pick up and move her litter to a new location. This sometimes happens during the first few days after birth. Establishing a new nest is part of your cat's instinctual behavior;

A KITTEN'S DEVELOPMENTAL MILESTONES

Birth	Kittens born blind, deaf, utterly dependent. Nursing is absolutely crucial over first 48 hours.
5–10 days	Eyes start to open.
8–20 days	Eyes fully open.
16–20 days	Crawling begins.
3–4 weeks	Solid food should be introduced. First juvenile teeth are cut. Toilet training begins.
6 weeks	Weaning begins.
8 weeks	Separation from the mother can begin.
6 months	First adult teeth are cut.

she is trying to safeguard her young by not staying in one place for too long.

If the mother cat decides to move, change the bedding of the maternity box and move it to the new location. Your feline family should soon settle comfortably into its new location.

If the litter is large, you can assist your cat in the weaning process as soon as the kittens can stand. This helps relieve the burden on the mother cat. The goal in weaning is to replace the mother's milk with an adult diet without upsetting the kittens' digestive system.

Before trying to wean the kittens away from their mother, familiarize yourself with foster parenting (see p. 221).

TAKING CARE OF YOUR KITTEN'S ESSENTIAL NEEDS

Rare is the mother cat who needs help caring for her new kittens; in fact, the less you do, the better. Too much handling of the kittens may cause the mother anxiety. After the kittens reach four weeks of age, however, social interaction with people and exposure to new and nonthreatening situations, such as toilet training, should begin.

GROOMING BY THE MOTHER CAT

Grooming plays a critical role in the maternal behavior of cats. In fact, few other animals lavish as much care and attention on their young as female cats do.

Not only does the mother cat take complete responsibility for the feeding and grooming of her litter, but she also guards her kittens against harm and patiently teaches them how to defend and care for themselves as they make the transition from kittens to young adults.

While your mother cat is still feeding her young, she will also attend to their toilet. The female cat will briskly lick the genital area of her kittens to stimulate urination and defecation. This is necessary because young kittens do not spontaneously do either.

Also, like many other carnivores, your cat will ingest the kittens' urine and feces for several weeks after birth in order to keep the nest clean. Once the kittens begin eating solid food, she will be more reluctant to clean up after them in this manner, but she will continue for some time to clean her kittens and thus show them how to groom themselves.

SEPARATING KITTENS FROM THEIR MOTHER

Do not begin separating kittens from their mother until they are at least six weeks old. The ideal is to wait until they are eight weeks old and fully weaned. Nor should a kitten be given away to a new owner until he is at least three months old, fully weaned, toilet trained, and settled into an adult diet.

You also should never give away or sell a kitten until he has gotten a clean bill of health from your veterinarian.

Your new kittens may be the offspring of a show-winning registered cat or the product of some dark-alley coupling. Whatever the case, all kittens are special. It is your responsibility to provide the best care possible for these young animals and to find them good homes and caring owners.

WEANING

Once the kittens are able to stand, you may begin the weaning process. Four weeks of age is about the right time to begin supplementing the kittens' diet with solid foods.

Begin the weaning process by offering the kittens one or two feedings a day of evaporated milk: the mix should be two parts milk to one part water. Make certain this mixture is warmed to body temperature (100 degrees Fahrenheit, 37.8 degrees Celsius) before serving. After a day or two, you may mix in some oatmeal and one raw egg. Place this gruel in a low-rimmed saucer. There is also a "mother's milk" product available commercially to supplement the kittens' diet until they are eating all-solid foods. Check with your veterinarian for more details.

The kittens may not at first get the idea, so dip your fingers into the gruel and let the kittens lick it off. Once they get to enjoy this new food, they will eat it out of the dish. During this period, the average kitten needs between 100 and 125 calories per pound of weight per day. Do not overfeed the kittens or they may get diarrhea.

As the kittens are being weaned, the mother's diet should be gradually reduced until by the end of eight weeks she should be receiving her normal prepregnancy amounts of food. This will aid the milk-drying process.

Once the kittens are accustomed to eating the gruel, you may switch to a canned meat product especially formulated for newly weaned kittens. As the kittens' solid diet increases, they will naturally turn away from mother's milk. This is helpful to the mother, since the appearance of teeth in the kittens will cause pain when they suckle.

TOILET TRAINING

When the kittens first begin to eat solid foods—or when they are about three to four weeks of age—the time has come to begin their toilet training. Take the litter box and put it in a convenient, easy-to-reach, and quiet spot. Place the kittens in the box frequently so that they can get used to it, especially when you see that they are ready to defecate—after meals or exercise and when they first wake up.

You can tell when a kitten is ready to relieve himself because he will crouch and raise his tail. If a kitten urinates or defecates in the wrong spot, do not rub his nose in the urine or droppings; this may in fact prompt the kitten to regard the spot as the place

to relieve himself. Instead, clean the area thoroughly so that no trace of odor remains.

FOSTER PARENTING

Sometimes a mother cat will turn her back on one of her offspring (see also Mother Cats Who Ignore Their Litter, p. 213). She may sense that something is wrong with the kitten and not want to have anything to do with it, or she may be unable to feed her new offspring because of illness or injury. (Some new mothers are chronically deficient in milk.)

In some cases a cat is unable to provide certain aspects of kitten care—for example, as above, being unable to breast-feed them due to milk deficiency—but can still take care of her new family in other ways. She will groom her kittens and keep them warm. If this is the case with your cat, you simply need to share with your cat the responsibility of raising her kittens. On the other hand, if your cat is too ill to care for her kittens, if she has died, or if she totally rejects the concept of motherhood, you have an important decision to make.

You can either become a foster parent, or you can take the orphaned kitten or kittens to your veterinarian, who will see that they are painlessly destroyed (see Euthanasia, p. 99). Another possibility is to check with your veterinarian, cat-owning friends, relatives, or neighbors to see if they have or know of any nursing cat with

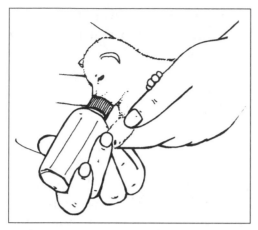

Only use sterile bottles when hand-feeding a kitten.

the capacity to care for one or more hungry mouths.

HAND-FEEDING

If you decide to become a foster parent, your most important task will be keeping your new charges warm and well fed.

When bottle-feeding kittens, you must make absolutely certain that any equipment you use is kept spotlessly clean. Newborn kittens have not yet developed immunity against many diseases and are highly susceptible to infection. All feeding utensils must be sterilized each time they are used, and fresh formula must be made up each day.

You must also provide each kitten with separate feeding and water dishes, and keep an eye on your new charges to make sure that one kitten is not stealing food from the others. If you are assisting the mother cat in the weaning process, when you hand out tidbits to the kittens, do not forget to feed the mother as well.

As a feline foster parent, you will need some kitten-friendly equipment and food supplies. Your local pet store will probably have all the items you may require, such as a specially designed curved kitten-feeder bottle. The pet store should also have the cat-milk substitutes you will need to feed the kittens, as well as food formulas. If milk substitutes are not available, you may use evaporated milk diluted with water, as is fed to human babies—except double strength.

Mix the milk substitute with hot water and then leave it to cool for five to ten minutes. Fill the nursing bottle with this milk and place it in a bowl of hot water for a few minutes. Before giving the kitten the milk, test it on the back of your wrist to make certain it is not too hot or too cool. The temperature of the formula you feed your kitten should be approximately 100–101 degrees Fahrenheit.

Next, gently grasp the kitten around the neck and push the teat of the bottle into his mouth. Take it easy and take your time. Do not push too hard; this will frighten the kitten. Light pressure on the bottle will work just fine if you have a little patience.

Whatever feeding formula your veterinarian recommends, you need to feed orphaned kittens every two hours for the first three weeks. Feeding every four hours until the kitten is full is usually adequate at night after the first few

---

MAKING AN INCUBATOR

Since chilling is one of the single greatest dangers to the newborn kitten's survival (see p. 218), you need to make an incubator to ensure that your hand-reared kitten will have adequate warmth.

Take a large cardboard box and place a small electric blanket or a heating pad on the bottom. Cover the blanket with some waterproof material, such as rubber or plastic.

Keep the incubator at eighty-five to ninety degrees Fahrenheit for the first week. During the second week, reduce the temperature to eighty to eighty-five degrees; after the second week, keep the temperature between seventy and seventy-five degrees.

---

days. As a general guide, one teaspoon of cat-milk substitute, diluted according to the directions on the package, is sufficient at first for each feeding.

HAND-WEANING

As would happen were a cat to wean from his mother (see Weaning, p. 220), after three weeks, gradually decrease the amount of milk you feed the kittens and begin adding a little gruel to their diet.

When the kittens are about four weeks old, you can put the food mixed with the milk substitute in a shallow saucer instead of a bottle. The kittens may eat as much of this as they want four times a day. At five weeks you can begin to substitute finely minced quality meat or finely chopped canned kitten food. Boiled or milk-poached fish should be added to at least one meal. The kittens are now being fed at least

once a day, and are being permitted to eat as much as they care to.

FEEDING AFTER WEANING

Beginning at six to eight weeks, increase the amount of solid minced food, preferably from nutritionally sound, canned kitten foods. Begin replacing the milk feeds with these solid meals. At eight weeks of age or older, the kitten or kittens should be normally weaned. Give them two to three solid meals daily. A saucer of cow's milk can now also be provided. If this causes diarrhea, however, discontinue it. When the kittens are six months old, you can switch from milk to water.

Multivitamin syrups for human babies should be mixed into each kitten's food once a day from the beginning of weaning until at least six months of age.

Check the product label for the amount to dispense.

After feeding, help the kittens get rid of waste products by gently stroking their lower abdomens to stimulate urination. Bowel movement can be encouraged by gently massaging the kittens' anuses with cotton wool moistened with mineral oil. If constipation develops, as evidenced by straining and possibly a swollen abdomen, consult your veterinarian. Normal kitten digestion results in about four bowel movements a day, but this number can vary from one kitten to the next.

YOUR KITTEN'S GROWTH AND DEVELOPMENT

Whether they are orphans that you have been caring for or kittens being raised normally, up to the age of three or four months your young cats have been very much waited upon. Most owners get so attached to these cute creatures that they cater to their every need, whether real or imagined.

The reality, of course, is that your kittens have quickly grown up from being the weak, defenseless creatures they once were. They are now completely independent. They are playing and developing hunting skills and are in complete control of their bodies.

By now the kittens have their second set of teeth; they have gained considerable weight and along the way have also acquired individual personalities. A hierarchy has most likely

evolved, with one of the kittens the dominant male.

When you feed the kittens now, the emphasis is not on what kind of food to give them, but how much. At age four months, kittens need a complete and balanced diet. They should be eating a combination of dry and wet commercial cat food specially formulated to meet a young cat's nutritional needs. The amount they are to be fed is usually specified on cans and packages of cat food, so all you need to do is follow the instructions.

Be careful not to overfeed any of your cats. Diarrhea (as well as unusual weight gain) often indicates overfeeding. Try to establish healthy and sensible eating habits during this period of their lives. Young kittens eat four or five small meals a day; by the age of six months, however, they should not be fed more than twice a day.

At this age pay attention to the amount of water you give your kittens. They may still love milk, but they should be encouraged to drink water primarily, since milk can cause digestive discomfort and diarrhea in adult cats. By the time kittens develop a taste for meat, poultry, and fish, they will have lost their taste for milk. When this happens, it is especially important that they get enough liquids. Make sure water is available at all times.

CLAWS

Trimming claws is never an easy job; no cat likes to have his feet handled. If you decide to undertake this task yourself, you can obtain special cat-claw clippers at your local pet store. Or it may be easier to have a professional cat groomer do the trimming for you.

Cats like to scratch with their claws. Chapter 2 contains tips on how to get your cat to use a scratching post instead of your favorite furniture. Many kittens and cats, however, prefer carpets or drapes to scratching posts.

If your kittens' claws are causing you grief, declawing is an option that should be carefully considered (see Declawing, p. 39).

CHEWING

Kittens love to chew. This is not bad behavior but, rather, instinctive behav-

ior. Chewing helps kittens shed their baby teeth. It also helps ease the pain and pressure of inflamed gums as the second set of teeth comes in. Clothes—especially your woolens—will be your kittens' favorite target.

It is unfair to punish your kittens for chewing up your favorite sweater. Instead, keep valuable things out of reach and purchase chewing toys from your pet store that are suitable for kittens.

If you have a four- or five-month old kitten who is the only pet in your home, he may be chewing out of loneliness. Try playing more with your young cat, and give him toys to amuse himself when you are not at home. Some kittens also chew because they are hungry. Make certain you are feeding your kitten properly and at the same time each day.

THE IMPORTANCE OF PLAY

Playing will take up much of your kittens' time. They will stalk one another, launch mock attacks, assume defensive positions, pounce, and in general have lots of fun. Play is a very important feline activity; it encourages the development of coordination, provides a source of exercise, and helps socialize the kittens. For a cat on his own, without the benefit of a warm and protective home, play serves as a training ground for learning how to survive.

Encourage play and enjoy it, but do not let them overdo it. Limit playtime sessions to fifteen minutes each day, two or three times daily. Rough play, in which a kitten nips or scratches, should also be discouraged. If it isn't, a kitten may begin to believe that aggressive, even violent, behavior is acceptable at home.

COMBING AND BRUSHING

While your kittens should have learned by now how to groom themselves, you can give them a little help—especially if they are long-haired cats. Your kittens are certain to enjoy being brushed and combed. Keep the grooming sessions short when you first begin, and do not be discouraged if your kittens become fidgety when you make the initial attempt. They will eventually become quite used to it.

Combing and brushing should be only part of your grooming duties. Cleaning your kittens' eyes and ears (see Ear Cleaning and Eye Cleaning, pp. 70, 71) if they need it and keeping their claws short (see Nail Trimming, p. 70) are also important. Grooming your cat is always a good time to be on the lookout for danger signals such as signs of mite infestation, unusual tenderness, or lumps under the skin.

TEETHING

Kittens usually get their second, or permanent, set of teeth in their fourth month, when their milk teeth are loosened and pushed out by the permanent teeth. If the baby teeth loosen but do not drop out, you may gently pull them out with your fingers.

This teething period is usually painful for kittens. Fortunately, it is generally short. In severe cases, kittens may develop diarrhea or experience other symptoms such as drooling, vomiting, or loss of appetite. Should such symptoms develop, have your veterinarian take a look at the kitten.

Even if no unusual symptoms develop, periodic dental checkups with your veterinarian are always a good idea. A visit to your veterinarian every six months will prevent a lot of problems.

To help keep your kittens'—or even your adult cat's—teeth healthy, you may wish to remove the buildup of tartar. (See Care of Your Cat's Teeth, p. 71, and Preventing Tooth Decay, p. 138.) This needs to be done at least once a month—weekly if there is a large tartar buildup.

WORMS

Many kittens suffer from roundworms; tapeworms and hookworms are also common internal parasites in kittens and cats. Diarrhea is one common symptom of worm infestation. (See Intestinal Parasites, p. 183)

You should have your veterinarian check your kitten's stools to make certain they are worm-free. Kittens with roundworms should be dewormed at two or three weeks of age. A second deworming treatment should be given at five to six weeks.

KITTEN ILLNESSES

Kittens are susceptible to various disorders, from digestive ailments to the deadly Feline Herpes Virus. You should familiarize yourself with the

SIGNS OF ILLNESS IN KITTENS

- A kitten who is rejected by his mother may be ill.

- Kittens who avoid nursing may be suffering from some disorder. Some kittens, however, simply need to be taught how to nurse. Such a kitten can be nursed by hand (see Hand-Feeding and Hand-Weaning, pp. 222, 223).

- A kitten who constantly cries is signaling that something is wrong. It may be either sick or hungry. Healthy kittens are usually quiet.

- If a kitten moves slowly and with great effort, it may be ill. Healthy kittens are vigorous and quick-moving.

- If the skin of a kitten is not resilient—meaning that when the skin is gently pulled it does not snap back into place—the kitten could be suffering from dehydration.

- Pale gums, instead of red or reddish-pink ones, may indicate malnutrition.

- A potbellied kitten may be suffering from constipation, parasites, or inadequate milk intake.

- Diarrhea is the symptom of a serious intestinal disorder. Mucus mixed with blood in the stools may indicate roundworm or hookworm infestation.

symptoms that may indicate something wrong with a young cat.

FELINE HERPES VIRUS
(see FADING KITTEN SYNDROME, p. 229)

IMPETIGO

CAUSES: Impetigo in kittens is usually caused by either *Pasteurella multocida* or *beta-hemolytic streptococcus*. Both organisms are found in a cat's mouth and spread to the kitten's skin while the mother carries it around. Impetigo affects the skin of kittens at least a week old. It is highly unlikely for impetigo to pass from cat to human.

SYMPTOMS: Puffy blisters on the body.

TREATMENT: Consult your veterinarian. The lesions are very infectious and the kittens may have to be put on oral antibiotics.

LEADING CAUSES OF EARLY DEATH IN KITTENS

Like human babies, kittens are extremely vulnerable to a variety of medical dangers during the first fifteen days of life. Two of the greatest killers of young kittens are chills and a disease known as Feline Herpes Virus.

CHILLING

CAUSES: When a kitten is first born, her body temperature is about that of her mother's. That temperature drops to about 92.5–96 degrees Fahrenheit over the first few days, rising to about 98 degrees by the end of the first week. In their first few days of life, kittens are unable to compensate for heat loss when the room temperature drops lower than the temperature of the nest. The body temperature of a kitten can drop quickly.

SYMPTOMS: The kitten becomes restless and starts to cry. The colder she becomes, the higher-pitched her crying. If she is not warmed up soon, the kitten will die.

TREATMENT: A chilled kitten must be warmed moderately—do not attempt to effect an instant, huge rise in temperature. Tuck the kitten beneath your

NUTRITIONAL ANEMIA

CAUSES: Nutritional anemia is the cause of 40 to 100 percent of deaths in some litters. If the mother is anemic—particularly in iron—her offspring will be anemic. Intestinal parasites (see p. 183) can also cause deficiency anemia due to chronic blood loss.

SYMPTOMS: Pale mucous membranes, slow growth, frequent lethargy.

TREATMENT: Consult your veterinarian. Nutritional anemia can be prevented by keeping the queen in good health during gestation.

TOXIC MILK SYNDROME

CAUSES: There are a number of reasons why the mother's milk sometimes becomes toxic. The main reason is mastitis (see p. 212), an infection of the milk glands. Improperly prepared formula can also bring on toxic milk syndrome.

SYMPTOMS: Kittens seem distressed

sweater or jacket next to your skin. To prevent chilling, the room temperature where the maternity box is located should be 70 to 72 degrees Fahrenheit and free from drafts.

Fading Kitten Syndrome (Feline Herpes Virus)

Feline herpes virus, also known as fading kitten syndrome, is a very insidious disease. Immediately after birth, the mother cat appears healthy, her milk production seems adequate, and all the kittens are nursing normally. Yet a few hours later, a kitten can be dead.

CAUSES: This deadly virus is believed to be acquired by kittens as they pass through the vagina at birth. It usually affects kittens one week after birth. Kittens affected by this virus who are older than three weeks will not die from it, but will suffer mild symptoms from the infection.

SYMPTOMS: Cessation of nursing, yellow-green diarrhea, acute abdominal pain, vomiting, pitiful crying, labored breathing.

TREATMENT: If you notice any of these symptoms, consult your veterinarian immediately. Treatment will depend upon the age of the kitten and the extent of damage incurred.

and cry constantly; diarrhea; bloating; dehydration.

TREATMENT: Consult your veterinarian. The kittens will need to be separated from their mother and hand-fed.

22

FIRST-AID GUIDE

CATS ARE CURIOUS, AGILE, and brave creatures with a splendid knack for getting themselves into trouble. Some of the many mishaps that happen to a cat are minor in nature, such as finding herself stuck on a tree limb. Others may be life-and-death situations, as when a cat is struck by a car.

If your cat does suffer a serious injury, you will need to act swiftly and effectively, making important snap decisions in order to save your cat's life.

This chapter will help you make the right decisions. It is divided into three sections:

Emergency Procedures
Common Emergencies
Poison Control

The first section explains how to perform lifesaving techniques such as cardiopulmonary resuscitation, heart massage, and controlling bleeding. It will also show you how to approach an injured cat, and how to safely transport her to safety.

The second section provides step-by-step first aid techniques that will help you through emergency situations common to cats, including catfights, electric shock, and frostbite.

The third section focuses on poison control, outlining the many substances toxic to cats, and detailing procedures for aiding a cat who has come into contact with them.

NOTE: This information is not a substitute for veterinary help, however. In an emergency, the best way to ensure your cat's survival is to get her to a veterinarian as quickly as possible.

231

EMERGENCY PROCEDURES

The basic steps outlined below will help you stabilize your pet while on your way to the veterinarian and will reduce the chance of further damage and complications. Familiarize yourself with these basics; better yet, practice them if you have the opportunity to do so.

Whatever feline emergency you may be confronted with, it is crucial that you keep calm. Assess the situation, approach the injured cat with caution, and be as gentle as you possibly can.

If you do not know how badly your cat is hurt or the nature of her injuries, it is sometimes best to do nothing at all except summon veterinary help; there are times when doing the wrong thing can cause more harm than good.

APPROACHING AND HANDLING AN INJURED CAT

If your cat is involved in an accident, your immediate response—even before any first-aid measures are applied—should be to assess the situation. Remain calm. Do not try to do everything at once. Take the following steps:

1. Cautiously approach your cat. Speak soothingly to her. If you have any gloves handy, put them on. They will protect your hands should your cat become uncooperative and aggressive.

2. If the injury looks serious, call your veterinarian immediately and get ready to transport your cat to the nearest animal hospital. Speak calmly to your veterinarian and describe the situation in detail. If a pet ambulance service is available in your community, call one. In the interim, try to get someone to assist you in handling and calming your cat.

3. If your cat is conscious, restrain her. Keep her lying down and as quiet as possible. How you restrain your cat depends on what part of the body needs to be treated, and whether the cat is cooperative or not. There are various ways to restrain a cat. If you need to treat any part of the cat's head or neck, one suggestion is to wrap the rest of the body in a thick towel. Another option is to pick him up from behind by the back of the neck and gently lower him into a laundry bag with only the head showing.

If the injury is to another part of the body, you will need help to restrain your cat. One person firmly grasps the scruff of the neck with one hand and the chest or forelegs with the other. The second person grasps the hind legs and administers whatever emergency treatment may be required.

Should your cat be cooperative enough to permit handling, grasp her by the scruff of her neck and press her down firmly against the top of the table so that she stretches out. This will prevent your being scratched by her rear claws.

In some emergencies your cat may

be in such pain that she will not coop-erate with you at all. One type of restraint is to make a noose of your belt or a thick piece of rope, slip it cau-tiously over your cat's head, and tighten it gently. Attach the free end of the noose to some fixed object so the cat cannot effectively move.

Next, grasp the cat's hind legs and extend the body. This immobilizes the cat and keeps her from biting or lashing out at you. Wrap a towel or cloth firmly around your cat's body; this often soothes an injured cat.

Remember that even a longtime feline companion, if injured, may revert to instinctual behavior and try to scratch or bite you if handled at this time. Accept this as part of animal behavior.

4. Check your cat's heartbeat. Do this by grasping the chest just behind the elbows with one hand (see How to Take Your Cat's Pulse, p. 83) while sup-porting the cat with the other. Move your hand until you feel the heartbeat. If there is none, follow the procedure for heart massage (see p. 236).

5. Check your cat's breathing. Put a mirror in front of his face and see if it clouds up with breath. Check to see if his chest is expanding and contracting. If there is breathing, listen to deter-mine if it sounds noisy and obstructed. If there is no breathing, begin the pro-cedure described on page 235 for arti-ficial respiration.

6. Check for bleeding. If there is any serious bleeding, begin the proce-dure described on page 237 for con-trol of bleeding.

7. Check your cat's mouth, lips, and tongue for burns, stains, or other symptoms of poisoning (see p. 255).

8. Check to make sure your cat is conscious and responsive. If she is not, treat for shock as described on page 251. (It is a good idea to study the section on shock, as treatment for shock is often the most urgent emer-gency procedure.) If your cat is con-vulsing do not move him (see Convul-sions, p. 244).

TRANSPORTING AN INJURED CAT

In an emergency, your veterinarian will advise you to bring your injured cat to his office, or to rush the cat over to the nearest animal hospital. Whatever you decide to do, the injured cat must be moved as quietly and carefully as possible.

Moving a critically injured animal must be done with care. Not only can such movement cause further damage, but a cat in pain may bite or claw you—so take precautions to protect yourself and your cat. If you are scratched or bitten while transporting your cat, make certain that you seek medical help.

If your cat has minor injuries, she should be handled in a normal man-ner. Lift the cat straight up while grasping her by the scruff of the neck. This does not hurt the cat; most go limp, as they did when their mothers carried them this way when they were kittens.

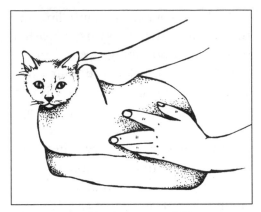

Use a towel or blanket to immobilize your cat and prevent shock.

Wrap a blanket, towel, or coat around your cat to keep her warm and guard against the possibility of shock (see Shock, p. 251). Wrapping a cat in a towel can also support an injured limb or cover a wound. Place your cat in her favorite carrier, a bowling bag, or a gym bag (with adequate air supply), making certain that you do not aggravate the injury.

Should your cat be critically injured, exercise extreme care in picking her up. A seriously injured cat may have a broken back, so support the back by placing a thick towel beneath her before lifting her up. If this is not possible, keep your cat's back straight when you lift her. With the towel in place, slide your hands beneath the towel and lift the animal in one smooth motion. Try to keep your cat's back facing you. Support the back with your hands and forearm as you place the cat in her carrier.

Place a cat with a broken leg on her side, keeping the damaged limb up. Utilize the lifting procedure described above, making certain that the side with the injured leg stays up.

If the cat is unconscious or paralyzed, lift her with one continuous motion without bending or twisting any part of her body.

NOTE: If an injured cat puts up a struggle, do not force the issue. Struggling with a weak or injured cat may

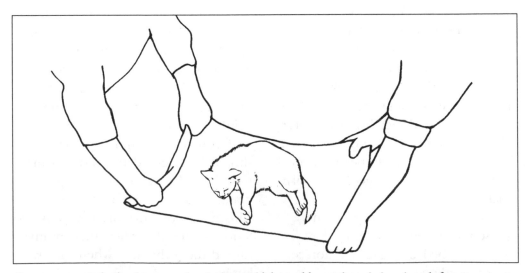

Support suspected spinal trauma by placing a thick towel beneath an injured cat before transporting her.

tire her out and produce shock and collapse. Call your veterinarian and follow her or his instructions.

RESUSCITATION

ARTIFICIAL RESPIRATION

Anything that causes your cat to stop breathing—drowning, inhalation of vomit, shock, or poisoning—will necessitate this emergency procedure. *Apply artificial respiration only if there is a heartbeat.* (If there is no heartbeat, heart massage or cardiopulmonary resuscitation as described following is required.) Artificial respiration should be administered immediately, because if no oxygen reaches your cat's brain for ten to fifteen minutes, permanent brain damage will result.

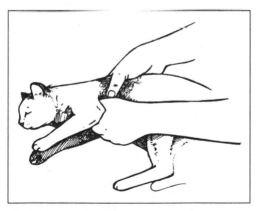

Artificial respiration requires you to squeeze the rib cage between your palms.

TECHNIQUE

1. Feel for pulse or heartbeat (see p. 83).

2. If there is a heartbeat, open the cat's mouth and check the air passage to make certain there are no obstructions. If there are any, remove them with your finger. Cautiously draw out the cat's tongue with your finger or a cloth. Hold the tongue to keep the airway open.

3. Lay the cat down on a flat surface, with the right side of the body down. Try to keep the head lower than the body.

4. Firmly but gently squeeze the rib cage, which you can feel behind the shoulders, between the palms of your hands. Release quickly. Repeat this procedure every four seconds. Keep looking and listening for signs of air moving in and out. If you can't detect any, begin mouth-to-nose resuscitation (see p. 236).

CARDIOPULMONARY RESUSCITATION (CPR)

Heart massage combined with mouth-to-nose resuscitation is called cardiopulmonary resuscitation (CPR). Because cessation of breathing is soon followed by cardiac arrest, and vice versa, CPR frequently is required to save a cat's life.

CPR on cats is not simple. If there is any way to get your cat to a veterinarian quickly before undertaking this procedure, do so. If that is impossible and it is clear that your cat's life is in imminent danger if nothing is done, try your best. Do not blame yourself if you fail. Often, even trained technicians cannot save a cat's life using CPR.

TECHNIQUE

1. Place the cat on her right side, either on the ground or on a table.

2. Check for breathing. Check for a heartbeat by pressing your fingers firmly against the lower side of the chest immediately below the elbows.

3. If there is no breathing and no heartbeat, begin CPR.

4. Perform mouth-to-nose resuscitation for ten seconds (see following).

5. Perform heart massage for fifteen seconds (see below).

6. Check for breathing and a pulse rate. If none, repeat the process until the heart begins to beat and your cat is breathing.

7. Seek emergency veterinary care immediately.

HEART MASSAGE

Heart massage is used when no heartbeat can be heard or felt.

TECHNIQUE

1. Lay the cat on her right side.

2. Put one hand on the back along the spine.

3. With your other hand, grasp the chest. Push in firmly but gently six times. Wait five seconds to let the chest expand.

4. Repeat, if necessary. Continue until the heart beats on its own.

5. Get your cat to the veterinarian as soon as possible.

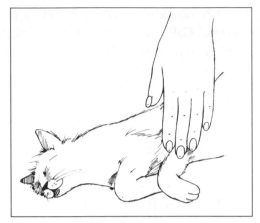

Heart massage is an essential component of CPR.

MOUTH-TO-NOSE RESUSCITATION

TECHNIQUE

1. Feel for pulse and heartbeat.

2. If heart is beating, close the lips and mouth. Cup your hands around the cat's muzzle to prevent air from escaping.

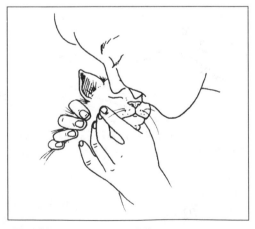

Mouth-to-nose resuscitation

3. Place your mouth against the cat's nose and blow in steadily, but gently, for three seconds.

4. Watch for the chest to expand. Remove your mouth and allow the air to come back out. Wait three seconds and repeat. Repeat this procedure every three seconds for one minute.

5. Recheck the breathing. If there still is no breathing, repeat the process.

CONTROL OF BLEEDING

Bleeding can be from an artery or a vein. Bright-red blood spurting in a pumping fashion is arterial bleeding. Flowing dark-red blood is from the veins.

PRESSURE DRESSING

Try to control bleeding by placing a pressure dressing over the wound. First, cover the wound using a clean cloth or heavy gauze compress. Place the gauze or cloth directly over the bleeding area. Apply direct pressure just firmly enough so that the bleeding stops. Take a fresh bandage and wrap it around the affected area to hold the gauze in place.

THE TOURNIQUET

If pressure dressing doesn't control bleeding, try using a tourniquet. An

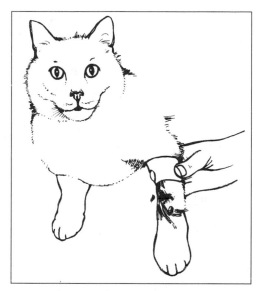

If a pressure dressing doesn't control bleeding, use a tourniquet.

emergency tourniquet can be made from anything available: a necktie, belt, shoelace, nylon hose, or rope. If the wound is arterial and on a limb, the tourniquet should be applied to the leg above the wound, between it and the heart.

Make the tourniquet by wrapping the material around the limb above the injury. Then insert a strong stick, pencil, or anything handy into the band. Tie a knot on top of the stick. Twist the stick until the bleeding stops. Secure the stick in place with adhesive tape. Do not keep a tourniquet tightened for more than five minutes. Loosen it for two or three minutes to let blood flow into the limb, and then reapply.

COMMON EMERGENCIES

This section covers the most common emergencies your cat may encounter. Use the information that follows in conjunction with the emergency procedures outlined previously.

ABDOMINAL PAIN

Severe abdominal pain can indicate a life-threatening condition. If your cat shows symptoms of such pain, get immediate veterinary assistance.

CAUSES: Urinary stones, internal injury, rupture of the bladder, poisoning, intestinal obstruction.

SYMPTOMS: A sudden onset of abdominal pain accompanied by vomiting, extreme restlessness, crying, labored breathing; abdomen extremely tender to the touch.

FIRST AID: There is none. Consult your veterinarian.

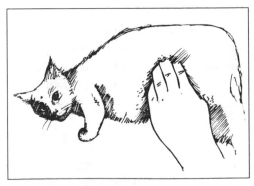

Gently press against your cat's abdomen to determine if she is experiencing abdominal pain, which may signal serious internal injury.

ALLERGIC REACTION

Two types of allergic reactions are common in cats; one is caused by substances in the air such as pollens, and the other by something in the food a cat eats.

HYPERSENSITIVITY REACTION

CAUSES: The immune system overreacts to certain substances that get into the blood system, such as pollens, powders, feathers, wool, and house dust.

SYMPTOMS: Sneezing, coughing, tearing, and swelling of the eyelids. You may see hair loss, oozing sores from constant scratching, diarrhea.

FIRST AID: Consult your veterinarian, who will conduct tests to determine the exact cause of your cat's distress.

FOOD ALLERGY

CAUSES: Some chemical substance in the food brings on an allergic reaction.

SYMPTOMS: Skin lesions, itchiness, redness. Gastrointestinal distress is rarely a sign of food allergy in cats.

FIRST AID: Because the symptoms of food allergy mimic those of other skin disorders, you should consult your veterinarian. He or she will probably advise you to use dietary measures to determine which food is affecting your cat adversely.

AMPUTATION (NONSURGICAL)

A cat may be struck by a car or get his leg caught in a piece of machinery, resulting in the loss of that limb.

SYMPTOMS: Uncontrolled bleeding, loss of limb.

FIRST AID: Remain calm and act quickly. The bleeding must be immediately stopped. Restrain your cat (see Restraining a Cat, p. 85) and try to control the bleeding by pressing a heavy compress over the wound (see Control of Bleeding, p. 237). Use adhesive tape to bandage the compress firmly in place. If the bleeding does not stop, tighten the tape. If serious blood loss continues, you may need to apply a tourniquet (see p. 237).

ASPHYXIATION

When oxygen is prevented from entering a cat's lungs and blood, asphyxiation—also called suffocation—can occur.

CAUSES: Carbon monoxide poisoning, inhalation of smoke or gasoline, drowning, foreign bodies in the air passages, injuries to the chest, smothering.

SYMPTOMS: Straining to breathe, gasping for air, extreme anxiety, dilation of pupils, tongue and mucous membranes begin to turn blue.

FIRST AID: Get your cat into fresh air immediately. If you keep oxygen at home, give your pet some. If your cat's breathing is shallow or absent, begin mouth-to-nose resuscitation (see Mouth-to-Nose Resuscitation, p. 236).

NOTE: In the case of drowning or the inhalation of vomit, liquid medication, or other fluids, hold your cat upside down by the hind legs for fifteen seconds. Give him a couple of downward shakes to help drain liquid from the air passages.

AUTOMOBILE ACCIDENTS

If your cat is allowed to roam freely outdoors, he runs the risk of being struck by a car. Most broken bones in cats are caused either by falling from great heights or by being hit by cars.

FIRST AID:

1. Approach your cat or any cat involved in a car accident cautiously. Speak to him in a reassuring tone of voice.

2. Evaluate the cat. Is he breathing? Does he have a heartbeat? If the cat is not breathing, proceed with artificial respiration (see Artificial Respiration, p. 235). If the animal has neither a heartbeat nor a pulse, administer heart massage (see Heart Massage, p. 236). If the cat is unconscious, check to make certain his airway is clear. Remove any secretions in his mouth and gently draw out the tongue using your fingers or a cloth. Keep the cat's head slightly lower than his body.

3. Stop any bleeding (see Control of Bleeding, p. 237).

4. Gently splint any injured or broken

limbs by tying or taping newspapers or a magazine around the limb so that he is kept motionless (see Fractures, p. 246).

5. If you are able to pick up the injured cat, remove him from the street or highway, where he may suffer further harm (see Transporting an Injured Cat, p. 233).

6. Place a coat or blanket over the injured cat to help prevent shock; wrapping also has a calming effect.

7. Prepare to transport the cat as quickly as possible to an animal hospital.

BITES (see CATFIGHTS)

BLOAT

Bloat is a serious, life-threatening condition in which the stomach becomes inflated with gas and then suddenly twists, trapping the gas inside. The swelling is rapid and acute, causing the stomach to stretch to twice or three times its normal size within an hour.

The causes of bloat are still not known, but swallowing air with food or vigorous exercise soon after feeding are thought to contribute to it.

SYMPTOMS: In the preliminary stage of bloat, the stomach is taut like a drum. The cat is restless and in severe pain. This is followed by a sudden and rapid swelling of the abdomen.

FIRST AID: Rush the cat to the nearest veterinary clinic.

BURNS AND SCALDS

Cats often fall victim to a variety of burns. Heat, electricity, radiation—such as sunburn—or corrosive chemicals all can cause burn injuries in cats. Cats sometimes burn their foot pads walking on hot surfaces, like tin rooftops. To a hungry cat, the kitchen is where the action is—especially when he smells something cooking. The kitchen is also a perfect

SEVERITY OF BURNS

TYPE	APPEARANCE	POSSIBLE CAUSES
First-Degree	Simple redness under fur	Quick contact with a hot pan or heater, light sunburn
Second-Degree	Deep redness, swelling, blisters	Splash of boiling liquid, deep sunburn
Third-Degree	Skin destroyed, appears white or charred. More than 15 percent of the body surface is burned	Fire, electrical burn

location for a cat to get underfoot and suffer scalds by steam or hot water.

A burn is the destruction of tissue by extreme and localized heat. The severity of a burn depends on how deeply the skin is affected and how much surface area is burned.

There are three categories of burns: thermal, chemical, and electrical.

THERMAL BURNS

CAUSES: Thermal burns occur most frequently. Scalding by hot water or contact with an open flame or stovetop results in a thermal burn injury. The skin usually turns red, and there may be some blistering. The hair around the burn may be singed.

SYMPTOMS: Redness of the skin; occasional blistering, some tenderness.

FIRST AID: It may be necessary for you to restrain your cat (see Restraining a Cat, p. 85). Apply cold compresses (that have been wrung out after being immersed in ice water) for 20 minutes to relieve pain. You can wash the area with bicarbonate of soda solution, following instructions on the package. Then an antibiotic jelly can be applied to the area to coat the injury, soothe him, and keep him clean. Ask your veterinarian to recommend a topical antibiotic ointment.

CHEMICAL BURNS

CAUSES: Chemical burns are caused by contact with corrosive materials. If your cat has contact with any substance containing an alkali, such as lye or ammonia,

the affected area will turn white or brown and have a slippery feel. Acid will cause the skin to dehydrate, contract and darken—a very painful injury.

SYMPTOMS: Skin appears white or brown, hair comes out easily when pulled, severe pain.

FIRST AID: Again, restraint may be necessary if the burning chemical was an acid (often found in drain cleaners, paint, and automotive products). Wash the wound with an alkaline solution— one teaspoon bicarbonate of soda mixed with one pint of lukewarm water. Flush any chemicals out of the mouth with a teaspoon of baking soda mixed with water (protect your hands with rubber gloves while you do this). If the burning chemical was an alkali (usually found in garden products), wash the area with soap and water. Sponge the mouth with vinegar or fruit juice. If the burn is extensive, treat for shock. Cover the burn area with petroleum jelly, bandage, and seek prompt veterinary attention.

ELECTRICAL BURNS

CAUSES: If your cat is a chewer—and many are—it may decide to sharpen his teeth on an electrical cord. If the cat succeeds in chewing through the cord, he may receive a dangerous or even life-threatening shock as well as burns. In most cases, the burn will affect the mucous membranes around the mouth, which eventually will heal by themselves. Cats also sometimes come in contact with exposed power lines or are struck by lightning.

SYMPTOMS: Burns around the mouth show a pale center surrounded by redness and swelling; excessive drooling.

FIRST AID: Such burns are usually caused by a cat or kitten chewing his way through an electrical cord. While these burns are painful, they generally heal by themselves. If such burns are accompanied by a shock to the cat's body, see Electric Shock, page 245.

NOTE: Keep electrical cords out of reach. If that is not possible, wrap those cords with the spiral-type telephone wires that cannot be bitten through.

CATFIGHTS

If your cat is permitted to go outdoors, sooner or later he may have a run-in with another cat and get into a vicious squabble over territory, females, or some other important feline matter. When your cat comes limping back home, he may be suffering from puncture wounds or lacerated wounds.

PUNCTURE WOUNDS

Puncture wounds are small, deep holes. They are potentially quite serious because of the likelihood of infection. If you do not treat puncture wounds, the skin will heal but an abscess will form beneath the skin. An abscess signifies infection, which could spread past the point of puncture to other parts of the cat's body.

Without proper cleansing, a lacerated wound can easily become infected.

FIRST AID: First, clean the wound and the area around it with a 10 percent solution of hydrogen peroxide. Then ask your veterinarian what type of antibiotics should be administered.

LACERATED WOUNDS

Lacerated wounds are jagged wounds with torn skin.

FIRST AID: Clean the skin with soap and water and a 10 percent solution of hydrogen peroxide. Large lacerations may require stitches, but that is a job for your veterinarian. It is wise to have a veterinarian inspect the wound to determine if stitches are necessary.

CHEST WOUNDS

BLEEDING

If your cat has been struck by a car, has fallen from a great height, or has been injured in battle with another animal, bleeding will accompany whatever wounds your cat suffers.

FIRST AID: To stop the bleeding, place a moistened gauze pad or other absorbent material directly over the wound. Put a plastic bag or sheet over the pad and secure it with tape. You have now created an airtight seal around the wound.

If the wound bleeds through the dressing, place another pad over it and bandage it more tightly, or apply direct hand pressure to the wound. Do not remove the first dressing; this will disturb the blood clot that has begun to form and will increase bleeding. Move your injured cat as little as possible when transporting him to the veterinarian.

NOTE: As a stopgap measure if the above materials are not available, wrap a towel or cloth around the cat and twist the ends snugly. Hold this makeshift dressing in place until you get help.

CHEST CRUSHED

If your cat's chest has been crushed in a car accident or fall, you will know it because your cat will have difficulty in breathing. He will stand with his neck stretched out, using his abdomen to breathe, with his elbows sticking outwards.

FIRST AID: Although it may be impossible to accomplish, try to determine visually which is the less injured side of the chest. Lay your cat down on that side. Clear the cat's airway by raising his head. Control any bleeding as described above. Then transport the injured cat to your veterinarian or animal hospital.

CHOKING

Curiosity, hunger, and activity can result in all kinds of problems for your cat—especially if he swallows something that gets stuck in his throat. Kittens are especially at risk because they often tend to swallow objects that they are chewing on when teething.

Choking occurs when a cat cannot breathe normally because some object is blocking his airway. If your cat is choking, you must take immediate action and not wait for veterinary assistance.

Be careful when handling a choking cat. The animal is confused and frightened. He may panic and try to bite you as you attempt to remove the object. Should this happen, get prompt medical attention for yourself.

SYMPTOMS: Cat not able to breathe, pawing at the mouth or throat, rubbing his face on the ground; extreme anxiety; violent coughing or gagging; eyes bulging; blue tongue; loss of consciousness.

FIRST AID: Wrap your cat in a thick towel with only the head showing. Open your cat's mouth wide. A good technique for doing so is by squeezing in the cheeks with your thumb and forefinger. Draw the tongue out, using

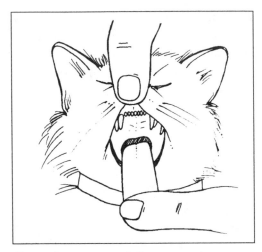

Draw the tongue out before attempting to remove an object that obstructs breathing.

a paper towel or a cloth. If you see the object, try to remove it gently with your fingers. Be careful not to force the object any farther down the throat.

NOTE: If this technique does not succeed, try picking your cat up by his hind legs and swinging him back and forth several times in a sideways motion. If still unsuccessful, try the Heimlich maneuver: Lay your cat on his side; place one hand on the spine behind the chest; grasp the lower part of the rib cage with the other hand; squeeze in and upward on the lower ribs. Repeat thrusts until object is expelled.

COMA (see UNCONSCIOUSNESS)

CONVULSIONS (FITS AND SEIZURES)

Convulsions are rarely fatal unless they are repetitive. Nonetheless, they are a frightening sight for any pet owner to observe. These severe, spasmodic jerkings of the entire body can last from two to three minutes and are caused by a burst of electrical activity in the brain. No matter how brief a fit or seizure your cat may be in, if convulsions recur within two hours, consult your veterinarian.

CAUSES: Excitement, ear mites, poison, disease, and other factors all can cause convulsions. Two of the most common causes in cats are epilepsy and distemper (see Epilepsy, p. 176). Quick-acting poisons such as strychnine can send a cat into a severe and prolonged convulsion.

SYMPTOMS: Sudden, uncontrolled bursts of activity; foaming at the mouth; champing and chewing; collapse; thrashing about on the ground; crying out in pain.

FIRST AID: The best policy is to leave your cat alone during the convulsion. Clear the area of sharp objects during such a seizure, because your cat may start to rush about the room in a blind frenzy. You may wish to cover your cat with a blanket to help keep him calm. When the convulsion ends, watch your cat's breathing carefully. If breathing stops, begin artificial respiration (p. 235).

DROWNING

Contrary to popular myth, not all cats detest swimming, although many cats do despise getting just their paws wet.

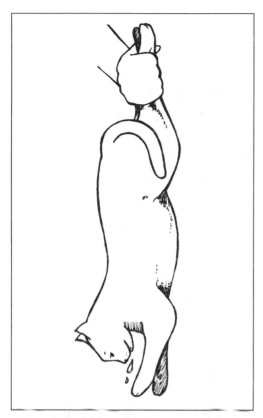

Lift a cat by his hind legs in order to clear his lungs of water.

In fact, cats are natural swimmers and can handle short distances quite well.

Drowning deaths are not common among the cat population because, as a general rule, cats do avoid water. But accidents happen. For example, a cat may fall into a swimming pool and not be able to climb out.

Drowning occurs when the lungs become flooded with fluid, which prevents inhalation of air. Even if breathing does not stop entirely, excess fluid can damage a cat's lungs.

SYMPTOMS: Panic in water, frantic efforts to swim, motionless in water.

FIRST AID: Try to reach the cat from land with a buoy, board, or anything that floats. Do not swim to a drowning cat without some rescue aid in hand for him to cling to, because you are likely to get seriously clawed. Once you bring the cat in, you must empty the lungs of water as soon as possible. Lift the cat up by his hind legs and let the water drain out of his mouth. Swing him gently back and forth in a sideways motion until water or other fluid stops coming out. Place the cat on the ground and try to keep his head lower than his body. Gently draw the tongue out of the mouth. Begin artificial respiration (see Artificial Respiration, p. 235). If the heart has stopped beating, begin CPR (see Cardiopulmonary Resuscitation, p. 235). Once the cat recovers, you may have to treat him for shock—basically this means keeping the animal warm and his body elevated (see Shock, p. 251). Take the cat to your veterinarian.

ELECTRIC SHOCK

Some cats and kittens love chewing on electrical cords. On occasion, a roaming cat may come in contact with a live power line after a storm. Each year, many cats are struck by lightning. Any of these close encounters with electricity can result in dangerous electrical shock.

SYMPTOMS: Burned or charred lips, difficulty in breathing, loss of consciousness, convulsions, collapsed or lying on one side, excessive drooling.

HOW TO PREVENT ELECTRIC SHOCK

As most cases of feline electrocution involve chewing on electrical cords, take steps in your household to prevent this. One bite-proof method is to cover electrical cords with those spiral plastic covers intended for telephone cords. Another is to tape the cords to the floor with duct tape and then cover the cords with carpet.

FIRST AID: Turn off the electrical supply. Check for heart and pulse rate. If the cat has no heart beat and is not breathing, and your veterinarian is not nearby, begin CPR immediately (see Cardiopulmonary Resuscitation p. 235). Furthermore, the lungs of a cat that has been electrocuted may fill with fluid. The sign is difficulty in breathing. Do not elevate the body above the head in an attempt to drain the fluid, because in this case it could worsen the condition. Get prompt veterinary attention.

WARNING: Do not touch the cat if he still has the cord in his mouth or is in contact with some other live power source. If you do, you can be electrocuted.

EYE INJURIES

A cat is exposed to a multitude of situations that can cause eye injuries, from foreign objects in the eye to puncture wounds. Any injury to your cat's eye should be considered an emergency. Most first aid procedures are too difficult for anyone but a vet-erinarian, as your cat will be fighting you all the way. Take your cat immediately to a veterinarian. If there is any bleeding, try to control it by applying direct pressure against the lid and bone with gauze or a clean cloth.

FRACTURES

Fractures are broken bones. In cats, the majority of fractures are caused by automobile accidents or falls from great heights—such as apartment building window ledges during the summer months.

Fractures can be open or closed. In an open, or compound fracture, the bone breaks and cuts through the skin. Closed, or simple, fractures do not break the skin. If your cat is limping badly, the muscles may be damaged but the leg probably is not broken. Cats with broken legs will put no weight on those legs at all.

Any type of fracture will cause your cat extreme pain. So approach the injured animal cautiously (see First Aid, p. 239). Restraints may be necessary while you apply first aid.

FRACTURES OF THE KNEE OR ELBOW

TREATMENT: Splints may be most effective, but your cat will probably resist any handling of his injured and painful limb. If you force the matter, you can cause even more damage. Instead, move the fractured leg as little as possible. If you see exposed bone, cover it with light gauze or a bandage. Shock may set in, so keep your cat warm by covering him with a blanket. Put a folded towel under the leg for support and take your cat to your veterinarian's office or the nearest animal hospital (see Transporting an Injured Cat, p. 233).

FRACTURES OF THE FOOT BONES

TREATMENT: Immobilize the foot by folding a magazine or piece of thick cardboard around the leg. Then wrap it with gauze or anything else handy

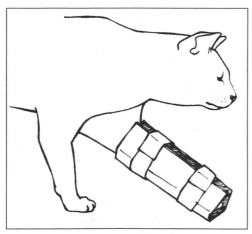

Immobilize a fractured foot by wrapping a magazine or newspapers around the entire leg.

such as a necktie. Take the cat to the nearest animal clinic.

FRACTURES OF THE JAW

If the lower jaw has been fractured, it will usually hang open. Your cat will drool. Tie a tight dressing under the chin and around the back of the head to support the jaw. Tie the knot behind your cat's ears so it cannot be removed by the cat. Summon veterinary help.

FRACTURES OF THE SKULL

Skull fractures result in impaired balance, unconsciousness, or nosebleeds. Your first response should be to control any external bleeding (see Control of Bleeding, p. 237). Handle skull injuries gently. Do not apply any bandages or administer any drugs or fluids. Transport the cat to your veterinarian or animal hospital immediately.

FRACTURES OF THE SPINE

Spinal cord injuries can occur after car accidents or falls. You should suspect a fractured spine if your cat has been involved in an accident and cannot move his hind legs, or if you pinch your cat's toes and there is no response. If you do suspect spinal area injury, do not move your cat unless absolutely necessary. If you must do so, slide the cat—do not lift him—on to a board large enough to support his back. Secure the cat to the board. Place the cat and board into your car or cab and take the cat to the nearest veterinary clinic.

FRACTURES OF THE TAIL

A tail fracture can occur when a car runs over a cat's tail or if the tail gets caught in a door. In such a case, the tail will hang straight down. If the fracture is at the root of the tail, do not attempt to bandage it. If the fracture is anywhere else along the length of the tail, you may apply an adhesive tape dressing to support the length of the damaged tail until you can get the cat to a veterinarian. If your cat's tail remains paralyzed after six weeks, your veterinarian may recommend that the tail be removed.

FROSTBITE AND COLD EXPOSURE (HYPOTHERMIA)

Prolonged exposure to the cold, also known as hypothermia, results in a drop of a cat's body temperature to a point much lower than the normal range of 101 degrees to 102.5 degrees. Hypothermia is most likely to occur in cats who are often wet. All cats are at risk, especially kittens and older cats.

Exposure to cold is very serious and can often result in frostbite or even death. In frostbite, the skin tissues begin to die. **Frostbite can develop without hypothermia.**

HYPOTHERMIA

SYMPTOMS: Stiff muscles, shivering, cold to the touch, dilated pupils, low pulse rate (below 150 beats per minute), low respiratory rate (below 10 breaths per minute), extremely low body temperature.

FIRST AID: Try to obtain veterinary care. If this is not possible, wrap your cat in a blanket or whatever else is available and bring him indoors. A wet cat may be dried off with a towel or blow-dryer. Use hot water packs or bottles that are warm—not scalding—to the wrist. You may also use a heating pad set on low. If no blankets are available, keep the cat cuddled against your chest inside your shirt.

FROSTBITE

SYMPTOMS: Scaling of the skin, loss of hair, pale white skin, leathery feel to the skin.

FIRST AID: Try to obtain veterinary care. If this is not possible, frostbitten parts of the cat's body should be thawed out thoroughly and efficiently, because the frozen parts have little blood circulation and gangrene can set in (see Gangrene, p. 249). Warm the frostbitten parts with warm water compresses for fifteen to twenty minutes. The temperature of the water should be about that of a baby bottle. In the recovery days, watch for gangrene (scabs and darkening of the skin) in the affected areas. If gangrene does develop, have your cat examined by your veterinarian—gangrene is a life-threatening condition.

GANGRENE

Gangrene is a condition in which the soft tissues of the skin die due to loss of blood supply. Severe frostbite can lead to such a condition.

FIRST AID: This is a veterinary emergency. Rush your cat to the nearest animal hospital.

HEATSTROKE

Cats do not tolerate high temperatures as well as humans do. When overheated, they utilize their respiratory system to cool down, inhaling cool air through the nose and exhaling hot air through the mouth. The faster they breathe, the more quickly they cool down. On a sweltering day there may simply not be enough cool air to effect this exchange. If a cat cannot effectively cool himself down, the excess body heat can result in a heatstroke.

CAUSES: The most frequent cause of heatstroke is leaving cats in cars on hot days or placing cats in traveling cages that are too small to accommodate them comfortably. Cats kept in overheated apartments or rooms with no ventilation or air conditioning also can suffer from heatstroke. And every once in a while a cat manages to get trapped in a clothes dryer in search of a warm place to take a catnap.

SYMPTOMS: Extreme panting, lethargy, staggering, sweating through the foot pads, excessive salivation, collapse, anxious expression on the face.

FIRST AID: In mild cases, simply relocate your cat to a cooler environment. If your cat is running a high temperature or is having difficulty standing upright, immerse her body in cool water. Be sure to shield her eyes. Keep cooling the cat until her temperature goes down. Other options include giving your cat an alcohol bath by soaking and rubbing her legs with rubbing alcohol. Rub a small amount of this alcohol on the body as well. (If your cat licks the alcohol, she will suffer no harm.) You can also apply ice packs all over the body and give your cat as much cold water as she wishes to drink. Vigorous massaging of the legs helps to increase blood flow and prevent shock.

INSECT STINGS

BEES, WASPS, AND YELLOW JACKETS

These and other insects are all capable of causing painful stings to your cat. Some especially foolhardy cats even invite trouble by attempting to catch bees in midflight.

While most insect stings are painful, they are usually harmless. However, if your cat is stung repeatedly, he could go into shock. Also, some cats experience an allergic reaction to insect venom, causing their airway passages to contract, and this can sometimes lead to cardiovascular problems and death.

SYMPTOMS: Swelling, usually around the face or legs; heat felt when the affected area is touched. If your cat is allergic to insect venom, symptoms may include: vomiting, diarrhea, swollen head and throat, possible shock.

FIRST AID: Use tweezers to remove the stinger at the point of entry to the skin. Pull stingers straight out. Make a paste of baking soda and lukewarm water and apply it to the sting. Use calamine lotion to relieve the itching. Ice packs generally relieve swelling and pain. If there are signs of shock, treat for it (see Shock, p. 251), and get immediate veterinary help.

SPIDERS

The bites of some species of spiders—like the brown recluse, black widow, or tarantula—cause toxic reactions in cats. Symptoms include sharp pain, followed by chills, fever, and labored breathing. Your cat may go into shock. Apply cold compresses, and consult your veterinarian.

INTESTINAL OBSTRUCTION

When a cat swallows a foreign object, the object can not only get stuck in the throat, but it sometimes lodges in the small intestine. When this happens, the intestinal blockage can be partial or complete.

The list of objects that can find their way down a cat's throat includes: pins, needles, rubber bands, feathers, and strings. Hair balls can also cause blockages.

The closer the blockage is to the stomach, the more acute the emergency. Sharp-edged objects are especially hazardous because they can puncture the intestine and cause peritonitis, a severe infection produced by leakage of gut contents into the abdomen. Foreign objects lodged in the small and large intestines can cause obstruction, constipation, or perforation.

SYMPTOMS: Acute vomiting, dehydration, lethargy, constipation; in later stages the abdomen becomes rigid to the touch and is extremely painful.

FIRST AID: None; get immediate veterinary attention.

PREVENTION: Do not allow your cat to play with string or with toys made of materials that he can tear apart. Be careful about giving your cat any toy that he can swallow. Hair balls can be prevented by giving your cat commercial hair ball preparations. Ask your veterinarian to recommend an effective product.

PARALYSIS

Paralysis usually begins in the rear legs. The animal drags himself, unable to walk.

CAUSES: This condition is generally

caused by disease, poison, blood clot, or an injury to the brain or spinal cord. Paralysis can also develop as a result of a slipped or ruptured disk. Tetanus or lockjaw (see Tetanus, p. 115) can also result in paralysis. Other contributing causes are injury to front leg nerves and tick infestation.

SYMPTOMS: Gradual onset of symptoms beginning with slight uncoordination in the rear legs; reluctance to move; an arched back, and pain when the back is touched. If nerves to the front legs are not severely damaged, the cat may be able to stand but staggers when he tries to take a step. In some cases, the nerves are only bruised, and the walking function will slowly return.

FIRST AID: Gently lift and transport the cat to an animal hospital.

RECTAL PROLAPSE (see p. 182)

SEIZURES (see CONVULSIONS, p. 244)

SHOCK

One of the most baffling and dangerous of all physiological phenomena is shock, or the lack of adequate blood to meet the body's needs. Shock can occur as a result of, or after, serious stress such as accidents or heart trouble. Scientists still do not fully understand its causes and function.

Shock can be fatal, which is why it is important for you to recognize some common symptoms. These include a drop in body temperature, shivering, lethargy, depression, weakness, cold legs and feet, pale and grayish gums, shallow and/or rapid breathing, thirst, vomiting, diarrhea.

Cats very often go into shock after falling from a great height or being struck by a car. The treatment for shock is as follows:

TECHNIQUE

1. First check to see if the cat is breathing and has a heartbeat; if not, undertake artificial respiration or heart massage immediately (pp. 235 and 236).

2. Put a blanket or a jacket under the cat if the ground is cold or damp. Make the animal comfortable, but do not force him to lie down—this may make breathing more difficult.

3. If the cat is unconscious, make certain his airways are clear of obstructions. Draw the tongue out and keep the head lower than the body.

4. Calm the cat. Speak soothingly to him.

5. Cover the cat lightly with a blanket.

6. Prepare to transport the animal to your veterinarian's office or to the nearest animal hospital.

SNAKEBITE

If your cat returns from his outdoor romp in the woods with a large swollen mass around his face, neck, or front legs, he may have been bitten by a snake.

INTERNAL BLEEDING

External bleeding may indicate that there is internal bleeding as well—a life-theatening emergency. You should familiarize yourself with the following symptoms and sources of internal bleeding and what they may suggest, as well as the accompanying first aid techniques.

BODY PART	CAUSES/SYMPTOMS	TREATMENT
The Eye	Can result from trauma to the head or eyeball.	See Eye Injuries, p. 246.
The Ear	Often seen after fights or car accidents. The bleeding may be from the earflap or from inside the ear.	Gently insert absorbent cotton through the ear opening into the ear canal—just enough to fill the ear. Consult with your veterinarian. If left untreated, such bleeding could develop into a serious middle-ear infection.
The Nose	Possible causes include a sharp blow, tumor, decayed tooth socket, foreign bodies in the nose, high blood pressure.	Sponge the nostrils dry with absorbent cotton. If you can see a foreign body, you may be able to remove it yourself with a pair of tweezers. Do not randomly poke around in your cat's nose, as the mucous membranes lining the nostrils can be easily damaged. If the cause of the nosebleed is not immediately evident, keep your cat as quiet as possible. Apply cold compresses to the bridge of the nose but do not pack the nostrils; this could cause your cat to sneeze and increase the bleeding. Most nosebleeds eventually subside on their own. This does not mean you should not be concerned. A nosebleed can be symptomatic of a disorder, and its cause should be determined by a veterinarian.

SYMPTOMS: A poisonous snakebite leaves two fang marks; the bite of a harmless snake will show tooth marks in the shape of a horseshoe, but no fang marks. Snakebite poisoning symptoms include intense pain in the area of bite, shortness of breath, vomiting, impaired vision, rapid swelling in bitten

BODY PART	CAUSES/SYMPTOMS	TREATMENT
The Mouth	May indicate a broken tooth, a broken jaw, a bitten tongue, or a cut gum. **Note:** Profuse bleeding usually stems from a bitten tongue, which is a serious injury. The tongue is moist and constantly in motion, which makes it difficult for a clot to form. A deep cut in the tongue can actually cause a cat to bleed to death.	If your cat has bitten his tongue—and if he will allow you to do so—hold the tongue in a cotton pad to reduce the bleeding while you take him to the veterinarian.
The Lungs	Indicated by vomiting of frothy blood. The froth is air mixed with blood.	Immediate veterinary attention is required.
The Lower Intestinal Tract	If a cat is bleeding bright-red blood from the rectum, he may be hemorrhaging from the lower intestinal tract.	Immediate veterinary attention is required.
The Stomach	If a cat is vomiting dark-red blood, he may be bleeding from the stomach. The blood is mixed with gastric juices, causing the darker-than-normal color.	Immediate veterinary attention is required.
The Upper Intestinal Tract	If a cat is bleeding dark brown or black blood, the hemmorhaging is coming from the upper intestinal tract. The blood is darker than normal because it is mixed with digestive juices.	Immediate veterinary attention is required.
The Urinary Tract	Blood in the urine can indicate bladder or kidney stones. In female cats, it can indicate tumors or cysts in the urethra or an infection of the uterus.	Immediate veterinary attention is required.

area, bleeding and oozing from the wound, dark bluish-purple discoloration in the area around the bite wound.

First Aid: Immediate first aid is the same as for humans. Apply a tourniquet between the bite wound and the heart. Do not tighten the tourniquet

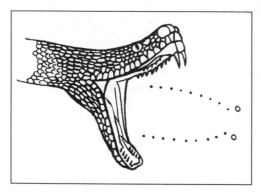

The bite of a poisonous snake leaves fang marks.

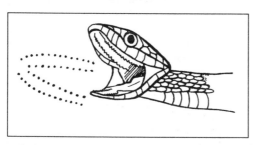

The bite of a nonpoisonous snake doesn't leave fang marks.

as much as you would to control bleeding, but keep it tight until a veterinarian sees your cat. Keep your cat quiet. Get veterinary help. Don't let the cat walk, as movement and exercise helps speed the flow of venom to the blood and lymph glands.

STROKE

Sometimes called *apoplexy*, a stroke is the sudden rupture or blockage of a blood vessel in the brain. While a cat of any age can suffer a stroke, they are more common in older animals.

SYMPTOMS: Sudden collapse, interference with bodily functions, partial to complete paralysis, walking in circles, droopy eyelids, flickering of eyes.

FIRST AID: There is none. Get immediate veterinary assistance.

UNCONSCIOUSNESS (COMA)

It is a shocking sight to come home and find your cat unconscious. Unconsciousness, or coma, has many causes, including heart attack as a result of circulatory failure, which causes the cat to faint. In addition, a stroke, poisoning, brain injury, or shock all can result in unconsciousness.

SYMPTOMS: Unconsciousness progresses in stages, from stupor and depression to complete loss of con-

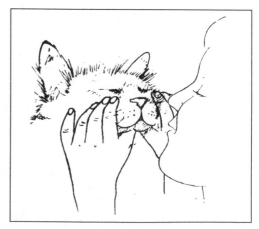

When aiding an unconscious cat, always check for breathing first.

sciousness. Coma accompanied by high fever is very dangerous.

FIRST AID: If your cat is unconscious, gently pull out his tongue and clear the airways. Wrap the cat in a blanket and transport him to the nearest animal hospital.

WOUNDS
(see CATFIGHTS, p. 242).

POISON CONTROL

Poisoning is one of the principal causes of pet deaths; in some locations it is second only to automobile accidents. It is important that you know something about how to counteract the effects of common poisons.

Any substance that can get into your cat's body and cause illness or death is considered a poison. Both indoor and outdoor cats are exposed to such toxins each day. These poisons include many common household items like sprays, paints, soaps, and medicines.

Cats can be poisoned by chewing, tasting, or even licking toxins such as excess flea and tick ointments from their skin. Cats also become poisoned by nibbling at poisonous weeds or plants or even scrounging in garbage pails.

Poisons can affect a cat suddenly if taken in large doses, or gradually if taken in small amounts. If poison has been ingested, some of the most visible signs may be excessive drooling, vomiting, pain, shivering, and impaired balance.

Fortunately, cats—unlike dogs—are finicky eaters. They do not bolt down everything in sight, and they have a marked distaste for spoiled food. The gastric acid in their stomachs is also quite effective in counteracting the bacteria that causes food poisoning. So food poisoning is not much of a problem for cats.

However, cats' compulsive cleanliness often brings them into contact with toxic chemicals. They will lick off any substance that gets on their coats. And, cats being curious creatures, they are likely to get into almost anything.

The outdoor cat is constantly in danger of poisoning. Plants, pesticides, fertilizers, even sidewalk salt can cause poisoning. After a winter outing, many a cat will lick the salt off her feet. If the cat swallows too much salt, she will suffer serious gastrointestinal upset.

Generally you will not see what your cat has ingested, and it may be hard to determine the specific poison from the symptoms alone. If you suspect that your cat has been poisoned follow the first-aid procedures listed on p. 256.

If, however, you see your cat ingest or come in contact with a known poison, take the cat to a veterinarian immediately and do not wait for symptoms to develop. If this is impossible, call the National Animal Poison Control Center at 1-900-680-0000 ($20.00 for five minutes).

Because many cases of cat poisoning result from ingesting poisonous houseplants or other household substances, you can do your cat and yourself a favor by practicing prevention. (Preventive techniques are listed on page 258.)

In addition to prevention, utilize caution. Do not overdo it, for example, when using flea and tick products. And be wary about giving medication to your cat. Aspirin may work wonders for people who are in pain, but it is toxic to cats.

GENERAL PROCEDURES

If your cat ingests acids, alkalis, or petroleum products *do not* induce vomiting. Without forcing your cat to do so, try to get her to drink as much milk or water as she will drink. This will help dilute the poison. For other types of poisons, your goals are as follows, but only if your cat is conscious:

1. Act with all haste, but don't panic. Get your cat to vomit so that the suspected poison can be eliminated from her stomach (see How to Induce Vomiting, p. 257). The more quickly the chemical is released from the stomach, the easier the treatment and the better the results.

2. Once the cat vomits, delay absorption of the poison by coating its stomach (see How to Prevent or Delay Absorption, below).

3. About thirty minutes after your cat vomits, administer a laxative to hasten elimination. One or two teaspoons of milk of magnesia will do nicely.

4. Get prompt veterinary help.

If your cat is unconscious, do nothing other than take her as quickly as possible to the nearest animal hospital.

HOW TO PREVENT OR DELAY ABSORPTION OF POISON

1. If your cat is conscious, and you know she hasn't ingested an acid, alkali, or kerosene, induce vomiting (see p. 257). Save the vomit and take it to the veterinarian to help determine the course of treatment.

2. Give one teaspoon of activated charcoal mixed with water per two pounds of body weight. Do not give charcoal if you have already administered syrup of ipecac—the two substances will counteract each other.

3. Half an hour later, give milk of magnesia or another coating product such as Kaopectate: one teaspoon per five pounds of body weight.

NOTE: Administer liquids slowly. Restrain your cat and pour the liquid down the side of the mouth, using an eyedropper or dosing syringe.

If your cat's skin or coat has come in

HOW TO INDUCE VOMITING (AND WHEN NOT TO)

Vomiting can be induced by giving your cat one teaspoon of a 3 percent hydrogen peroxide solution every ten minutes. One-fourth of a teaspoon of table salt placed at the back of the tongue or mixed in one tablespoon of water is also effective. Also good for inducing vomiting is syrup of ipecac: one teaspoon per ten pounds of body weight. If your cat doesn't vomit within thirty minutes, try it again. (Hydrogen peroxide is most effective.)

When your cat has finished vomiting, give her one heaping teaspoon of activated charcoal tablets (available in drugstores) dissolved in one ounce of water. Charcoal absorbs many poisons. Thirty minutes later, give your cat milk of magnesia or Kaopectate, one teaspoon per five pounds of body weight.

Do not induce vomiting if your cat has swallowed an acid or other corrosive. Symptoms of such poisons include sores on your cat's mouth, a swollen mouth or tongue, and burns around the mouth, lips, and tongue. In such a case, if your cat is conscious, encourage her to take in as much milk or water as she will drink to dilute the poison.

contact with a poisonous substance, wash the poison off using a lot of mild hand soap and water. Wear rubber gloves to avoid contaminating yourself. You may want to give your cat a complete bath using lukewarm water (see Bathing a Cat, pp. 68–69). Lather and rinse your cat's coat well, using mild hand soap or shampoo. Repeat the process until all traces of the toxic substance have been washed away.

NOTE: If your cat begins to show extreme anxiety or convulsions—symptoms of poisons such as strychnine, which affect the nervous system—it is in serious trouble. Rush your cat to your veterinarian or nearest animal clinic. Try to bring with you a sample of vomitus or, ideally, the poison itself.

FIRST AID FOR SPECIFIC POISONS

In the following guide, substances toxic to cats are divided into these categories:

Automotive Products
Food
Gardening Products
Household Cleaners
Insecticides
Medicines
Pesticides
Plants

PREVENTING POISONING

Minimalizing your cat's exposure to toxic agents is an important responsibility for any cat owner. Every room in the house—including the garage—spells potential trouble for your pet. Here are some commonsense measures you can take to help prevent accidental poisoning:

1. Keep medications out of reach, preferably in a locked cabinet.
2. Never store poisons in old food or drink containers. Your cat may think she has found food or water.
3. Check on the quality of any ceramic food or water dishes you use to make certain they do not leak lead when holding food.
4. Whenever possible, use nontoxic fertilizers and weed killers. If this is not possible, keep your cat off treated lawns until they have dried.
5. Keep poisonous plants out of your cat's reach.
6. If you use insecticides indoors, keep your cat out of the room until it has aired out and the poison has dried.
7. Keep pesticides out of your cat's reach.
8. Keep garbage cans tightly covered.

Remodeling Products
Miscellaneous

If you know the identity of the poison ingested by your cat, take the steps outlined here.

AUTOMOTIVE PRODUCTS

BATTERY ACID

SYMPTOMS: Abdominal pain, blood-stained vomit, shock; possibility of mouth, lip, and tongue burns.
FIRST AID: Administer a 5 percent sodium bicarbonate solution or milk of magnesia, one teaspoon per ten pounds of body weight. If nothing else is available, provide your cat with as much water or milk as she will drink. Treat for shock if necessary (see Shock, p. 251). Get veterinary help as soon as possible.

ANTIFREEZE

Cats love the sweet taste of deadly antifreeze. They will lap up the liquid spilled from the car radiators or get into open containers of this product.

SYMPTOMS: If a lot of antifreeze has been consumed, acute poisoning occurs. Signs are lethargy, staggering, coma, paralysis of hind legs, vomiting. Lesser amounts will produce signs of kidney damage, such as frequent voiding.

FIRST AID: Induce vomiting. Give milk of magnesia or Kaopectate to coat the stomach and intestines. Remove any antifreeze from the coat with lukewarm water and a mild soap; wrap your pet in a towel afterward. Get veterinary help.

MOTOR OIL

SYMPTOMS: Same as Antifreeze.

FIRST AID: Do not induce vomiting. Get prompt veterinary assistance.

GASOLINE

SYMPTOMS: Vomiting, difficulty in breathing, tremors, convulsions, coma.

FIRST AID: Do not induce vomiting. Give your cat one ounce of mineral oil, vegetable oil, or olive oil. In thirty minutes, give one teaspoon per ten pounds of body weight of milk of magnesia. Inhalation of gasoline fumes can lead to respiratory failure, so be ready to administer artificial respiration (see Artificial Respiration, p. 235).

FOOD

Because cats are such fastidious eaters, they usually avoid food poisoning. But some cats are scavengers and may not hesitate to poke their heads into the neighbor's garbage can and sample some spoiled foods.

If that food happens to be contaminated with salmonella or clostridium bacteria, a serious case of food poisoning for your pet can result (see Salmonella, p. 114).

SYMPTOMS: Initial signs are vomiting and stomach pain. In severe cases, blood-streaked diarrhea. Shock may develop. *Clostridium poisoning:* Partial to complete paralysis for a period of a few days to two or three weeks. The bacteria gives off a toxin that affects the nervous system. Constant nursing care is required.

FIRST AID: Induce vomiting. Give one teaspoon of milk of magnesia per five pounds of body weight. Observe for shock. Get prompt veterinary help.

GARDENING PRODUCTS

FERTILIZERS

SYMPTOMS: Difficulty breathing, blue tongue and mucous membranes, congested lungs.

FIRST AID: Give one ounce of mineral oil, olive oil, or vegetable oil by mouth. Get veterinary assistance.

WEED KILLERS

Most weed killers are toxic only if they are ingested in large amounts. Some can be absorbed through the skin. If your cat likes to nibble on grass, herbicides used to kill weeds can eventually build up in your cat's system and produce toxic symptoms. (Nontoxic weed killers are available at gardening stores.)

SYMPTOMS: Vomiting, pain, impaired balance, panting.

FIRST AID: Induce vomiting. Observe for shock. Get veterinary help.

HOUSEHOLD CLEANERS

TOILET-BOWL CLEANERS AND DRAIN UNCLOGGERS

Materials to keep your toilet bowl clean and bathroom drains free of grit can be harmful to cats who like to drink out of such fixtures.

SYMPTOMS: May include pain in the stomach and vomiting.

FIRST AID: Do not induce vomiting. These substances are corrosive, and vomiting will cause further damage. Give as much milk or water as your cat will drink. Observe for shock. Get immediate veterinary assistance.

FURNITURE POLISH

SYMPTOMS: Same as for Toilet-Bowl Cleaners.

FIRST AID: Do not induce vomiting. Give as much milk or water as your cat will drink to dilute the poison.

Observe for shock. Get prompt veterinary help.

LAUNDRY OR DISHWASHING DETERGENTS

Dishwashers, washing machines, and clothes dryers should be off limits to your cat, not only because of the danger of the cat falling into the machinery, but because residues of bleaches and detergents can get on cats' paws and coats. Cats will lick themselves clean of these toxic substances.

SYMPTOMS: May include vomiting, pain, lack of coordination.

FIRST AID: Induce vomiting. Wipe off as much of the material as possible with lukewarm water and mild soap. Observe for shock. Get prompt veterinary help.

PINE OIL CLEANER

SYMPTOMS: Same as for Detergents.

FIRST AID: Induce vomiting. Observe for shock. Get veterinary help.

INSECTICIDES

Insecticides are a growing hazard to both indoor and outdoor cats. We increasingly use insecticides to kill everything from mosquitoes to cockroaches. Roach traps, flypaper, bug sprays, and flea collars are all insecticide products. Even cats who have no direct contact with an insecticide can ingest toxins by eating dead bugs.

SYMPTOMS: Twitching of the mouth, convulsions, coma, collapse. Symptoms are the same for insecticides absorbed through the skin.

FIRST AID: Induce vomiting if insecticide is ingested. Observe for shock. Seek prompt veterinary attention. On the skin: Wash product off with mild soap and lukewarm water.

PYROPHOSPHATES

These are compounds usually used in flea and tick dips. A cat dipped for too long in such a compound can absorb this toxin.

SYMPTOMS: Excess salivation, dilated pupils, abdominal cramps, vomiting, diarrhea, muscle spasms, convulsions.

FIRST AID: Wash your cat's coat with mild soap and lukewarm water. Seek prompt veterinary aid.

MEDICINES

ANTIBIOTICS, AMPHETAMINES, ANTIHISTAMINES, BARBITURATES, TRANQUILIZERS

There is a huge veterinary pharmacopia for animals. Sometimes these pet medications are overused or abused. Or your cat may find an open bottle of your pills or other medication that is to her liking. Veterinarians are frequently summoned to aid a cat who has swallowed pills intended for her owner. Because cats are unusually sensitive to drugs or medications, any of these substances can create a medical emergency.

SYMPTOMS: May include vomiting, pain, impaired balance, convulsions, coma.

FIRST AID: Induce vomiting only if the animal is conscious; otherwise, she may choke on her own vomit. Give one teaspoon of milk of magnesia per five pounds of body weight.

ASPIRIN

Aspirin is extremely toxic to cats. One aspirin tablet a day for three or four days could result in poisoning and death. While some veterinarians recommend aspirin in small doses and on occasion, as a cat owner you should be aware that there is professional diversity of opinion about the use of aspirin for cats.

SYMPTOMS: Loss of appetite, depression, convulsions, vomiting, excess salivation, dehydration, staggering.

FIRST AID: If your cat has gotten into a bottle of aspirin, induce vomiting. Call your veterinarian.

PESTICIDES

Rat and mouse products are a common cause of poisoning in cats, who do not necessarily have to ingest such pesticides directly in order to become ill. If a cat eats a rodent or a squirrel that has been poisoned by a pesticide, the toxin will get into the cat's system.

ARSENIC

Arsenic, a swift cat killer, is an impurity found in chemicals used to make ant poisons, weed killers, and insecticides. It is also found in slug and snail bait.

SYMPTOMS: This poison is so quick-acting that there is often no time to observe symptoms. In small doses the signs are thirst, excessive drooling, vomiting, staggering, intense abdominal pain, cramps, diarrhea, paralysis, and death. The breath of a cat poisoned by arsenic smells like garlic.

FIRST AID: If your cat is conscious, induce vomiting. Get quick veterinary help. Your veterinarian has a specific antidote for arsenic poisoning.

STRYCHNINE

Most of those coated and color-dyed pellets used to poison mice and rats contain strychnine.

SYMPTOMS: Initial anxiety, restlessness, twitching of the muscles. These symptoms are followed swiftly by painful seizures during which the cat throws back her head and turns blue as a result of not being able to breathe. These convulsions are sporadic but become progressively more frequent until the slightest external stimulation—even a tiny noise or touch—will bring on another seizure.

FIRST AID: If your cat displays these symptoms but has not vomited, induce vomiting. If convulsions have begun, wrap the cat in a blanket until they subside. Seek prompt veterinary aid.

WARFARIN

Warfarin is one of the most common rat poisons today and a leading cause of cat and dog poisoning. It causes death by interfering with the blood-clotting mechanism and producing spontaneous bleeding.

SYMPTOMS: Blood in stools or urine, nosebleeds, hemorrhages beneath the gums and skin, fast and weak heart rate. In later stages, staggering, collapse, and death.

FIRST AID: Handle your cat gently, because any rough treatment will increase bleeding. Keep the cat warm and get veterinary assistance.

PLANTS

Cats are not big plant eaters. Occasionally, however, cats' curiosity or—in

Keep all plants toxic to cats out of your pet's reach.

the case of house cats—their craving for a little greenery will lead them to nibble on house and garden plants and weeds, some of which may be poisonous.

Symptoms of plant poisoning vary. In general, when a cat ingests some poisonous plant, signs include irritation of the mouth and skin, excessive drooling, abdominal pain, cramps, vomiting, and diarrhea.

Poisonous plants can also cause other symptoms, ranging from tremors to heart, respiratory, and kidney problems. In severe cases, some species can cause coma and even death.

REMODELING PRODUCTS

PAINT THINNER AND TURPENTINE

SYMPTOMS: **Paint thinner**: Burns around the mouth, lips, and gums. **Turpentine**: May include vomiting, difficulty in breathing, tremors, and convulsions.

FIRST AID: If on the skin, wash thoroughly with lukewarm water and mild detergent. Apply a mild baby oil. **If paint thinner is ingested**, give the cat as much milk or water as she will drink. Observe for shock and get veterinary help. **If turpentine is ingested**, induce vomiting. Observe for shock. When the cat has finished vomiting, give one heaping teaspoon of activated charcoal mixed in one ounce of water.

LEAD AND OIL POISONING

Cats can suffer lead poisoning by licking or chewing on wet paint or drinking water out of paint cans. Lead poisoning can also occur when cats feed from glazed pottery dishes that have not been sufficiently fired. Acid from food in these dishes can cause lead to seep in. Cats most often suffer from oil poisoning when oil-based paints are used, or if artists' oil paints are left around the house.

SYMPTOMS: In chronic cases of lead poisoning, bluish discoloration along the gum line. More acute symptoms are excessive drooling, vomiting, muscular spasms, fast breathing, convulsions. Cat will walk in circles with her head down, or go into a corner and hold her head against the wall. Oil poisoning victims exhibit similar symptoms, as well as difficulty in breathing and diarrhea.

FIRST AID: If left untreated, lead poisoning can be fatal. If the cat has eaten

PLANTS POISONOUS TO CATS

There are many potentially poisonous plants and shrubs—more than 700 types of plants in the Western hemisphere alone. Identification of all these species is not possible here, but a selected list of common plants that can be toxic follows:

TOXIC HOUSEPLANTS

SYMPTOMS: Some cats who eat these plants will exhibit no symptoms; others may drool, vomit, have diarrhea, swelling on side and around the mouth, or difficulty in breathing.

Amaryllis	Ivy
Asparagus fern	Japanese yew
Azalea	Lily of the valley (can be fatal)
Bird of paradise	Mistletoe (can be fatal)
Castor bean (can be fatal)	Needlepoint ivy
Cherry (Jerusalem and ordinary)	Ornamental yew
Creeping Charlie	Philodendron (can be fatal)
Crown of thorns	Poinsettia (leaves can be fatal)
Dieffenbachia (can be fatal)	Pot chrysanthemum
Easter lily (nontoxic in humans	Rhubarb
but often fatal in cats)	Ripple ivy
Elderberry	Spider chrysanthemum
Elephant ears	Sprangeri fern
Glocal ivy	Umbrella plant
Heart ivy	

FIRST AID: Induce vomiting, unless your cat is unconscious or having convulsions. Get immediate veterinary assistance.

substances containing lead within the previous half-hour, induce vomiting. Obtain prompt veterinary aid. For **oil-based paints**, induce vomiting and get veterinary help.

NOTE: If your cat gets paint on her fur or claws, *do not* use turpentine to remove it. Turpentine can severely burn a cat's skin and mouth. Use mild hand soap or shampoo.

TOXIC OUTDOOR PLANTS

SYMPTOMS: Unless otherwise noted, most of these plants cause vomiting, abdominal pain, cramps, and diarrhea.

American yew
Angel's trumpet
Apricot, almond
Arrowgrass (can be fatal)
Azalea
Bird of paradise
Bittersweet (the berries can be
   fatal)
Black locust
Buttercup
Cherry tree (foliage and bark can
   cause cyanide poisoning)
China berry (causes convulsions)
Corlara (causes convulsions)
Daffodil
Delphinium
Elderberry (can cause cyanide poi-
   soning)
English holly
English yew
Foxglove
Hemlock (can be fatal)
Jasmine

Jimsonweed (can be fatal)
Larkspur
Lily of the valley
Locoweed (can be fatal)
Lupine
Mescal bean
Mistletoe
Mock orange
Moonweed (causes convulsions)
Mushrooms and toadstools (cats
   like to eat them; can be fatal)
Peach tree (leaves and bark can
   cause cyanide poisoning)
Pokeweed
Privit
Rhododendron
Rhubarb (can cause convulsions
   and death)
Skunk cabbage
Soapberry
Spinach
Tomato vine
Wisteria

FIRST AID: Unless your cat is having convulsions, induce vomiting. Follow the procedures outlined at the beginning of this section to delay absorption and speed elimination. Get prompt veterinary assistance.

MISCELLANEOUS POISONS

GOLF BALLS

Some golf balls have liquid centers that are potentially toxic. If your cat chases after one of these balls and manages to pierce it with her teeth, problems can develop.

SYMPTOMS: May include vomiting, pain, impaired balance.

FIRST AID: Induce vomiting. Seek veterinary attention.

GLUES AND PASTES

SYMPTOMS: Discomfort in mouth, excessive drooling, smacking of lips.

FIRST AID: Induce vomiting. Give as much milk or water as your cat will drink. Get veterinary assistance.

KITCHEN MATCHES

Your cat or kitten may decide to make the acquaintance of your kitchen matches or matchbox. Matches contain potassium chlorate and phosphorus that, if ingested, can cause stomach irritation.

SYMPTOMS: Vomiting, diarrhea, cramps, pain in the abdomen.

FIRST AID: Induce vomiting. Consult your veterinarian if symptoms persist.

NAIL POLISH

SYMPTOMS: Vomiting, impaired balance, panting, convulsions, coma.

FIRST AID: Induce vomiting. Give your cat or kitten as much milk or water as she will drink. Give one teaspoon of activated charcoal mixed in one ounce of water. Get veterinary help.

SHAMPOO

SYMPTOMS: Same as in Nail Polish.

FIRST AID: Same as in Nail Polish.

SHOE POLISH

SYMPTOMS: Burns around the mouth, lips, and tongue.

FIRST AID: Do not induce vomiting. Give milk or water. Observe for shock. Obtain veterinary assistance.

SIDEWALK SALT

SYMPTOMS: Sore, swollen feet; vomiting; diarrhea.

FIRST AID: Give plenty of milk or water. Thoroughly wash pads. Ice packs can reduce swelling.

SKIN CREAMS AND OTHER COSMETICS

SYMPTOMS: May include vomiting, impaired balance, panting, convulsions, coma, slimy mouth.

FIRST AID: Induce vomiting. Give as much milk or water as cat will drink. Give one teaspoon of activated charcoal mixed in one ounce of water. Get veterinary help.

TALCUM POWDER

Studies have shown that infants who inhale or ingest talcum powder can suffer damage to internal organs. The same can hold true for cats.

SYMPTOMS: Same as in Skin Creams and Other Cosmetics.

FIRST AID: Same as in Skin Creams and Other Cosmetics.

RECORDING YOUR CAT'S HISTORY

NAME _____

SEX _____

DATE OF BIRTH _____

DATE OF ADOPTION _____

PLACE OF ADOPTION _____

BREED _____

PARENTS' NAMES AND BREEDS _____

_____

APPEARANCE

COAT COLOR _____

EYE COLOR _____

PHYSICAL DISTINCTIONS _____

NORMAL WEIGHT _____

TASTES

BELOVED FOODS _____

DESPISED FOODS _____

FAVORITE TOYS AND GAMES _____

FEARS _____

VACCINATIONS

	TYPE	*FIRST VACCINATION*	*BOOSTER*
DISTEMPER			
RABIES			
UPPER RESPIRATORY			
OTHERS			

MEDICAL

NAME OF VETERINARIAN _____

ADDRESS _____

PHONE NUMBER(S) _____

DATE OF ANNUAL CHECKUP _____

OTHER VISITS _____

SPECIAL CONDITIONS _____

FOOD ALLERGIES _____

ALLERGIES/SENSITIVITIES TO MEDICATIONS _____

INJURIES _____

RESOURCES

Adoption Information:
Defenders of Animal Rights, Inc.
P.O. Box 4786
Baltimore, Md. 21211

Allergy Information:
The Associated Humane Societies, Inc.
124 Evergreen Ave.
Newark, N.J. 07114

Animal Ambulances:
The Associated Humane Societies, Inc.
124 Evergreen Ave.
Newark, N.J. 07114

Animal-Assisted Therapy Programs:
San Francisco SPCA
2500 16th St.
San Francisco, Ca. 94103

The Humane Society of New York
306 E. 59th St.
New York, N.Y. 10022

The Chicago Anti-Cruelty Society
157 W. Grand Ave.
Chicago, Il. 60610

Anti-Cruelty Societies:
The American Society for the Prevention
of Cruelty to Animals
442 E. 92nd St.
New York, N.Y. 10028

Associations:
American Animal Hospital Association
P.O. Box 150899
Denver, Co. 80215

American Cat Association, Inc.
10065 Foothill Blvd.
Lake View Terrace, Ca. 91342

International Cat Association
211 East Olive St., 201
Burbank, Ca. 91502

United Cat Federation, Inc.
6621 Thornwood St.
San Diego, Ca. 92111

Attorneys:
Animal Legal Defense Fund
333 Market St.
San Francisco, Ca. 94105

Animal Behaviorists:
Animal Behavior Therapy Clinic
Animal Medical Center of New York
510 E. 62nd St.
New York, N.Y. 10021

Breed Clubs:
The American Dog and Cat Breeders
Association and Referral Service
33222 N. Fairfield Rd.
Round Lake, Il. 60073

Cemeteries:
Bide-A-Wee Pet Memorial Parks
Wantagh & Beltagh Avenues
Wantagh, N.Y. 11793

Los Angeles SPCA
Pet Memorial Park
5068 North Old Scandia Lane
Calabasas, Ca. 91802

Crematories:
Marble Hill Crematory for Pet Animals, Inc.
418 W. 219th St.
New York, N.Y. 10034

Death of a Pet: Free brochure from
The American Animal Hospital Association
P.O. Box 150899
Denver, Co. 80215-0899

American Veterinary Medical Association
930 N. Meacham Rd.
Schaumburg, Il. 60196

Euthanasia: Free brochure from
American Veterinary Medical Association
930 N. Meacham Rd.
Schaumburg, Il. 60196

Geriatric Cats: Free brochure from
The Carnation Research Center
5045 Wilshire Blvd.
Los Angeles, Ca. 90036

Health Information:
The American Animal Hospital Association
P.O. Box 150899
Denver, Co. 80215-0899

Animal Health and Nutrition Council
P.O. Box 184
Pennsauken, N.J. 08110

Hospitals:
The American Animal Hospital Association
P.O. Box 150899
Denver, Co. 80215-0899

Animal Medical Center
510 E. 62nd St.
New York, N.Y. 10021

Angell Memorial Animal Hospital
180 Longwood Ave.
Boston, Ma. 02115

Grand Avenue Pet Hospital
1602 N. Grand Ave.
Santa Ana, Ca. 92702

Hotlines:
Animal Rescue League
(617) 426-9170

Nationwide Health Line
(212) 895-5175

Toxicology Hotline
(217) 333-3611

Tree House Animal Foundation
(312) 784-5480

Housing Discrimination:
Humane Society of the United States
2100 L St., N.W.
Washington, D.C. 20037

Immunization: Free brochure from
American Veterinary Medical Association
930 N. Meacham Rd.
Schaumburg, Il. 60196

Legislative Groups:
United Action for Animals
205 E. 42nd St.
New York, N.Y. 10011

Society for Animal Protective Legislation
P.O. Box 3719
Georgetown Station
Washington, D.C. 20007

Loss Counselors:
Carole C. Wilbourn
The Cat Practice
230 W. 13th St.
New York, N.Y. 10011

Jamie Quackenbush
Center for the Interaction of Animals and
Society
University of Pennsylvania
Philadelphia, Pa. 19104

Natural Cat Food: Free brochure from
Veterinary Nutritional Associates, Inc.
229 Wall St.
Huntington, NY 11743

Registries National:
American Cat Association
10065 Foothill Blvd.
Lake View Terrace, Ca. 91342

American Cat Fanciers Association, Inc.
P.O. Box 203
Point Lookout, Mo. 65726

Cat Fanciers Association, Inc.
1309 Allaire Ave.
Ocean, N.J. 07712

Publications:
Animals Magazine
350 South Huntington Ave.
Boston, Ma. 02130

The Cat Fanciers' Almanac
1309 Allaire Ave.
Ocean, N.J. 07712

Cat Fancy Magazine
P.O. Box 2431
Boulder, Co. 80321

Cats Magazine
P.O. Box 83048
Lincoln, Ne. 68501

CFA Yearbook
1309 Allaire Ave
Ocean, N.J. 07712

**Spaying and Neutering Clinics, Low
Cost:**   Nationwide listing provided by
Friends of Animals
1 Pine St.
Neptune, N.J. 07753

Veterinarian, Selecting:
American Animal Hospital Association
P.O. Box 105899
Denver, Co. 80215-0899

INDEX

Page numbers in *italics* refer to illustrations.

AAHA (American Animal Hospital Association), vii, 59
abdomen, distended, 55
abdominal pain, 238, *238*
abscesses, 148–149
Abyssinian, 9, 11–12
acne, 149–150
aggressiveness, 32–33
    as behavior problem, 42–43
aging, 95–98
    accident-proofing efforts and, 97
    dental health and, 96, 98, 140
    diet and, 97–98
    hearing loss and, 96, 127
    litter box problems and, 41, 96
    process of, *95*, 96–97
    vision problems and, 96, 132
AIDS, 117
airplane travel, 73
allergic bronchitis (asthma), 160
allergic reactions, 149
    bronchial, 160
    of cat owners, 51
    contact dermatitis, 149, *149*
    emergency first aid for, 238
    to flea saliva, 155, *155*, 156
to foods, 144, 149, 180, 238
hypersensitivity reactions, 238
nasal, 144
pulmonary edema as, 163
of skin, 149, *149*, 156–157
American Animal Hospital Association (AAHA), vii, 59
American Humane Association, 76
American Shorthair, 6, 11, 12, 13, 14
American Wirehair, 11, 12
amino acids, 62
amputation:
    accidental, 239
    adjustment to, 93
anal problems, 55, *55*, 180–182
anal sacs, 29, 30, 181
ancylostoma (hookworms), 183, 184, *184*, 226
anemia, 173, 228
    feline infectious (FIA), 113–114, 172
anger, body and facial expressions of, 24–25, *25*, 27–28, *28*
"Animal-Assisted Therapy" programs, 52
animal shelters, 49, 50
animal welfare groups, 77
Ankara cats (Turkish Angora), 6, 10–11

antibiotics, 113
antifreeze, ingestion of, 258–259
aortic thrombosis, 172
apoplexy, 254
appetite:
  weather changes and, 35
  see also eating
arsenic, 262
arthritis, 167, 169
artificial respiration, 235, *235*
ascarids (roundworms), 111, 183,
  184–185, *184*, 226
ascites, 188
ash, 63, 64, 65
asphyxiation, 239
aspirin, 261
asthma (allergic bronchitis), 160
attack, body language for, 26, *26*
auditory ossicles, 126
auto accidents, 239–240
automotive products, poisonous, 258–259
auto travel, 72–73, 188
awareness, sensory, 23
AZT, 117
Aztecs, 5

bacteria, 112–113
bacterial diseases, 112–115
bacterial skin infections, 149–150
bad breath (halitosis), 138–139, 140
balance, sense of, 126
balanoposthitis, 199–200
balding, 156
Balinese, 6, 7
bandaging techniques, 86–87, *87*
Bast (Bastet), 4
bathing, 68, 69, *69*, 158
  see also grooming
beds, 55–56
bee stings, 249–250
behavior, 21–43
  body language and, 24–27
  facial expressions and, 27–28
  problematic types of, 37–43
  social, 30–37
bereavement, 100–101
beta-hemolytic streptococcus, 227
Birman, 6, 7–8

birth control, 201–202
birth process, 203, 206–210, *207, 208,*
  214
biting, 42
Bitter Apple Jelly, 38
bladder infection (cystitis), 41, 193,
  194
bladder stones (urinary calculi), 63, 194
bleeding:
  external, 237, *237,* 242–243
  internal, 252–253
blepharitis (irritated eyelids), 135–136
blindness, 131, 134, *134*
bloat, 240
blocked bowel, 186, 250
blood:
  clots, 172, 174
  physiology of, 171–172
  in stool, 181
boarding facilities, 74
body language, 24–28
  for anger, 24–25, *25*
  for attack, 26, *26,* 32
  for contentment, 24
  defensive, 25–26, *25,* 32
  for desire, 26–27, *27*
  for fright, 24–25, *25*
  illness conveyed by, 26
"Body of Liberties, The," 77
body temperature:
  fever levels for, 112, 178
  regulation of, 176
  taking of, 82–83, *83*
Bombay, 11, 13
bone development, 165–166
bone infection (osteomyelitis), 167
bones, chewing on, 71, 139
bowel, blocked, 186, 250
brain function, 175–176
brain infection (encephalitis), 176, 178
breast cancer, 202
breasts, inflammation of, 212
breathing:
  abnormal, 160
  see also respiratory system
breeders, 49–50, 52
breeding, 96, 202–205
  see also mating

breeds, 5–19
  Abyssinian, 9, 11–12
  American Shorthair, 6, 11, 12, 13, 14
  American Wirehair, 11, 12
  Balinese, 6, 7
  Birman, 6, 7–8
  Bombay, 11, 13
  British Shorthair, 6, 11, 13
  Burmese, 11, 13–14, 19
  cat purchase and, 48–49
  Colorpoint Shorthair, 11, 14
  Cornish Rex, 11, 14–15
  Cymric, 7
  Devon Rex, 11, 14–15
  Egyptian Mau, 11, 15
  established, 11
  Exotic Shorthair, 11, 15–16
  five basic categories of, 6
  Havana Brown, 11, 161
  Himalayan, 6–7, 9
  hybrid, 11, 13
  Japanese Bobtail, 11, 16
  Javanese, 7
  Kashmir, 6–7, 9
  Korat, 11, 17
  long-haired, 6–11
  Maine Coon, 6, 8–9
  Manx, 11, 17
  mutations, 11, 12
  natural, 11
  Norwegian Forest cat, 7
  number of, 5–6
  Oriental Shorthair, 6, 11, 17–18
  Persian, 6–7, 9, 12, 71
  Ragdoll, 7
  Russian Blue, 11, 18
  Scottish Fold, 11, 18
  short-haired, 11–19
  Siamese, 7, 11, 14, 16, 18–19, 204
  Somali, 6, 9–10
  tail-less, 17
  Tiffany, 7
  Tonkinese, 11, 19
  Turkish Angora, 6, 10–11
British Shorthair, 6, 11, 13
bronchitis, 160–161, *161*
bruises, 151

brushing, 67–68, *69*, 158, 226
  see also grooming
bulging eye (exophthalmos), 131, *131*
bunting, 30
burial, 99–100
Burmese, 11, 13–14, 19
burns, 240–242
bursitis, 169

calcium, 165–166, 169, 213, 215
calici virus, feline (FCV), 121
camping, 74
cancer, 195–197
  aging process and, 96
  of breast, 202
  feline leukemia, 112, 114, 117–119, 136, 137, 162, 172, 197
canned food, 64–65
carbohydrates, 62–63
cardiopulmonary resuscitation (CPR), 235–236, *236*
carpal hair, 158
carriers, 71–72
car travel, 72–73, 188
cataracts, 131–132, *132*
Cat Fanciers' Association (CFA), 6–7
catfights, 31, 32–33, 34, 242
Catholic Church, 5
catnip, 144
cat owners:
  allergy problems of, 51
  children as, 52–53, 66
  choice of pet for, 48–53
  death of, 101
  expenses of, 48
  grieving process of, 100–101
  grooming by, 51, 67–68, 158, 224–225, 226
  handling methods used by, 67, *67*, 232–235, *234*
  home-nursing techniques used by, 81–93
  household moves by, 76
  lost cats and, 75–76
  name response taught by, 58
  pet health insurance for, 78
  preparation of home by, 53–58
  redecorating disruptions and, 76–77

cat owners *(continued)*
 responsibility of, 47–48
 socialization aided by, 58–59
cat repellent, 42
cats:
 aging process of, 95–98
 ancestry of, 3–5
 basic care for, 61–78
 behavior of, 21–43
 breeds of, 5–19
 cult worship of, 4, 5
 death of, 99–101
 disabled, 93, 126, 131
 disruptive home events and, 76–77
 dogs in home with, 52
 domestication of, 4
 essential supplies needed for, 55–57
 fights between, 31, 32–33, 34, 242
 indoor, 31, 42–43, 58, 66
 longevity of, 95
 lost, 75–76
 male vs. female, *see* female cats; male cats
 new home adjustments for, 58–59
 outdoor, 30, 31–32, 58, 96
 owner's allergies and, 51
 pedigree, 5–6; *see also* breeds
 traveling with, 71–74
 wild, 30, 33
 working, 12
Cats, 49
cats, purchase or adoption of:
 health check for, 53, 54–55, *54, 55*
 home preparation for, 53–59
 other house pets and, 51–52, 57
 sources for, 49–51
cat scratch disease (CSD), 113
cat shows, 49
cerebrovascular disease, 178
cestodes (tapeworms), 152, 183,
  185–186, *185,* 226
CFA (Cat Fanciers' Association), 6–7
chemical burns, 241
chest wounds, 242–243
chewing, 225
chiggers, 151
children, cats' relations with, 52–53, 66
chilling of kittens, 228–229
chlamydia psittaci, 133

Chloromycetin, 114
choking, 243–244, *244*
chronic bronchitis, 161
circulatory system, 171–174
claws:
 grooming of, 39, 70, 224–225, 226
 physiology of, 148
 removing of, 39–40
 scratching and, 39, *39,* 56, 113, 225
clostridium poisoning, 259
Clostridium tetani, 115
coccidia, 183
coccidiosis, 123
cochlea, 126
cold exposure (hypothermia), 248
colds, 161
colitis, 186–187
collars:
 Elizabethan, 88, *88*
 flea problems and, 153, *155*
 identification tags for, 72
 resistance to, 73
color blindness, 130
Colorpoint Shorthair, 11, 14
colostrum, 218
coma (unconsciousness), 176, 254–255, *254*
communication, 23–30
 body language for, 24–27
 facial expressions for, 27–28
 smell used in, 29–30
 by touch, 28–29
 vocalization in, 28, 29
conjunctivitis (pinkeye), 132–133, *133,*
  136
constipation, 98, 181–182
contentment, body and facial expressions
  of, 24, 27, *27*
convulsions, 176–177, 244
cornea, 130
corneal disorders, 133–134, *134*
Cornish Rex, 11, 14–15
Cort, organ of, 126
cosmetics, ingestion of, 265
coughs, 161–162
CPR (cardiopulmonary resuscitation),
  235–236, *236*
cracked pads, 167–168
cremation, 99–100

cryosurgery, 196–197
cryptococcosis, 122
cryptococcus, 162
CSD (cat scratch disease), 113
Cymric, 7
cystitis (bladder infection), 41, 193, 194
cysts, 122, 157, 214
cytauxzoonosis, feline, 123

dandruff, 158
deafness, 126
death, 99–101
declawing, 39–40
defensiveness, body language of,
     25–26, 25, 32
dehydration, 136
dental health, 137
     abscesses and, 139, 140
     bone chewing and, 71, 139
     cleaning procedures for, 71, 138, 140
     dry food for, 64, 71, 138
     in general health check, 54, 55
     gingivitis and, 138, 140, 141–142, 141
     of kittens, 54, 55, 218, 219, 221, 225,
          226
     of older cats, 96, 98, 140
     periodontal disease and, 138, 140
     tooth decay and, 138
depression, 88–89
desire, body language for, 26–27, 27
Devon Rex, 11, 14–15
diabetes, 98, 188–189, 189
diarrhea, 55, 180
dietary requirements, 62–66
     see also eating
digestive system, physiology of, 179–180,
     180, 186, 187–188
digestive system problems, 180–189
     anal, 180–182
     of intestinal tract, 186–187
     in liver, 187–188
     in mouth, 138–142, 137, 253
     pancreatic, 188–189
     parasites, 183–186
Dinictis, 4
Dirofilaria immitis (heartworm), 174
disabled cats, adjustments made by, 93,
     126, 131

disc, herniated, 177
dishwashing detergents, ingestion of, 260
dislocated joint, 168
distemper, 59, 79, 80, 119
dogs:
     cats' relationships with, 52
     history of, 3, 4
dreams, 37
drowning, 244–245
drug toxicity, 178
dry food, 64, 71, 138

ear problems:
     bandaging procedures used for, 87
     deafness, 126
     foreign bodies in, 127–128
     fungal infections, 128
     hematoma, 128, 128
     injuries, 87, 252
     medication procedures for, 92, 92
     mite infestations and, 54, 70, 127, 127
     of older cats, 96, 127
     otitis, 128–129
     sunburn, 129–130
     of white cats, 126, 129
ears:
     balance abilities and, 126
     cleaning of, 70–71, 70
     health check for, 54
     physiology of, 125–126, 125
eating, 61–66
     aging process and, 97–98
     allergic reactions and, 144, 149, 180, 238
     dental health concerns and, 64, 71, 138
     dishes for, 56
     evolutionary behavior in, 61–62
     finicky behavior in, 66
     flatulence due to, 182–183
     food intake quantities and, 62, 65,
          217–218, 220–221, 223
     food refusal and, 66
     food temperature for, 65, 66
     force-feeding techniques and, 89–90, 90
     frequency of, 65
     hand-feeding and, 222–223, 222
     illness and, 89–90
     kitten's dietary needs and, 65, 217–218,
          220–221, 222–224

eating *(continued)*
   nutritional requirements and, 62–64,
     165–166, 169
   obesity problems and, 65, 66, 203
   predatory behavior and, 61–62
   pregnancy and, 65, 205
   quiet atmosphere for, 66
   sleep after, 38
   of snacks, 65–66
   as social behavior, 35
   of special diets, 65
   of table scraps, 62
   three types of cat food, 64–65
   in travel situations, 72, 73
   variety in, 62, 65
   weather changes and, 35
eclampsia (milk fever), 213
Egypt, cat cult in, 4, 11
Egyptian Mau, 11, 15
elbow fractures, 247
elderly, feline companions for, 52,
   100–101
elderly cats, *see* aging
electrical burns, 241–242
electrical cords, cats attracted by, 38, 78
electric shock, 163, 245–246
Elizabethan collars, 88, *88*
emergencies, common types of, 231,
   238–255; *see also specific emergencies*
emergency procedures, 231, 232–237
   for control of bleeding, 237, *237,*
     242–243
   for handling of injured cat, 232–235,
     234
   resuscitation, 235–237, *235, 236*
encephalitis (brain infection), 176, 178
endocrine alopecia, feline, 157
endocrine system, 175
enteritis, 186–187
epiglottis, 137, *137,* 145–146
epilepsy, 176–177
epiphora (watery eye), 134
essential fatty acids, 62
estrus (heat), 33–34, 202, 203–204, *203*
euthanasia, 99
exercise needs:
   illness and, 89
   for indoor cats, 66

   for older cats, 98
   for pregnant cats, 205
exophthalmos (bulging eye), 131, *131*
Exotic Shorthair, 11, 15–16
eyelids:
   folded, 134–135
   irritated, 135–136
   ringworm check for, 54
   third (nictitating membrane), 130,
     136
eye problems, 131–137
   abrasions, 133
   blindness, 131, 134, *134*
   bulging eye, 131, *131*
   cataracts, 131–132, *132*
   conjunctivitis, 132–133, *133,* 136
   corneal disorders, 133–134, *134*
   dark stains in corners, 134
   eyelid irritation, 135–136
   folded eyelid, 134–135
   foreign object in eye, 135
   glaucoma, 135, 137
   injuries, 246, 252
   keratitis, 131, 133–134
   medication procedures for, 92, *92*
   retinal diseases, 136
   subjunctival hemorrhage, 136
   sunken eye, 136
   ulcers, 134, *134*
   uveitis, 131, 136–137
   watery eye, 134
   wound bandaging method for, 87, *87*
eyes:
   cleaning of, 71
   health check for, 54
   physiology of, 130–131, *130,* 133, 136

facial expressions, 27–28
fading kitten syndrome (feline herpes
   virus), 229
false pregnancy, 213–214
fats, dietary, 63, 64
feeding, *see* eating
feeding dishes, 56
feet, *see* foot
feline calici virus (FCV), 121
feline cytauxzoonosis, 123
feline endocrine alopecia, 157

feline herpes virus (fading kitten syndrome), 229
feline immunodeficiency virus (FIV), 117
feline infectious anemia (FIA), 113–114, 172
feline infectious peritonitis (FIP), 116–117, 137, 162
feline leukemia virus (FeLV), 112, 117–118, 137, 162, 197
feline panleukopenia (FPL), 112, 118–120
feline urological syndrome (FUS), 191
feline viral rhinotracheitis (FVR), 121
Felis catus, 3
Felis lyhica, 4
FeLV (feline leukemia virus), 112, 117–118, 136, 162, 197
female cats, 201–215
    aging process and, 96
    birth process and, 206–210, *207, 208*
    breeding of, 96, 202–205
    in heat, 33–34, 202, 203–204, *203*
    maternal behavior of, 210–213, 217–220, 221
    mating behavior of, 33–35, *34,* 202, 203–205
    postpartum problems of, 211–213
    pregnancy and, 65, 119, 205–206, 213–214
    reproductive problems in, 96, 213–215
    in social order, 30–31
    spaying of, 33, 48, 201–202
feral (wild) cats, 30, 33
fertilizers, ingestion of, 259
fever, 112, 178
FIA (feline infectious anemia), 113–114, 172
fights:
    combative behavior in, 32–33
    over females in heat, 34
    injuries from, 242
    over male social order, 31
FIP (feline infectious peritonitis), 116–117, 137, 162
first-aid guide, 231–267
    for common emergencies, 231, 238–255; *see also specific emergencies*
    for control of bleeding, 237, *237,* 242–243
    to emergency procedures, 231, 232–237
    for handling of injured cat, 232–235, *234*
    for poison control, 251–267
    for resuscitation, 235–237, *235, 236*
first-aid kit, supplies for, 82, 84–85
fits, 176–177, 244
FIV (feline immunodeficiency virus), 117
flatulence, 182–183
flea allergy dermatitis, 155, *155*
fleas, 111, 151–153, *152, 157*
flies, 156
flower vases, drinking from, 63–64
folded eyelids, 134–135
follicular conjunctivitis, 133
food:
    allergies to, 144, 149, 180, 238
    nutritional requirements for, 62–64, 165–166, 169, 223–224
    types of, 64–65
    see also eating
food poisoning, 259
foot:
    bandaging procedure for, 86, *87*
    claw grooming and, 39, 70, 224–225, 226
    cracked pads on, 167–168
    declawing of, 39–40
    foreign objects in, 168
    fractures of, 247, *247*
    physiology of, 148
    swollen, 169
force-feeding technique, 89–90, *90*
foreign objects:
    in ear, 127–128
    in eye, 135
    in mouth, 139
    in paw, 168
    swallowed, 146
FPL (feline panleukopenia), 112, 118–120
fractures, 246–248, *247*
fright, body and facial expressions of, 24–25, *25,* 28, *28*
frostbite, 248
fungal infections, 122–123, 128, 156–157
fur, 55, 147–148, *147,* 158
    brushing of, 67–68, *69,* 158, 226

furniture polish, ingestion of, 260
FUS (feline urological syndrome), 191
FVR (feline viral rhinotracheitis), 121

Gaines Professional Services, 73
gangrene, 249
gardening products, poisonous, 259–260
gasoline, ingestion of, 259
gastritis (upset stomach), 187
gastrointestinal tuberculosis, 115
genital tract, female, *see* female cats
genital tract, male, 199–200
gestation period, 205
giardia, 183
gingivitis, 138, 140, 141–142, *141*
glaucoma, 135, 137
glossitis, 143
glue, ingestion of, 266
glycogen, 63
golf balls, toxic materials in, 265–266
grass-eating, 187
grief, 100–101
grooming:
    bathing, 68, 69, *69,* 158
    brushing, 67–68, *69,* 158, 226
    cat owner's responsibility for, 51
    cat's procedures for, 36
    of claws, 39, 70, 224–225, 226
    dental care, 71, 138
    ear cleaning, 70–71, *70*
    eye cleaning, 71
    hairballs and, 67, 186
    of kittens, 219–220, 224–225, 226
    mutual, 28, 36–37, *36*
    of older cats, 96
    pregnancy and, 206
    professional services for, 69–70
gum care, 64, 71
gums, problems with, 140–142, *141*

hair, 55, 147–148, *147,* 158
    brushing of, 67–68, *69,* 158, 226
hairballs, 67, 181–182, 186
halitosis (bad breath), 138–139, 140
handling procedures, 67, *67,* 232–235, *234*
harnesses, 72, 73
Havana Brown, 11, 16
Hayes, Mrs. Rutherford B., 18

head and neck problems, 125–146
    ears, 125–130
    eyes, 130–137
    head injuries, 176, *176*
    head mange, 135, 154
    injuries, 176, *176*
    mouth, 137–142
    nose, 143–145
    throat, 145–146
    tongue, 142–143
health care, preventive, 77–78
health insurance, 78
hearing, 125–126
    see also ear problems
heart, physiology of, 171, *171*
heart massage, 236, *236*
heart problems, 98, 160, 162, 163,
    172–174
heartworm (*Dirofilaria immitis*), 174
heat (estrus), 33–34, 202, 203–204, *203*
heating pads, 89
heatstroke, 249
hematoma, 128, *128*
Hemobartonella felis, 113
hemorrhoids, 182
herniated disc, 177
herpes virus, 120, 122
herpes virus, feline (fading kitten syn-
    drome), 229
Himalayan, 6–7, 9
hip dysplasia, 168
HIV, 117
hives, 156–157
home-nursing techniques, 81–93
    for administration of medicine, 90–93,
    91, 92
    for bandaging, 86–87
    first aid kit for, 82, 84–85
    force-feeding, 89–90, *90*
    protective collar construction, 88
    restraint measures for, 85–86, *86*
    sick room atmosphere and, 89
    after surgery, 93
    for taking pulse, 83–84, *83*
    for thermometer use, 82–83, *83*
    for urine samples, 84–85
    for warming of cat bed, 89
home safety, 78, 97

hookworms (ancylostoma), 183, 184, *184,* 226

hormonal skin disorders, 157

hormonal system, 175, 176, 203, 214

hotels, cats admitted in, 72–73

hot water bottles, 89

household cleaners, poisonous, 260

household moves, 76

houseplants, 40

humane societies:
   animal-assisted therapy programs of, 52
   animal shelters operated by, 50
   pets for elderly from, 52

Humane Society of the United States, 77

hunting behavior:
   eating habits and, 61–62
   facial expression and, 28
   in kittens, 22, *23*
   mouse catching and, 62

hybrid breeds, 11, 13

hydrocephalus, 177

hydrogen peroxide, 85

hypothermia (cold exposure), 248

illness:
   body signals for, 26
   house veterinary calls for, 81
   signs of, 81
   see also specific health problems

immune system, 111–112, 113
   of kittens, 58, 112, 113, 218, 222

immunization, *see* vaccinations

immunodeficiency virus, feline (FIV), 117

immunotherapy, 197

impetigo, 227

incubators, 223

indoor cats:
   on camping vacations, 74
   exercise needs of, 66
   problem behavior between, 42–43
   social order for, 31
   special needs of, 58
   territorial behavior of, 31

infectious anemia, feline (FIA), 113–114, 172

infectious diseases, 111–123
   bacterial diseases, 112–115
   cat scratch disease (CSD), 113

coccidiosis, 123

cryptococcosis, 122

feline cytauxzoonosis, 123

feline immunodeficiency virus, 117

feline infectious anemia, 113–114, 172

feline infectious peritonitis, 116–117, 137, 162

feline leukemia virus, 112, 117–118, 136, 162, 197

feline panleukopenia, 112, 118–120

fever and, 112

fungal diseases, 122–123, 128

human susceptibility to, 111, 113, 114, 118, 123

immune system and, 111–112

nocardiosis, 122

protozoan diseases, 123–124

pseudorabies, 120, *120*

salmonella, 114, 259

tetanus, 115

toxoplasmosis, 111, 123, 137

tuberculosis, 111, 115

upper respiratory, 79, 80, 121–122

viral diseases, 111, 116–122

infertility, 199, 200, 214

injuries, handling procedures and, 232–235, *234*

inner ear, 126

insecticides, poisonous, 260–261

insect stings, 163, 249–250

intelligence, 22–23, 175

internal bleeding, 252–253

intestinal parasites, 55, 152, 183–186

intestinal tract disorders, 123, 186–187, 250, 253

ipecac, syrup of, 85

Japanese Bobtail (Mi-Kee), 11, 16

jaundice, 188

Javanese, 7

jaw, fractures of, 247

joints:
   dislocation of, 168
   swollen, 169
   see also musculoskeletal system

Kaopectate, 85

Kashmir, 6–7, 9

kennels, boarding facilities at, 74
keratin, 148
keratitis, 131, 133–134
kidney problems, 98, 193–194, *193*
kitchen matches, ingestion of, 266
kitten mortality complex, 116
kittens:
    adoption of, 51, 53, 54–55, *54, 55*
    bathing discouraged for, 69
    birth process for, 206, 207–211
    caring for, 217–229
    developmental stages for, 218, 219,
        225–226
    dietary needs of, 65, 217–218,
        220–221, 222–224
    foster parenting of, 218, 221–224, *222*
    frequency of meals for, 65
    general health check for, 54–55, *54, 55*
    grooming of, 219–220, 226
    hand-feeding of, 222–223, *222*
    human interaction with, 219
    hunting skills taught to, 22, *23*
    illnesses of, 116, 226–229
    immune systems of, 58, 112, 113, 218,
        222
    maternal care of, 210–213, 217–220,
        221
    mother separated from, 220
    newborns, 210–213, 217–219, *217*
    optimal room temperature for, 206,
        218, 223
    as outdoor cats, 58
    ownership responsibility for, 51
    play behavior among, 36, 225
    rejection of, 218, 221, 227
    teeth of, 54, *55,* 218, 219, 221, 225,
        226
    toilet training of, 221
    vaccinations for, 60, 79, 80
    veterinary care for, 60
    washing abilities of, 37
    weaning of, 218, 219, 220–221, 223
kitty litter, 56
knee, fractures of, 247
kneecap, slipped (patellar dislocation),
    169–170
Korat, 11, 17
Kübler-Ross, Elisabeth, 100

labor, 206–210, *207, 208*
lameness, 168
landlords, 77
laryngitis, 146
laundry detergents, ingestion of, 260
lead poisoning, 263–264
leashes, 72, 73, 74
legal issues, 77
leg wounds, bandaging techniques for, 87
leukemia, 114, 118–119, 137, 162, 172,
    197
    feline leukemia virus (FeLV), 112,
        117–118, 136, 162, 197
lice, 152, 153, *153*
lick granuloma, 150
life span, 95
lip granuloma (rodent ulcer), 141
lips, inflammation of, 139
lip tumors (squamous cell carcinoma),
    139–140
liquid consumption, 63–64
liquid medication, administration of,
    90–91, *91, 92*
litter box:
    care of, 56
    kittens introduced to, 221
    older cats and, 41, 96
    problem behaviors and, 40–42
littermates, adoption of, 51–52
liver problems, 187–188
lockjaw (tetanus), 115
long guard hair, 147–148, 158
long-haired cats:
    anal plugs developed by, 181
    ancestry of, 7
    Balinese, 6, 7
    Birman, 6, 7–8
    breeds of, 6–11
    Cymric, 7
    grooming requirements of, 51, 68
    Himalayan, 6–7, 9
    Javanese, 7
    Kashmir, 6–7, 9
    Maine Coon, 6, 8–9
    Norwegian Forest cat, 7
    Persian, 6–7, 9, 12, 71
    Ragdoll, 7
    Somali, 6, 9–10

Tiffany, 7
Turkish Angora, 6, 10–11
lost cats, searches for, 75
lung, ruptured, 162
lungs, *see* respiratory system
lungworms, 160, 162
lymphosarcomas, 118, 196

maggots, 154
Maine Coon, 6, 8–9
male cats:
    fights among, 31, 34
    genital tract of, 199
    mating behavior of, 33–35, *34,*
        199–200, 202, 204–205
    neutering of, 31, 33, 41, 48, 52, 200
    sexual disorders of, 199–200
    social hierarchy among, 30, 31
mange, 135, 154
Manx, 11, 17
Massachusetts Bay Colony, 77
mastitis, 212, *212*
matches, ingestion of, 266
maternity box, 203, 206, 219
mating, 33–35, *34,* 111, 199–200,
    202–205, 214
Mayflower, cats aboard, 5, 12
medications, administration of, 90–93, *91,*
    92
medicines, poisonous, 160, 261
memory skills, 23
meningitis, 178
metritis, 212
Miacis, 3
mice, as prey, 62
Microsporum canis, 156
middle ear, 126
Mi-Kee (Japanese Bobtail), 11, 16
milk, water consumption vs., 64
milk fever (eclampsia), 213
milk of magnesia, 85, 98
milk supply, 212, 228–229
minerals, 63
miscarriage, 214
mite infestation, 54, 70, 127, *127,* 135,
    154, *154,* 158
molar abscess, 140
motels, cats permitted in, 73

motherhood:
    birth process and, 206–210, *207, 208*
    breeding and, 96, 202–205
    maternal care and, 210–213, 217–220,
        221
    postpartum problems for, 211–213
    pregnancy and, 65, 119, 205–206,
        213–214
    reproductive problems and, 96,
        213–215
    social order affected by, 31
motion sickness, 72, 126, 188
motor oil, ingestion of, 258
mouth, physiology of, 137–138, *137*
mouth, problems of, *137,* 138–142
    bad breath, 138–139
    bleeding, 253
    dental abscess, 139, 140
    foreign object in, 139
    gum problems, *55,* 140–142
    lip granuloma, 141
    lip inflammation, 139
    lip tumors, 139–140
    peridontal disease, 138, 140
    pyorrhea, 141
    stomatitis, 141, 142
    upper P4 syndrome, 142
mouth-to-nose resuscitation, 236–237,
    236
moving, disruptions of, 76
muscle strain, 168–169
musculoskeletal system:
    of older cats, 98
    physiology of, 165–167, *166*
musculoskeletal system problems,
    167–170
    arthritis, 167, 169
    bone infection, 167
    cracked pads, 167–168
    dislocated joint, 168
    foreign object in foot, 168
    hip dysplasia, 168
    lameness, 168
    muscle strain, 168–169
    nutritional secondary hyperparathy-
        roidism, 169
    rickets, 170
    slipped kneecap, 169–170

musculoskeletal system problems *(continued)*
    sprains, 170
    swollen joints, 169
    tendon injuries, 170
mutations, 11, 12

nail polish, ingestion of, 266
nail trimming, 70, 224–225, 226
name, cat's response to, 58
narcotic poisoning, 160
National Animal Poison Control Center,
    256
national parks, 74
National Research Council, 97
nervous system, 175–178
neutering, 200
    feline population problem and, 48
    optimal age for, 52
    sexual behavior and, 33
    social standing affected by, 31
nictitating membrane (third eyelid), 130,
    136
night vision, 130
nipping, 42
nipples, sore, 213
nocardiosis, 122
Norwegian Forest cat, 7
nose:
    bleeding from, 145, 252
    health check for, 55
    nasal problems and, 144–145
    physiology of, 143–144, *143*
    rubbing of, 28
nutritional anemia, 228
nutritional requirements, 62–64,
    165–166, 169, 223–224
    see also eating
nutritional secondary hyperparathyroidism
    (paper bone disease), 169

obesity, 65, 66, 98, 202
ocelots, 5
odor counteractant, 42
oil poisoning, 263, 264
ointments, application of, 91, *92*
olfactory system, 143–145
On Death and Dying (Kübler-Ross), 100
oocysts, 123

optic nerve, 131
organ of Cort, 126
Oriental Shorthairs, 6, 11, 17–18
osteoarthritis, 167
osteomalacia, 170
osteomyelitis (bone infection), 167
otitis externa, 128–129
otitis interna, 129
otitis media, 129
outdoor cats:
    aging process and, 96
    owner's precautions for, 58
    social order among, 30
    territorial behavior of, 31–32
ovarian cysts, 214
ovulation, 204

pads, 148, 167–168
paint, poisonous, 263–264
pancreatic problems, 188–189
panleukopenia, feline (FPL), 112,
    118–120
paper bone disease (nutritional secondary
    hyperparathyroidism), 169
papillae, 36, 142
paralysis, 250–251
paraphimosis, 199, 200
parasites:
    external, 54, 70, 127, *127*, 135,
        151–155, *154*, 158
    intestinal, 55, 152, 183–186
parks, pet behavior in, 74
Parrovirus, 119
Pasht, 4
passive immunity, 112
pastes, ingestion of, 266
Pasteurella multocida, 227
patellar dislocation (slipped kneecap),
    169–170
paws:
    bandaging of wound on, 86, *87*
    claw grooming and, 39, 70, 224–225,
        226
    cracked pads on, 167–168
    declawing and, 39–40
    foreign objects in, 168
    fractures of, 247, *247*
    swollen, 169

penis, 199–200
periodontal disease, 138, 140
peritonitis, feline infectious (FIP),
    116–117, 137, 162
Persians, 6–7, 9
    in crossbreeding, 12
    tear ducts of, 71
pesticides, poisonous, 262
pet cemeteries, 100
pet registry, tattoo identification listed
    with, 76
pet shops, cats purchased from, 49, 52
pet sitters, 74–75
pharyngitis, 146
pharynx, 145
pheromones, 29
phosphorus, 166, 169
pills, administration of, 91–93, 91
pine oil cleaner, ingestion of, 260
pinkeye (conjunctivitis), 132–133, 133, 136
pinna, 126
plants, eating of, 40
plants, poisonous, 262–263, 263,
    264–265
plaque, 140, 141
play behavior, 35–36, 36
    facial expression for, 28
    kitten development and, 36, 225
pleurisy, 160, 162
pneumonia, 144, 146, 162
pneumonitis, 59
pneumothorax, 163
poisons, 231, 251–267
    automotive products, 258–259
    food poisoning, 259
    gardening products, 259–260
    gastritis reaction to, 187
    general procedures for, 256–257
    household cleaners, 260
    insecticides, 260–261
    medicines, 261
    paint products, 263–264
    pesticides, 262
    poisonous plants, 262–263, 263,
        264–265
    preventive measures for, 258
    from snakebites, 251–254
porcupine quills, 157

postpartum problems, 211–213
pouncing, 22
pregnancy, 65, 119, 205–206, 213–214
pressure dressing, 237
preventive health care, 77–78
problem behavior, 37–43
    of aggression, 42–43
    declawing procedure and, 39–40
    destructive scratching, 39, 39
    excess energy and, 38–39
    between indoor cats, 42–43
    plant eating, 40
    punishment discouraged for, 38
    soiling, 40–42
    stress as source of, 37–38
proctitis, 182
progesterone, 214, 215
prolapse of uterus, 214–215
protein requirements, 62, 65
protozoan diseases, 122–123
pseudorabies, 120, 120
ptyalin, 179
puberty, 33
pulmonary edema, 163, 172
pulse, 83–84, 83
puncture wounds, 111, 114, 162, 163,
    242
punishment:
    physical, 38
    watergun deterrent and, 40, 42
    with whistle sounds, 42
pupils, 130
purebred cats:
    breeder's papers on, 49–50
    see also breeds
Puritans, humane statutes passed by, 77
purulent conjunctivitis, 133
pyoderma, 150
pyometra, 202, 215
pyorrhea (tooth infection), 141
pyothorax, 163
pyrimethamine, 123
pyrophosphates, 261

queens, see female cats

rabies, 111, 120–121
rabies vaccinations, 79, 80

Ragdoll, 7
rectal problems, 180–182
rectal thermometers, 83–84, 85
redecorating, disruptions of, 76–77
reovirus, 121
reproductive problems, 96, 199–200,
    213–215
respiratory infections:
    fever as sign of, 112
    nasal symptoms of, 144
    tuberculosis, 111, 115
    viral, 116–117, 121–122, 136
respiratory system:
    physiology of, 121, 159–160, *159*
    problems of, 158–163, 172, 253
    see also respiratory infections
restraint techniques, 85–86, *86*
resuscitation, 235–237, *235, 236*
retina, 130, 131
retinal diseases, 136
Rhabdoviridae, 120
rheumatism, 169
rhinotracheitis, feline viral (FVR), 121
rickets, 170
ringworm, 54, *54,* 111, 122, 135, 156
rodent ulcer (lip granuloma), 141
roundworms (ascarids), 111, 138,
    184–185, *184,* 226
Russian Blue, 11, 18
rut, 33

safety, in home environment, 78, 97
saliva, 137–138, 179
salmonella, 114, 259
salt, sidewalk, 266
scent-marking, 29, 32, 41
Scottish Fold, 11, 18
scratches, infectious disease from, 113
scratching, 39, *39*
scratching posts, 39, 56, 225
sebaceous cysts, 157
sebaceous glands, 147
seizures, 176–177, 244
semimoist foods, 64
senior citizens, feline companionship for,
    53
senses, acuity of, 23, 66, 96, 125–126,
    143, 148

serious conjunctivitis, 133
sexual behavior, 33–35, *34,* 111, 199–200,
    202–205
    see also female cats; male cats
shampoo, for cats, 68
shampoo, ingestion of, 266
sharp objects, swallowing of, 146
shedding, 158
shipping services, animal, 73
shock, 251
shoe polish, ingestion of, 266
short-haired cats:
    Abyssinian, 9, 11–12
    American Shorthair, 6, 11, 12, 13, 14
    American Wirehair, 11, 12
    Bombay, 11, 13
    breeds of, 11–19
    British Shorthair, 6, 11, 13
    Burmese, 11, 13–14, 19
    Colorpoint Shorthair, 11, 14
    Cornish Rex, 11, 14–15
    Devon Rex, 11, 14–15
    Egyptian Mau, 11, 15
    established breeds of, 11
    Exotic Shorthair, 11, 15–16
    four basic groups of, 11
    grooming for, 68
    Havana Brown, 11, 16
    hybrid breeds of, 11
    Japanese Bobtail, 11, 16
    Korat, 11, 17
    Manx, 11, 17
    mutations, 11
    natural breeds of, 11
    Oriental Shorthair, 6, 11, 17–18
    pet purchase decisions and, 51
    Russian Blue, 11, 18
    Scottish Fold, 11, 18
    Siamese, 7, 11, 14, 16, 18–19, 204
    Tonkinese, 11, 19
Siamese cats, 11, 18–19
    in heat, 204
    other breeds developed from, 7, 14, 16,
        19
sidewalk salt, 266
sinusitis, 145
skeleton, *166*
    see also musculoskeletal system

skin:
    communication functions and, 28, 30
    glandular secretions from, 29, 30
    health check for, 55, *55*
    physiology of, 29, 30, 147, *147*, 148
    sensory acuity of, 28
skin creams, ingestion of, 266
skin disorders, 148–158
    bacterial infections, 149–150
    external parasites, 150–155
    fungal infections, 156–157
    hormonal, 157
skull fractures, 247
skunk odor, 157
sleep:
    accommodations for, 55–56
    patterns of, 37, *37*, 38
smell:
    communicative function of, 29–30
    olfactory system and, 143–144
snacks, 65–66
snakebite, 251–254, *254*
sneezing, 145
social behavior, 30–37
    aggressive, 32–33
    eating as, 35
    in play, 35–36, *36*
    sexual, 33–35, *34*
    social order and, 30–31
    territoriality, 31–32, *31*
    with visitors, 76
    of washing, 36–37, *36*
socialization, 58–59
soft eye (uveitis), 131, 136–137
soft-moist foods, 64
soiling, 40–42
Somali, 6, 9–10
sore mouth (stomatitis), 141, 142
spaying:
    advantages of, 201–202
    feline population problems and, 48
    optimal age for, 201
    sexual behavior and, 33, 202
spider bites, 163, 250
spinal injuries, 247
spleen, 172
sprains, 170
spraying (urine markings), 29, 32, 41

squamous cell carcinoma (lip tumors),
    139–140
stalking, 22
state parks, 74
stings, 249–250
stomach, upset (gastritis), 187
stomatitis (sore mouth), 141, 142
strays, adoption of, 50–51, 79–80
stress, behavioral problems and, 37–38
stroke, 254
strychnine, 262
stud tail, 150
subjunctival hemorrhage, 136
sulfamethazine, 123
sulfonamides, 123
sunburn, 129–130
sunken eye, 136
surgery, home-nursing care after, 93
surviving-pet maintenance programs,
    101
sweat glands, 148

tabby, 8
tail, disorders of, 150, 168
tail injuries, 87, 248
talcum powder, ingestion of, 267
tapetum lucidum, 130
tapeworms (cestodes), 152, 183,
    185–186, *185*, 226
tartar buildup, 64, 138, 140, *141*, 226
tattooing, 75–76
taurine, 173, 174
TB (tuberculosis), 111, 115
tear ducts, 71
teeth:
    abscesses and, 139, 140
    bone chewing and, 71, 139
    cleaning procedures for, 71, 138, 140
    dry food for, 64, 71, 138
    in general health check, 54, *55*
    gingivitis and, 138, 140, 141–142,
        141
    of kittens, 54, *55*, 218, 219, 221, 225,
        226
    number and types of, 137, *138*
    of older cats, 96, 98, 140
    periodontal disease and, 138, 140
    tooth decay and, 138

temperature:
    fever levels and, 112, 178
    regulation of, 176
    taking of, 82–83, *83*
tendon injuries, 170
territoriality, 29–30, 31–32, *31*, 41, 181
tetanus (lockjaw), 115
tetracycline, 114
Thailand, Korat ownership restricted by, 17
thermal burns, 241
thermometer techniques, 82–83, *83*
third eyelid (nictitating membrane), 130, 136
throat, 145–146
thrombosis, 172, 174
thyroid deficiency, 156
ticks, 85, 152, 154–155
Tiffany, 7
toenails, *see* claws
toes, extra, 168
toilet bowl, drinking from, 63–64
toilet-bowl cleaners, ingestion of, 260
toilet training, 221
toms, *see* male cats
tongue, 36, 38, 142–143
Tonkinese, 11, 19
tonsilitis, 146
topical medications, administration of, 90–91, *91*, *92*
touch, communication by, 28–29
"Touring with Towser," 73
tourniquets, 237, *237*
toxic milk syndrome, 228–229
toxoplasmosis, 111, 123, 137
toys, 42, 56–57
tranquilizers, 72, 73
transneptalactone, 144
travel, 71–75
    on airplanes, 73
    camping and, 74
    by car, 72–73, 188
    carriers for, 71–72
    home cat care and, 74–75
    leash use and, 72, 73, 74
    tranquilizers for, 72, 73
    veterinary checkup before, 71
trembling, 178

tuberculosis (TB), 111, 115
tumors, 118, 139–140, 160, 181, 195–196
Turkish Angora, 6, 10–11
tympanic membrane (eardrum), 126

ulcers, corneal, 134, *134*
unconsciousness (coma), 176, 254–255, *254*
underfur, 148, 158
upper P4 syndrome, 142
upper respiratory infections, vaccinations against, 79, 80
upper respiratory viral diseases, 121–122
upset stomach (gastritis), 187
urinary calculi (bladder stones), 63, 194
urinary system disorders, 191–194, *192*
urine markings (spraying), 29, 32, 41
urine samples, collection of, 84–85
urological syndrome, feline (FUS), 191
uterine inertia, 215
uterine infections, 202, 212, 215
uterus, prolapse of, 214–215
uveitis (soft eye), 131, 136–137

vaccinations, 60
    for distemper, 59, 79, 80, 119
    for FeLV, 118
    for rabies, 79, 80, 121
    for respiratory diseases, 79, 80, 116, 122
    schedule for, 80
    for tetanus, 115
vaginal infection, 215
vases, drinking from, 63–64
vestibular disease, 178
veterinary care:
    house calls for, 81
    for older cats, 96
    regular checkups for, 59–60, 77
    selection of, 59–60
    before traveling, 71
vibrassae (whiskers), 28–29, 148
viral infections, 111, 116–122
viral rhinotracheitis, feline (FVR), 121
virus, feline calici (FCV), 121
viruses, 116, 121–122
vision, 29, 130–131
    see also eye problems

visitors, cat's behavior with, 76
vitamin D, 147, 170
vitamins:
   from dietary fats, 63
   for kittens, 223–224
   for older cats, 97
   overdoses of, 63
   supplementary, 63, 97, 223–224
   water-soluble vs. fat-soluble, 63
vocalization, 28, 29, 33
vomeronasal gland, 142
vomiting, 187
   induced, 85, 256, 257

warfarin, 262
warts, 158
washing, 36–37, *36*
water bowl, 56
water consumption, 63–64, 72, 73
water pistol, as cat deterrent, 40, 42
watery eye (epiphora), 134
weaning, 218, 219, 220–221, 223
weed killers, ingestion of, 259–260

weight:
   cyclical fluctuations in, 35
   of older cats, 98
   reduction programs for, 65, 66, 98
   sunken eye from rapid loss of, 136
wheezing, 160
whiskers (vibrassae), 28–29, 148
whistles, for problem behaviors, 42
white cats, ear problems of, 126, 129 130
wild (feral) cats, 30, 33
window screens, 78
wire cages, 71–72
Wong Mau, 13–14
working cats, 12
worming, 79, 183–186, 226
   see also specific worms
wounds, 242–243, *242*
   bandaging techniques for, 86–87, *87*
   chest, 242–243
   lacerated, 242, *242*
   puncture, 111, 114, 162, 163, 242

yeast infection, 122